RIVALS

RIVALS

75 Years of the Lions v. the All Blacks

The New Zealand Herald

RANDOM HOUSE
NEW ZEALAND

Acknowledgments:
The publishers would like to thank Don Cameron, Bob Luxford at the New Zealand Rugby Museum and Lauri Tapsell of the *New Zealand Herald*.

Reproduction of work from the New Zealand Press Association is by kind permission of the NZPA.

Cover images:
Front cover
Top: Tom Lister and Willie John McBride come to blows during the third test in 1971.
Below left: Ian Kirkpatrick tries in vain to tackle J.P.R. Williams in the third test in 1971.
Below middle: Welshman, W.B. Cleaver dons a Maori skirt to entertain onlookers during the Lions tour in 1950.
Below right: Chris Laidlaw clears the ball from R.M. Young on the ground. Watching on are Waka Nathan, Brian Lochore and Colin Meads at Carisbrook in 1966.

Back cover: The 1930 All Blacks trying to keep warm at a snowy Carisbrook during the first test match.

National Library of New Zealand Cataloguing-in-Publication Data

Rivals : 75 years of the Lions v. the All Blacks / [from the
archives of the] New Zealand Herald.
ISBN 1-86941-731-3
1. All Blacks (Rugby team) 2. Lions (Rugby team) 3. Rugby
Union football—Tournaments—New Zealand. 4. Rugby
Union football—Tournaments—Great Britain. I. New Zealand
Herald.
796.33365—dc 22

A RANDOM HOUSE BOOK
published by
Random House New Zealand
18 Poland Road, Glenfield, Auckland, New Zealand
www.randomhouse.co.nz

First published 2005
© New Zealand Herald 2005
© photographs Auckland Weekly News and New Zealand Herald

ISBN 1-86941-731-3

Cover, text design and layout: Nick Turzynski, RedInc, Auckland
Printed by APN, Wellington

CONTENTS

FOREWORD

The *New Zealand Herald* has been covering rugby in this country for well over a century, and among the most closely contested games in any era have been the All Blacks taking on the Lions.

We are delighted that *Rivals* has brought together 75 years of some of the *Herald*'s finest rugby coverage, with contributions from such well-known names as T P McLean, D J Cameron and Wynne Gray, not to mention all the photographers who have captured history from the sidelines.

Rivals looks back over some of the most exciting contests in rugby history. I am sure the 2005 Lions v All Blacks series will be as memorable as those that have gone before.

Tim Murphy
Editor
The New Zealand Herald

INTRODUCTION

D J Cameron

It makes even the weariest rugby heart skip a beat. The Lions are coming — still roaring, still likely to add lustre to the golden patches they have stitched into the fabric of New Zealand rugby.

Since the Great Britain side first brought the Lions' pride to New Zealand in 1930 eight British Isles sides have built a special tradition, distinctive styles of play and opened New Zealand eyes to new rugby cultures. The Australians and South Africans used to share this tradition, but their impact has been diminished through over-familiarity in recent years.

The fascinating thing about the Lions (the nickname came just after the First World War and more recently the words 'British and Irish Lions' have replaced the familiar 'British Isles') is that they have flourished for so long. The four 'Home' countries cherish their own distinctive attitudes to sport, and the men who played it could wear either cloth cap or coronet.

And over the decades the Lions remain the one major sport that every now and then unites the lords and the lads, and distils from the four cultures a spirit and comradeship not found in any other significant sport.

And the arrival this year of the Lions is also the signal that this special tradition can withstand the modern perils of international/commercial sport.

When in the mid-1980's New Zealand and Australia were demanding the formation of a World Cup, a strong counter argument from the conservative north was that the strong focus on a World Cup would mean that Lions tours would fade away in the shadows.

Similarly, when rugby took the plunge into professionalism in 1995 there were persuasive voices saying that the Lions would be shunted aside as irrelevant to the overall commercial interests, and weakening the traditional co-operation of four Home unions, each with different financial profiles.

But, blessedly, the historic ties that bind rugby men are still strong enough to find a place for Lions' tours and their glorious traditions.

For New Zealand, each Lions' tour has been a refresher course in the playing and the philosophy of the game, and often the scene for the occasional rowdy difference of opinion on some rugby matter or another.

When 'Bim' Baxter managed the 1930 side in New Zealand he came rather like a stern headmaster intent on bringing the Colonials back under the strict laws established in Britain. He railed against the way the 2-3-2 scrum left a roving forward not possible under the 3-2-3 British formation. He stirred up New Zealanders about their allowing substitutes, their taking teams from the field at halftime, their amended kick-into-touch rules.

New Zealanders listened, but then found that after losing the first test they were strong and clever enough to win the next three.

A section of the Athletic Park crowd at the fourth test in 1930.

Baxter's British supporters did remove the 2-3-2 soon afterward, but soon afterward the All Blacks were introduced by the Springboks to the superior alternative of the 3-4-1 formation.

The 1950 Lions brought a mixture or rugby talent and genuine good humour. They had not long before been entertained by the 2nd NZEF Kiwis, and were eager to repay the debt. They started the four tests with a draw, finished with Ken Jones' brilliant try in the fourth. The All Blacks won the last three tests, but the really wrinkled ones among us will still maintain the 1950 Lions were perhaps the real gentlemen of the game.

Before their 1959 tour of New Zealand the Lions had shared a test rubber with South Africa in 1955, and the mellow mood of 1950 had wafted away. The Lions' good humour was further eroded when they scored four tries and still lost the first test 17-18 to Don Clarke's six penalty goals. They had potent backs, useful forwards and were embroiled in all manner or argument against the All Black forwards wearing shoulder-pads, the quality of New Zealand referees, and managed to win only the fourth test 9-6 when Clarke, of all people, missed a late penalty goal attempt.

The Lions of 1966 brought their own leadership and selection problems, they met an All Black team of immense confidence and skill and, sadly, were doomed to lose all four tests.

Five years later the Lions were revived by the planning and managership of Dougie Smith, the turning of coaching into an art form by Carwyn James, and the regal five-eighths and goal-kicking style of Barry John. New Zealand were still recovering from losing to South Africa in 1970, and the Lions deserved their rubber win of 2-1, with the fourth test drawn.

The 1971 Lions left behind the skills of counter-attacking play and the Lions of 1977 brought the new style of power-scrummaging. They also attracted a very wet winter, they lost the rubber 1-3 to a lucky last-minute try to the All Blacks in the fourth test, and they only raised a cheer among their ranks when their plane carried them off New Zealand soil.

Willie John McBride, the most famous Lion of all, brought the 1983 Lions to New Zealand, with

Lions' fullback Gavin Hastings set to tackle All Black fullback John Timu at Eden Park in 1993.

high hopes of spreading his glory among the players. Sadly, they were not consistent enough and gradually Andy Dalton's All Blacks knitted together to finish the 4-0 win with a shattering 38-6 demolition at Eden Park.

England formed a strong backbone and confidence to the 1993 Lions. They lost the first test 18-20 to a last-minute penalty goal by Grant Fox, struck back to win the second test at Wellington, but were outplayed by the All Black pack in the third.

And now, 12 years later, we await the new chapter of this great saga. It will be a different tour — the money-makers busy in the rugby temple, the rugby-man-in-the-street sitting in front of a television set instead of queuing overnight for standing room.

But let us hope that this Lions rugby tour, no matter how squashed and squeezed into new commercial shapes, will perhaps mark the start of a new tradition, even more dramatic than the legends so nobly etched in the past.

Blankets were well in evidence among onlookers at the first test in Dunedin.

1930

21 June – Dunedin
5 July – Christchurch
26 July – Auckland
9 August – Wellington

16 May 1930

CHOICE OF COLOURS

Mr Baxter's Explanation

By Telegraph — Own Correspondent

WELLINGTON, THURSDAY.

When asked why dark blue had been chosen as the colour for the British team in view of the possible confusion with the All Black uniform, Mr Baxter the British manager, said that dark blue was the international colour of Great Britain's Rugby representatives. It was the colour worn on the Argentina tour and on the South African tour, with the difference that the monogram on those tours had been a combination of the rose, thistle, Prince of Wales' feathers, and shamrock. For this tour the monogram would consist of three golden lions.

A Press Association message from Masterton states that the management committee of the Wairarapa Union has decided to make an emphatic protest against the decision that the New Zealand team will play in white jerseys. It asks all unions to support the protest and to request the New Zealand Union to reconsider its decision.

17 May 1930

BRITISH RUGBY TEAM

Enthusiastic Golfers
Some Good Players
Departure for Wanganui

By Telegraph — Press Association

WELLINGTON, FRIDAY.

The 'plus fours' worn by half the members of the British Rugby team as an everyday garb are no mere affectation. A Wellington resident who was apprised of their liking for golf arranged to take some of them out to the Miramar links. He called for them at their hotel soon after 1pm, on Thursday, and when he announced his mission they abandoned the idea of luncheon, rushed for their clubs, and in a few minutes had taken their seats in the waiting cars.

When at about 3.30pm it was suggested that they should adjourn for afternoon tea they would have none of it. 'This is too good to be true,' said one.

'They like golf,' said their host. 'Indeed, I am inclined to think they like it better than football. Some of them play a rattling good game, too.'

Members of the visiting British rugby football team take 'time off' to go on a hare drive in North Canterbury.

22 May 1930

VISITORS' RULINGS

Definition of a Mark
Play With One Ball Only
Referee Must Keep Own Time
By Telegraph — Athletic Reporter

WANGANUI, WEDNESDAY.
Mr James Baxter, manager of the British Rugby team, and F.D. Prentice, captain, held a long consultation this morning with Mr J.H. McKenzie, the referee, regarding interpretation of rules. Mr McKenzie was handed a book of rules as set out by the international board. It is very interesting to New Zealanders to note differences of interpretation, in some cases only slight, as compared with the prevailing custom throughout the Dominion.

The definition of a mark has created a great deal of controversy in New Zealand of late. The British attitude is that a mark can be claimed if a fair catch is made with one or both feet on the ground, and a mark made.

The visitors refuse absolutely to play with more than one ball, unless the one in use is kicked right out of the ground. It was pointed out to them that the custom in New Zealand was to have a spare ball on either touch-line, but they will not agree to the use of either of those unless the ball in play is kicked over the fence.

The British interpretation of Rule 19B is going to be a difficult one for New Zealand referees. The rule in the New Zealand handbook reads: 'A player overtaking an opponent also running for the ball must not shove him from behind.' The British ruling gives further, adding the words: 'Unless he is stooping to pick up the ball.' This means that referees will have to determine when a player is actually stooping. The Britishers consider that a man in such a position

23 May 1930

BRITISH RUGBY
TEAM

Colours For The Tests
No All Black Jerseys
Decision of the Union
By Telegraph — Press Association

WELLINGTON, THURSDAY
The New Zealand Rugby Union has decided to adhere to its original decision on the question of colours for the All Black team in test matches with the British team. The New Zealand representatives, therefore, will take the field in white jerseys, black shorts and black stockings with white tops. This decision was made at a meeting of the New Zealand Union this afternoon, proceedings being held in

C.G. Porter leading the white-jerseyed All Blacks on to Carisbrook.

committee.

A letter is to be sent to Mr James Baxter, manager of the British team, expressing the union's appreciation of the sportsmanlike action of he and his team in offering to play in white jerseys, but stating that the union considers its original decision should stand.

is attempting to play the ball.

The visitors will not recognise the time-bell, and insist on the referee keeping his own time.

Regarding the knock-on rule, the slightest fumble and recatch is permissible, but the least propelling forward and recatching must be ruled a knock-on. The custom in the Dominion is that the player putting the ball in the scrum shall not indicate from which side it is coming. The British rule allows such a practice, the half-back calling out which side, so as to put the front row men on the alert. The visitors are very strict on the tackle rule, in that the player tackled must immediately part with the ball.

---

23 June 1930

WIN FOR BRITAIN
First Rugby Test
Six Points to Three
All Blacks Disappoint
Scoring Chances Missed
Sensational Conclusion

By Telegraph — Press Association

DUNEDIN, SATURDAY.

A sensational last-minute try by the speedy little British threequarter, Morley, converted a certain draw in the first test match between Britain and New Zealand into a well-deserved and popular win for the visitors by 6 points to 3. The game was played under conditions that did not make for the best exhibition of the game, in spite of the fact that for an hour preceding the commencement of the game there was an unprecedented fall of snow, which left the surrounding hills with a mantle of white to an extraordinarily low level.

There were about 26,000 people present by the time the big match was begun. The ground was very slippery and heavy and it was a matter of a few minutes before the ball became disconcertingly greasy. The contest resolved itself into a struggle between two well-matched packs of forwards. It

was a great game in spite of everything and the crowd recognised early in the match that the New Zealanders, who, it must be admitted, were firm favourites, had the hardest part to do to win.

The British forwards, led by Ivor Jones, Hodgson and Beamish, were superb in both the tight and loose and in the first spell were consistently on the offensive. In the latter stages of the game, without overwhelming its opponents, the New Zealand vanguard held its own. The All Black inside backs failed dismally and it must be confessed that the Lilburne-Cooke combination at five-eighths cannot be expected to be effective against the skill of the Englishmen.

Wing-threequarters Starved

Mill was far from impressive. He was slow behind the scrum, and far too many of his passes were aimed at the feet. The crowd did not like this in such an experienced player. Lilburne's transfers to Cooke were scarcely any better. Cooke was the life and soul of the backs, but that is a doubtful compliment in that the New Zealand backs lacked life and initiative.

Perhaps one of the most regrettable features of the game from a New Zealand point of view was the starving of the wing-threequarters, neither of whom had half the opportunities they might have had. Hart had one good chance which he used to excellent effect, scoring one of the prettiest tries of the afternoon. Oliver, too, had one which he missed badly, dropping the ball through his hands when he was a few yards from the line with nothing to beat. Nepia, at fullback, delighted the crowd. He was sure in defence, and his line-kicking could not be faulted. His one mistake was when he refused to go down to a forward rush. He tried to stop the ball with his foot and was swept along with the ball. Only Cooke's surprising anticipation saved trouble on that occasion. The day was a bad one for goal-kicking, and Nepia had few chances in that direction, anyhow.

Forwards Below Standard

The forwards accomplished very much less than was expected of them. Porter was everywhere and did a lot of good, hard work, but somehow lacked finish. He was continually offside, and, although

Cheerful spectators undaunted by the snow and sleet.

he attracted the referee's attention often, he got away with too much in the opinion of the crowd, who resorted several times to the expedient of urging in chorus that he should get back on side. Finlayson was the hero of the day, as far as the forwards were concerned, and Steere was generally in the picture, but the former was brilliant. He broke through time and again and could always be seen hard at work in both defence and offence. Batty was prominent frequently and earned some applause, but the crowd had few laurels to spare after they had recognised the performances of Cooke, Finlayson and Nepia. Hazlett proved to some extent the justice of the charge of shining that has been levelled against him lately and most of the others did nothing more than was asked of them.

Great Play by British

The British team played an inspiring game. It was a case of 'Even the ranks of Tucany could scarce forbear a cheer.' The crowd simply had to cheer the work of both backs and forwards. Spong, Murray, Bowcott, Aarvold, Reeve and Morley were a delight throughout. Both halves exhibited rare resource and the wings made the best use of their opportunities. Bassett, at fullback, distinguished himself. On last Saturday's showing [against Otago] he was unimpressive and generally considered to be a weak link in the British side, but, although a shade on the slow side today, he was sure and certain always. His side owed him much.

The backs played sparkling football of a kind that seemed foreign to the All Blacks. Playing behind hard-working forwards they were

The British team take the field during the snow fall.

Mr S. Hollander, the referee, and George Nepia partake in the usual refreshment at half-time.

encouraged to open up the game and they did it. They outclassed the New Zealanders, of whom Cooke alone could teach them anything. His uncanny knack of anticipating defence was remarkably demonstrated this afternoon. Reeve's first try for Britain was a great effort. Hart's score brought the crowd to its feet enthusiastically, but Morley's exciting run of 50 yards, finishing off a movement that began in the British twenty-five, sent the crowd into raptures.

Visitors' Opening Try

Porter led New Zealand out to the accompaniment of vociferous applause and the home team kicked off. After a scrum at half-way Finlayson led a forward rush to the British twenty-five. Play was in midfield until Hodgson found the line well in New Zealand's twenty-five. Batty led the New Zealand pack in a strong rush, but Bassett saved. Mill secured and kicked through to Bassett, who fumbled. The New Zealand forwards packed round, but Murray eased a difficult position. The British backs handled in a promising movement, but Aarvold was grassed in possession. A free kick to each side saw little change in play. The British backs were then sent away by Murray, who achieved a smart back pass to Spong, who cross-kicked to Reeve. The fast winger accepted the chance and outran Hart to score at the corner after seven minutes' play. Black's kick failed. Britain, 3; New Zealand, 0.

New Zealand forwards get the ball off their backs after one of the lineouts. Ivor Jones is about to tackle Mill, the New Zealand halfback.

Spong headed another British offensive but the attack was repulsed. Offside play by the British in front of the goal gave New Zealand a free kick, but Nepia's effort was poor, the ball failing to rise. The British forwards came away again, led by Beamish and Hodgson, but Irvine found touch with a lucky speculator. The visitors kept up a strong attack, carrying play right to the New Zealand line. The New Zealand forwards bullocked their way through, however, but their progress was stopped when New Zealand was penalised. Black's kick fell short.

Nepia found the line with a good kick, and from the line-out Porter dribbled through to Bowcott, who picked up and found touch. The weather had now cleared, but the ground was heavy and the ball greasy. Bowcott cut through, beating Lucas badly, and passed in to Ivor Jones, who was well taken by Lilburne. Play was returned to midfield when Lilburne found the line with a good kick. Ivor Jones went through with the ball at his toes, Nepia putting up an extremely weak defence. Bowcott stopped a counter forward movement by Finlayson, Porter and Steere.

The British team was well adapted to the conditions. Murray sent Spong and Bowcott away, the last-named cutting in cleverly, but Lilburne was in the right place at the right time. Nepia was fielding cleanly and, kicking without a mistake, saved his side twice in almost as many minutes.

Porter was caught badly offside, and Black found touch well in the New Zealand twenty-five.

The New Zealand backs handled, Cooke kicking through to Bassett, who fielded well and found touch in the New Zealand twenty-five. Murray secured and sent his backs away, Aarvold dummying Porter cleverly and passing on to Morley, who was brought down by Oliver. The crowd heckled Porter for offside play, but the referee was not looking.

Very Sound Defence

Cooke was playing a magnificent game, but the defence was as sound as a rock. The Britishers were having the better of the game territorially and at the same time were making all the play. Lilburne started a passing movement, but Cooke dropped his pass although he carried on with the ball at his toes. Ivor Jones was always prominent and led Britain to the New Zealand twenty-five. An infringement in the scrum gave New Zealand a free kick, Nepia finding the line at halfway. A further free kick to New Zealand saw Porter kick through to Bassett, who returned play to the New Zealand twenty-five. Finlayson broke through and passed to Cooke, who was brought down ten yards from the line. A free kick to Britain saved an awkward situation. Mill secured from a scrum and sent the backs away in one of the most promising movements of the game

on the New Zealand side. It collapsed when Lucas was caught in possession. Britain was easily on top in the set scrums, but the line-outs were slightly in New Zealand's favour. New Zealand was going much better when the whistle sounded for halftime. The score then being: Britain, 3; New Zealand, 0.

Finlayson broke through from the first scrum in the second spell and from the rough Porter secured, dashing up to be pushed out at the corner. Mill secured from the scrum and passed to Lilburne, who sent on to Cooke, who kicked over the line, Britain forcing. From the next scrum Mill sent his backs away again, Lilburne, Cooke and Lucas handling before the last-named transferred to Hart, who dashed across at the corner, beating both Reeve and Bassett. Within five minutes of resumption New Zealand had equalised the score. Nepia's kick hit the post. Britain, 3; New Zealand, 3.

Some Faulty Passing

The New Zealand forwards were now battling to good effect, but Bassett at fullback was playing superlatively, in marked contrast to last Saturday's performance [against Otago]. Lilburne passed out to Cooke, who cross-kicked to Oliver, but the winger failed to connect. Batty and Porter led a forward rush to the British twenty-five, but Bassett again saved. Mill

sent out to Lilburne, who gave Cooke a bad pass, the latter kicking. A minute later the same thing occurred, Bassett finding the line with a hasty kick.

Faulty passing by the New Zealand inside backs spoiled some good efforts. New Zealand was having all the better of the game now and only Bassett's sure defence was preventing scores. Hard tactics by Britain moved the sphere of action to the New Zealand twenty-five, where an infringement by one of the British forwards gave Nepia a chance to find touch well down with a magnificent kick.

Bassett was caught in possession five yards from his line, but he passed back in time for Aarvold to find the line. Spong picked up in a handy position and passed to Morley, who moved right up to Nepia. His pass to Ivor Jones went astray and the movement broke down.

Injury to McWilliams

With the spell half gone New Zealand still held the upper hand, although unable to pierce the defence. A three-minutes' stoppage occurred as the result of an injury to McWilliams, who was eventually taken off. Lilburne went down to a British forward rush, but it was only a temporary check, and the heavy pack moved on, sweeping Nepia right off his feet. Cooke, however, came across in time to save. McWilliams' return at this stage was the cause of tumultuous applause.

Hazlett broke through with the ball at his toes, and reached Bassett, who picked up cleverly to kick into touch at halfway. A free kick to New Zealand was taken by Porter, who tried the dangerous experiment of up and under, Cooke retrieving what proved to be a blunder by picking up from the toss of the advancing British vanguard. From a scrum Mill sent a bad pass to Lilburne, who, however, picked up and sent Cooke away toward the touchline, where Bassett threw the ball out. Nepia's kick at goal failed. A minute later Nepia found the line from a free kick, and a struggle ensued five yards from the British line. Mill tried to get over on his own, but failed, and a second time he just missed again. Porter dived round the back of a scrum, but Bassett cleared. Cooke got away, to be pulled down after a good run.

Victory Gained

Then Hart cut through and passed to Lucas, who kicked out of bounds just before he was taken by Reeve. Lucas charged down a kick by Aarvold, and New Zealand looked like scoring until Oliver let the ball fall through his hands. New Zealand was still pressing hard when the end came with sensational suddenness. What appeared to be a certain draw was suddenly converted into a decisive victory by the redoubtable Ivor Jones, who secured possession in his own twenty-five and set out for the line 75 yards away. He reached the halfway line before he was seriously challenged, and in the nick of time he transferred to Morley, who had come up fast. The little winger then set off for the line with Cooke in hot pursuit. Morley outpaced Cooke by about a yard, the pair finishing up on the grass a yard from the corner, and just across the line, the wing scoring the most sensationally unexpected try that has been seen on Carisbrook since Steel made his never-to-be-forgotten run against the Springboks nine years ago.

The stand, the tiers outside, and every part of the ground was in an uproar at the unexpected termination to the game. When Jones picked up there was less than half a minute to go, and Black's unsuccessful attempt at goal was made after time had expired. Round after round of tumultuous applause echoed around the ground. The Britishers had snatched a drawn game from the fire in a manner that could not but appeal to every sporting instinct of the crowd. The try was of the kind that is seen seldom, and the visitors deserved to win for the remarkable opportunism they exhibited in that effort. The opening was there, and quick as a flash, Jones jumped into the breach. Morley followed up in perfect style, and there was scarcely a yard between him and Cooke. But the Briton was just too fast, and at the end of a great run had the satisfaction of knowing he had won the game for his side. The final score was therefore: Britain, 6; New Zealand, 3.

Mr S. Hollander, Christchurch, was referee.

The 1930 'All Blacks' who met the British rugby team in the first test in Dunedin.

10 July 1930

RE-SALE OF TICKETS

Enhancement of prices

The opinion that any scheme for the resale of test match tickets at enhanced prices was wrong in principle was expressed today by Mr S.F. Wilson, a past president of the Canterbury Rugby Union.

Mr Wilson voiced the belief that, if there were any suggestion of such trafficking the Auckland and Wellington Rugby Unions would probably apportion the tickets among the clubs, which would see that the football section of the public was not exploited. Mr Wilson's remarks were in reply to a recommendation by Mr A.F. Stacey whose scheme in regard to the sale of tickets for the second test match at Christchurch realised £200 for the Returned Soldiers' Association's unemployment fund.

19 July 1930

QUESTION IN PARLIAMENT

Presumably having in mind the large queues which have been formed in Wellington in connection with the booking of seats for the fourth rugby test match between Britain and New Zealand, Mr J.T. Hogan (Independent — Rangitikei) addressed an urgent question to the Minister of Labour, the Hon. S.G. Smith, in the House of Representatives today.

Mr Hogan asked if the Minister would look into the matter of the employment of young boys to take part in all night queues, a practice that was likely to be detrimental to their health during cold, wintry weather.

The Minister said he had only just received notice of the question, but he would take immediate steps to have the matter investigated.

July 21 1930

ALL BLACKS WIN THE SECOND TEST THIRTEEN POINTS TO TEN

Britain unfortunate
Loss of halfback
I. Jones versatility

New Zealand beat Britain in the second test by 13 points to 10 in a hard-fought game full of exciting incidents, but unmarked by brilliance on either side. There was light rain during the night and early morning which made the surface of the ground greasy, although not really heavy, and about midday the misty rain ceased, the match being played in sunshine. It was estimated that the crowd in Lancaster Park numbered 35,000.

The teams were:—

All Blacks
Nepia, Hart, Lucas, Oliver, Cooke, Nicholls, Corner, Porter, Cottrell, Hore, Finlayson, McWilliam, Steere, Stewart, Hazlett

Britain
Bassett, Morley, Novis, Aarvold, Bowcott, Spong, Murray, Rew, Parker, O'Neill, Black, Farrell, Prentice, Beamish, Ivor Jones

The teams took the field promptly at 2.30pm in brilliant sunshine. Porter won the toss and New Zealand played with the sun behind them. The kick-off went out of bounds and a scrum was formed at halfway. New Zealand won the ball quickly but Nicholls' pass to Cooke went wrong. In the early forward clashes the British pack concentrated on keeping the ball at its toes by which means it repeatedly gained definite advantages.

The opening score

The best move of the match to date was a passing bout in which Cooke, Lucas and Oliver were

A panorama of the vast crowd at Lancaster Park. Inset: F. Prentice and C. Aarvold.

prominent. Oliver just failed to get over, being pulled down by Bassett a little short of the line. Britain cleared momentarily, but the New Zealand backs attacked immediately on the other wing. The passing, however, was faulty at a critical moment and the ball did not reach Hart. An offside breach gained New Zealand a free kick and Nicholls scored first blood with a good penalty goal.

New Zealand 3

Great Britain 0

After the kick-off the territorial advantage was with Britain, due mainly to faulty kicking by the New Zealand backs. Both sides, in fact, seemed unable to kick accurately. A bad pass by Spong, who had been given the ball from a scrum on New Zealand's side of halfway, gave Cooke an opportunity. He made a good breakaway, but his pass to Lucas was far astray. Britain escaped with a piece of bright passing.

The British backs were getting a great deal of ball and throwing it about with the utmost daring, but without that accuracy essential to success. Offside play by McWilliams, after some shocking passing by the British backs, gave the visitors a free kick in a fair position, but Black's kick was wide. Splendid passing by the British rearguard failed

Porter grappling with Ivor Jones, who succeeded in kicking clear notwithstanding the desperate efforts of McWilliams and Stewart to smother the ball.

Corner going down pluckily to the feet of the onrushing British forwards with Parker almost on top of him.

when Prentice stumbled and fell with the ball in his hands a few yards short of the line, a certain try being lost. A second later Britain got the ball from a loose rush. Crisp passes went out, Murray, Morley and Aarvold all racing at top speed, and the last-named scored a splendid try. It was brilliant work, which left the New Zealanders standing. Prentice goaled from the easy position.

Great Britain 5
New Zealand 3

All Blacks lead again

Much forward play followed the kick-off, mostly on New Zealand's side of halfway. Passing by the New Zealand backs broke down when Cooke was well tackled with the ball, but in a loose scramble Lucas got away and passed to Corner, who gave Hart an excellent pass when the fast three-quarter was at full speed near the line. Hart ran round to a good position and Nicholls goaled.

New Zealand 8
Great Britain 5

After a passing bout in midfield, Murray was left lying on the field following a hard tackle. He had to go off nursing his left shoulder. It was found to be dislocated. Britain played for the rest of the game short of one of its best backs. Ivor Jones came out of the pack to replace Murray. The remainder of the spell was without important incident, but the advantage was with the British backs, who continually opened up the game. Their passing, however, was not quite accurate enough.

The spell ended with the score:–
New Zealand 8
Great Britain 5

The New Zealand backs got moving well and the ball went out to Hart, but Novis pushed him out 10 yards from the line. A free kick to Britain allowed Bassett to clear to halfway. A long kick by Lucas was well followed up, and Bassett was pushed out near the corner. A scrum was formed near the British goal. A free kick should have let Britain out, but the kick was called back for a man being in front. A series of scrums followed near the British goal. Corner had a sharp shot at goal but the ball went outside the post.

Oliver prominent

The New Zealand backs dominated play at this stage, the forwards getting the ball consistently. Corner let it away speedily. Oliver kicked well to the line when stopped after a good run. Following up fast, he took the ball well, but was caught just short of the line. He tried to rabbit over and was penalised. The New Zealand backs came again, and the forwards took up the movement with a loose scrambling charge, from which Bassett just saved Britain on the line. A free kick allowed Britain to clear.

From halfway Aarvold broke away on a good run. He slipped Lucas and ran to Nepia. He had Novis on his flank, but he tried to side-step and Nepia grassed him on the twenty-five line. Corner, first by good line kicks and then smart passing, put New Zealand on attack. Nicholls ran to the right wing, centred well, and the New Zealand backs, charging up in echelons, had the defence at their mercy. The ball went to Cooke, Lucas and Oliver, but the pass to Oliver was low and he failed to get hold of the ball, the easiest of tries being lost. Cooke had made a beautiful opening, giving the other backs a sitting shot.

Goal from the side line

The British forwards cleared with a good dribbling rush. Britain opened up an attack, but the New Zealand tackling was too deadly. Good play by the home side, and a lucky kick took play down for the British line again. There Nicholls worked the blind side very cleverly. Taking the defence completely by surprise he ran to Bassett and gave Oliver a beautiful pass to allow the three-quarter to trot over. It was a brilliant piece of work by Nicholls. The kick was taken by Nicholls, who landed a beautiful goal from the sideline.

New Zealand 13

Great Britain 5

New Zealand pressed relentlessly after the kick-off, and Corner never lost an opportunity of setting the backs going. The New Zealand backs were taken by surprise when from his own side of halfway Aarvold was given the ball by Ivor Jones, who beat Nicholls and the speedy three-quarter beat everybody in yards in the race for the line. He grounded the ball unopposed between the posts. Prentice goaled, making the final score:—

New Zealand 13

Great Britain 10

---

26 July 1930

INFLUX OF VISITORS TO THE CITY

Thousands of visitors
Accommodation fully taxed
Train and Steamer traffic

Trains, motor-cars and buses brought thousands of visitors to Auckland yesterday for the third rugby test match between Britain and New Zealand, which is to be played at Eden Park this afternoon. The accommodation at Eden Park is estimated to be sufficient for about 49,000 people. From the indications yeasterday it would seem that all the accommodation possible will be needed, for Auckland was a crowded city.

Accommodation at the leading hotels is fully taxed. They were booked up to the limit last night and they are fully booked for the weekend. Many people who had failed to make previous arrangements for their accommodation were prepared yesterday to accept anything that was available in the way of a 'shakedown'. Most of the visitors from the south arrived yesterday morning, many of them from as far distant as Christchurch and Dunedin. How many more will arrive today is a matter for conjecture. Queen Street yesterday had the appearance common to the few days before Christmas, and every entertainment in the city last evening had its full share of patronage.

Traffic by train to Auckland yesterday was particularly heavy. Both expresses from Wellington were crowded and trains from the north also brought hundreds of people. The Whangarei express last evening had three extra carriages, two from Maungatoroto and one from Helensville. More country visitors will be brought to the city today by special trains from Whangarei, Tauranga, Rotorua and Taumarunui. Cheap fares are available on all trains arriving at Auckland before 2.15pm.

The Northern Company's steamer *Clansman*, which arrived from Russell yesterday morning, was a full ship, many people realising that trains and later boats would be crowded. A special permit to carry extra passengers has been obtained from the Marine Department for the steamer *Claymore*, which will arrive from Whangarei early this morning. Many people who went north after the match last week took the precaution of booking their seats by train to arrive back yesterday.

It is expected that there will be an early rush today for the best vantage points on the terraces at Eden Park. Last week there was a large crowd by ten o'clock for the match between Britain and Auckland, many people taking boxes and portable stands for their convenience. There will no doubt be a greater rush today, but boxes and portable stands will be prohibited; as it is considered not fair that late arrivals should obscure the view of hundreds who have been waiting on the banks for hours.

Special trams will commence running to Eden Park about 8.30am to cater for the early arrivals. As was the case last week tickets admitting to the park will be sold from boxes at the approaches and no money will be taken at the gates. Holders of grandstand tickets are advised to use the entrance at Reimers Avenue at the back of the stand. Special trams will be in readiness at Eden Park and in Dominion Road at the finish of the match.

There was a constant stream of traffic to Auckland along Great South Road last evening and motorists arrived from as far south as Wellington.

The Mount Albert Borough Council has arranged for a kite bearing the words: 'Welcome to Mount Albert' to be flown over Eden Park today as a welcome to the many visitors expected from other districts.

28 July 1930

ALL BLACKS WIN THIRD RUGBY TEST

Defeat of Britain Fifteen to Ten
Hard-fought game
Keen forward play

In a game which was strenuously contested and in which incidents both thrilling and spectacular occurred at fairly frequent intervals, the New Zealand rugby team took the lead in the test series by defeating Britain in the third test at Eden Park on Saturday afternoon by 15 points to 10. A crowd of over 40,000 — the largest that has ever witnessed a football match in New Zealand — fully taxed the capacity of the ground.

Test football is rarely continuously spectacular and in this respect Saturday's game was no exception. There were periods of rugged forward play alternated with sudden loose rushes by the packs and bursts of passing among the backs. Against a heavier British pack the New Zealand forwards struggled gamely and if anything won the honours of the game. The backs on both sides were evenly matched, and it was a rare treat to see the elusive brilliance of R.S. Spong, and the spectacular speed of the British three-quarter line pitted against the coolness and experience of M.F. Nicholls and A.E. Cooke. New Zealand was a more versatile team on the day and it was this coupled with the leadership of C.G. Porter that resulted in Britain's second test defeat.

Rousing cheers for the teams

In spite of fairly heavy rain earlier in the week the ground was in excellent order. The huge crowd rose and sang the National Anthem after the teams had filed out, and then as the players took up their positions there was a roar of cheering. Following were the teams:—

All Blacks
Fullback: G. Nepia (East Coast)
Three-quarters: G.F. Hart (Canterbury),
A.E. Cooke (Wellington), F.W. Lucas (Auckland)
Five-eighths: W.A. Strang (South Canterbury),
M.F. Nicholls (Wellington)
Halfback: M. Corner (Auckland)
Wing forward: C.G. Porter, captain (Wellington)
Hookers: A.L. Cottrell (Canterbury), J. Hore
(Otago)
Lock: E.R.C. Steere (Hawke's Bay)
Sides: R.G. McWilliams (Auckland), W.E. Hazlett
(Southland)
Back Row: W. Batty (Auckland), H.F. McLean
(Wellington)

Britain
Fullback: J.Bassett (Wales)
Three-quarters: J.C. Morley (Wales), C.D. Aarvold
(England), H.M. Bowcott (Wales), J.S.R. Reeve
(England)
Halfbacks: R.S. Spong (England), N. Poole
(Wales)

The two teams lined up on the field during the singing of the National Anthem prior to the commencement of the match.

Forwards: H. Rew (England), D. Parker (Wales), H. O'H. O'Neill (Ireland), R.H. Black (England), J.L. Farrell (Ireland), J. McD. Hodgson (England), G.R. Beamish (Ireland), Ivor Jones (Wales)

Nicholls kicked off into the sun, and after an exchange of kicks a penalty against the British forwards for offside play gave Strang a fruitless long range shot. It was not long before the British backs opened out, in a spectacular passing bout, throwing the ball about with rare abandon. The New Zealand backs, however, were running inside their men and forcing them across, and when Morley dropped the ball Lucas and Cooke broke away in a dash for the corner. Bassett was wonderfully cool and intercepted Cooke's pass to clear.

Penalty kicks fail

Britain was awarded a penalty in mid-field and Black essayed what was well-nigh an impossible shot at goal, the kick failing. There was some ill-directed kicking at this stage but the game was brightened when Reeve dashed away. He kicked too hard and the ball went over the dead-ball line. A loose rush by the New Zealand forwards, led by Porter, brought play back to mid-field, but in two passing movements the backs could gain little ground. New Zealand was penalised again and Black missed narrowly from long range.

Britain was dominating the scrums but the New Zealand forwards were countering by breaking fast and worrying the inside backs. Spong was sending the ball out quickly when he received it from Poole, and on one occasion Aarvold broke through

strongly but was forced into touch. The British forwards, led by Parker and Beamish, came away from a line-out and bustled Nepia, but Cooke raced across in a flash and saved brilliantly.

Then Spong altered his tactics and gave the Auckland public the first taste of his attacking genius. Securing from the scrum he dashed past Strang, drew the defence beautifully and then sent on a pass to Bowcott. The Welshman gathered up in his stride and scored between the posts. Ivor Jones made no mistake with the kick.

Britain 5

New Zealand 0

Strong British attack

Short bursts by Hart placed New Zealand on attack, but Aarvold blocked Strang when he was working Lucas into position on the other wing. Well placed punts by Morley and Poole transferred play to the other side of the field and Ivor Jones failed with a penalty given against Porter for offside play. Aarvold was making strenuous efforts to break through, ignoring his wings at times, but one back movement in which Bassett joined had New Zealand defending desperately. Corner broke away from a scrum in the New Zealand twenty-five and with Ivor Jones in pursuit raced across the field and saved by kicking into touch.

A quick pass by Morley sent Spong away in a corkscrew run, but Aarvold knocked on in a promising position. Hart and Cooke countered, but at this stage New Zealand was not backing up well. Poole dashed away from a scrum in great style and Morley and Ivor Jones placed Britain in a strong

Faces among the densely packed crowd on the terrace.

attacking position when a penalty held them up. Porter, Steere and Lucas were next associated in a fine piece of combined play, but Steere's final pass to Lucas was forward.

The New Zealand backs were now playing with more dash and Lucas came in from the wing to make an extra man in one passing bout. Cooke put through beautifully, and it seemed that New Zealand must score. However, Hart was beaten for the touch down. The New Zealand backs continued to throw the ball about but Nicholls was well marked. Then came an inspiring break away from Ivor Jones and Hodgson. They beat Nepia, but Cooke appeared from nowhere, snapped up the ball and found safety in touch.

New Zealand attacked again when Porter broke through and kicked for a gap. Bassett was nearly in trouble through waiting for the bounce, but he managed to elude McLean who had followed up well. Bassett was working like a Trojan and shortly afterwards cleverly blocked a short punt by Cooke.

One of the finest pieces of play of the match followed — a movement engineered by Nicholls, and one which probably only Nicholls could

conceive and carry out. There was some delay over a scrum, and noticing that Morley was standing well infield, Nicholls signalled to Lucas to stand well out. He went in to first five-eighths in place of Strang, and when New Zealand secured the ball, punted almost straight across the field. Lucas was under the ball in a flash, caught it on the full and dashed round to score between the posts with the British defence still wondering what had happened. It was a wonderful piece of co-operative play. Strang's kick equalised the scores.

Britain 5

New Zealand 5

There was a short delay owing to an injury to Corner and when the game resumed New Zealand was penalised for a scrum infringement. Parker hit the posts with a great kick. An even first half ended.

An unusual incident occurred shortly after the resumption of play. While attempting to run from a scrum Corner was overwhelmed by the British forwards and was penalised for holding the ball. Black took the kick about 40 yards in front of the goal and the British captain, Mr F.D. Prentice, who was acting as a line umpire, raised his flag. However the other line umpire, Mr G. Nicholson,

The British backs secure the ball from a line-out.

signalled no goal and was upheld by the referee. It was stated later that Mr Prentice had raised his flag only to signal that the ball had passed inside the goal post which he was watching. Mr Nicholson said the ball went outside the other post.

A long line kick by Lucas followed by a short burst on the blind-side of a scrum, placed New Zealand in an attacking position but a typical run by Spong turned the tables very effectively, allowing Bowcott and Aarvold to make determined assaults on the New Zealand line. The forwards packed around quickly and Hart secured to beat Reeve. Nicholls, following up fast with an eye for a great opening, was ruled offside but Parker failed with the kick.

New Zealand takes the lead

Cooke took the ball as it dropped and cut past three British forwards before gaining 60 yards with a powerful punt to touch. The line-out play of the New Zealand forwards had improved. They were dropping the ball and packing instead of attempting to knock it back to Corner, and the British forwards were not able to break through so often and fluster the halfback. Gaining the ball from one line-out, Nicholls kicked accurately for a gap and in a magnificent loose rush the forwards swamped Bassett, McLean scoring a good try. Strang failed at goal.

New Zealand 8

Great Britain 5

The British backs now made every effort to regain the lead and with the crowd cheering impartially they swung the ball from one side of the field to the other. Resolute tackling was New Zealand's reply although once Aarvold made a dangerous burst, only to lose touch with his supports. New Zealand was now penalised in its own twenty-five, but the forwards were doing their share on defence, struggling hard against the heavier opposition.

After a great forward tussle New Zealand won the ball and Nicholls and Hart cleared. Porter then robbed Spong of the ball after Britain had secured in mid-field and the New Zealand forwards fanned out again. The movement broke down when McWilliams' pass was blocked.

Nicholls' potted goal

Once more New Zealand heeled quickly and the ball came out to Nicholls. He ran as if to work Cooke and Lucas into position, but then sold a perfect dummy cut infield for a few yards and steadied himself before sending the ball sailing between the posts with a great drop kick. It was another brilliant movement and fully deserved the thunderous applause with which it was greeted.

New Zealand 12

Great Britain 5

The British forwards made Herculean efforts to break through and Beamish broke away from a scrum only to be tackled by Strang. Spong then took a pass well above his head from Poole and Aarvold came through behind Bowcott to take a scissor pass. The mercurial Porter was backing up, however, and intercepted Aarvold's pass. Back came Morley in a brilliant sideline run. He pushed past Nepia and dodged the fullback's delayed tackle, but Cooke had anticipated the movement and kicked to touch. Spong had to receive attention to his injured thumb but was able to resume.

Nepia and Corner held up a strong British forward rush only a matter of feet off the line, and Batty, who was playing a magnificent game at the head of the New Zealand pack, took the ball to midfield in a solid rush, defying the efforts of three British forwards to hold him back. Poole then had to receive attention for a minor injury.

A little diversion was caused when one ball was kicked high up on the terrace. As Lucas threw the other ball in for a line-out, the first was returned to the field, and with Corner holding on to the ball which was in play, Parker made a great breakaway with the other.

McLean's second try

New Zealand now held the upper hand with Porter transferring his attentions from Poole to Spong, the British backs made little headway. At the break-down of one back rush, Lucas kicked through to find the line. Corner secured and dashed round the blind-side to send the forwards away. In a solid body they forced their way through the defence and over the line, the try being awarded to McLean. Nicholls failed with the kick.

New Zealand 15

Great Britain 5

New Zealand was now marking Spong at all costs, and even when he beat Porter he was generally surrounded by forwards before he had time to go far. On one occasion he carried Porter on his back for several yards before he was downed. Aarvold then made an attempt to cut through but Cooke's tackling was deadly. The British pack was playing a great game and it was not its fault that the backs lacked the power to penetrate. Time and again it seemed that Britain must break through but the New Zealand pack succeeded in opening up the play, a forward pass robbing McWilliams of a try.

Britain's final effort

Britain now pinned its faith in its two wingers for the final onslaught. The ball was flung out to Morley, and he sprinted down the line with the crowd cheering madly, Cooke and Nepia forcing him into touch. Twice the British backs tried to use the short punt, but on both occasions Corner came across to kick clear before the forwards could get the ball.

Loose play in midfield, and Spong broke away to kick for the centre when he was blocked. Cooke was badly obstructed when he was running for the ball, but the breach was not noticed and Ivor Jones picked up to give Aarvold a perfect pass. The British captain ran through to score between the posts. Black converted.

As a last resort the British pack tried to break through in solid formation, Lucas stopping one rush by bringing Beamish down heavily and Corner another with a neat mark. He kicked to touch and the game ended with the score:—

New Zealand 15

Great Britain 10

ENTHUSIAST'S LONG VIGIL

Waiting at Gates All Night

By Telegraph — Press Association

WELLINGTON, FRIDAY

At least one man is determined that he will not miss the Rugby test match tomorrow for before 10 o'clock this evening he sat down on a box outside the gates at Athletic Park and commenced a vigil of 16 ½ hours.

The weather remains fine, as it has been for the last two days.

11 August 1930

ALL BLACK'S VICTORY FINAL RUGBY TEST

Britain Outplayed
Twenty-two to Eight
Fast, Exciting Game
Bright Play By Backs

By Telegraph — Press Association

WELLINGTON, SATURDAY

Before a crowd of over 40,000 people New Zealand had a decisive victory in the fourth and last Rugby test against Britain this afternoon, the score being 22 points to 8. The game was an exhilarating one from start to finish, with the New Zealand team attacking for two-thirds of the time. It was remarkable for the number of times the home forwards secured the ball, thus allowing Conner to set his backs going frequently. With the exception of brief spells in the first half and the opening 10 minutes of the second half the British forwards were defending, although it was not until fairly late in the game that the New Zealanders could be said to have the game well in hand.

Porter scored twice for New Zealand, Cooke twice, and Batty and Strang once each. Strang converted two tries. For Britain Novis scored a magnificent try after cutting in and leaving the defence completely beaten. Parker kicked a penalty goal and Black converted the try by Novis. There was no doubt as to which was the better team on the day.

The teams were:—

BRITAIN

Fullback: J.A. Bassett (Wales).

Threequarters: A.L. Novis (England), D. Aarvold (England), H.M. Bowcott (Wales), J.S.R. Reeve (England).

Fly Half: R.S. Spong (England).

Scrum half: P.F. Murray (Ireland).

Forwards. H. Rew (England), D. Parker (Wales), H.O'H. O'Neill (Ireland), B.M. Black (England),

J.I. Farrell (Ireland), Ivor Jones (Wales), G.R. Beamish (Ireland), W.B. Welsh (Scotland).

NEW ZEALAND

Fullback: G. Nepia (East Coast).

Threequarters: F.W. Lucas (Auckland), A.E. Cooke (Wellington), G. Hart (Canterbury).

Five-eights: H. Lilburne (Canterbury), W.A. Strang (South Canterbury).

Halfback: M. Corner (Auckland).

Wing-forward: C.G. Porter (Wellington).

Forwards: A.L. Cottrell (Canterbury), J. Hore (Otago), E.R.G. Steere (Hawke's Bay), R.G. McWilliams (Auckland), W. Hazlett (Southland), W. Batty (Auckland), H.F. McLean (Wellington).

Mr F.E. Sutherland, of Auckland, referee.

Britain Starts Well

Britain won the toss and there was a thrill from the start when Porter kicked off and caught the ball on the rebound from one of the British forwards, whose comrades, however, packed around and a line-out was formed on the halfway line. Britain hooked the ball, and after Murray, Spong, Bowcott and Aarvold had handled it, Reeve found the line in New Zealand's twenty-five where both forwards and backs combined in returning play to halfway, Lilburne and McWilliams being prominent.

From the first set scrum Britain hooked the ball neatly and when Spong received it from Murray he got in one of his characteristic runs, but was held up and McLean and Cottrell were to the fore in heading a dribbling rush that took play back to halfway. McLean and McWilliams got the ball from the line-out, but a penalty for offside play let Britain clear, Nepia allowing the ball to go over the line, thus giving his side a drop off from the twenty-five. Farrell got offside when the forwards were scrummaging in neutral territory and Nepia found the line.

New Zealand's First Try

From the scrummage Corner sold the 'dummy' and, although he was smothered by the British forwards, he managed to send the ball on to McWilliams, who forged ahead for a few yards and passed to Porter. He later hurled himself across the line. Nepia took the kick but missed.

His Excellency, the Governor General, Lord Bledisloe shaking hands with players before the match.

Within three minutes Britain had equalised. Murray and Spong combined well in an exchange of passes until Cooke intercepted. Following a scrum New Zealand was penalised and Parker kicked a splendid goal from five yards inside the halfway line.

New Zealand   3

Britain   3

When Murray got offside Nepia found the line well down and from a scrum Corner was given the ball. It was passed out along the line to Cooke, who clapped on the pace and passed to Hart, but the latter was pushed out by Reeve. Again getting the ball Corner worked the blind-side and passed to Hart and McWilliams. There was a forward struggle only a few yards away from the British line until an infringement allowed Britain to clear.

Good Score By Strang

A passing bout by the New Zealand backs looked dangerous, but it broke down and Aarvold forced. A rush by the British forwards gained 50 yards before Nepia stopped it. From a scrum in New Zealand's twenty-five Murray sent the ball out along the line to Novis, but the latter's pass in was well intercepted by Nepia who brought off a great save. Spong was again prominent in evading Strang and

Corner, but Porter headed a counter rush. Cooke was clean away with Hart in support when he was called back for infringement.

Ivor Jones broke away supported by several forwards, but Porter and Lucas stopped the movement. Corner at length set his backs going. Lilburne cut in and sent a pass back to Strang who went over the line for a great try. He failed to convert. Corner worked the blind side of the scrum to advantage on several occasions and New

Waiting for the ball to drop after a short kick by Murray (seen kneeling).

Zealand steadily gained ground until in a scrum not far from Britain's line McLean was penalised. For the remainder of the spell Britain was defending and half-time came with the scores:—

New Zealand   6
Britain   3

Murray put the ball in action in the second half and the British forwards, following up quickly, gained a good deal of ground until Corner took a neat mark and found the line. Britain secured the ball from a scrum and the ball went out along the line to Reeve who was held up, and Aarvold, who was in support, was smothered by Cooke. Murray went through the pack in a solo effort but lost possession. A hot British attack ended when Murray was penalised and Nepia found the line well up.

Lilburne, Cooke and Lucas were associated in a passing rush which ended well in British territory. A scrum was formed and the ball again came along the line to Cooke, who sent out a long pass to Hart, cutting out Lilburne. Hart was collared but in the scrummaging that followed the ball was kicked over Britain's line and Cooke showed a great turn of speed to win the race for possession and score well out amid wild enthusiasm. Strang's kick failed.

New Zealand   9
Britain   3

The game went with even greater pace after the kick-off. From a line-out after a great kick by Bassett, a British forward kicked high and Nepia was tackled by Rew, who had followed up quickly. Both Nepia and Rew were hurt and the game was stopped for some minutes. From a scrum the ball was sent along the line to Novis, who had come in to centre, Aarvold having taken the wing position. Novis cut in beautifully and left the defence completely beaten. He ran 40 yards for a splendid try and scored between the posts. Black converted.

New Zealand   9
Britain   8

Three minutes later New Zealand scored again. From a line-out Corner secured the ball and sent out a beautiful pass to Lucas just as the British forwards were breaking through. Lucas performed a feat similar to that by Nicholls in the third test, and cross kicked. Unfortunately for Britain Bassett fumbled the ball and before the backs in support could retrieve the mistake Cooke had come up, kicked across the line, followed up and scored. Strang converted.

New Zealand   14
Britain   8

Playing safe in the face of a hot forward attack. Porter (left) has just kicked into touch.

Mishaps to Spong

Play was held up for a few minutes when Spong hurt his thumb. The next excitement was when Corner brought off a wonderful save after Beamish, Rew, Farrell and Welsh had broken through to New Zealand's twenty-five. Spong was hurt again and took some time to recover from the effects of a kick on the thigh. Murray evaded Porter and Corner in coming round a scrum and punted over Nepia's head. Lucas took the ball on the bounce but was smothered in goal as he forced.

The British forwards were playing much better at this stage. Aarvold was given the ball on the blind-side and cross-kicked, but New Zealand just managed to force in time. Strang, Lilburne, Cooke and Lucas were seen in a bright passing bout until Lucas was pushed out. From the line-out Cooke had a shot at goal but missed. Porter scored a wonderful try when he secured the ball about 10 yards out, dodged through to the line and threw himself over with two defenders hanging on him. Strang converted.

New Zealand   19

Britain   8

Britain won applause when Ivor Jones scored the ball from the scrum and Spong, Reeve and Novis set off at top speed with the ball. In a flash they took play to the New Zealand line where a heap of New Zealand and British players went over the line together. A scrum was ordered and Porter and Corner cleared to the twenty-five. Seven minutes before time was called Lucas hurt his knee, and although he carried on he was limping badly. He changed places with Hart, but was immediately faced with the task of bringing down Reeve after the British threequarter line had handled the ball.

Batty Scores Last Try

A trick kick from a penalty after Porter had got off-side failed to produce results, Porter smothering the movement at its start. Corner and Cooke followed up a short punt and caught Bassett in possession. A line-out was formed and McWilliams, Batty and Lucas, and again Batty, handled the ball in quick succession, Batty going over for a try which Strang did not convert.

New Zealand   22

Britain   8

A series of line-outs saw New Zealand gain ground. McLean went over the line with British players on top of him. A scrum was ordered and time was called with New Zealand still hammering

on the line.

The crowd stormed the field when the players were walking off and several of them were 'chaired'. There was wild cheering long after the teams had reached their dressing rooms and the scene was one of the most enthusiastic ever witnessed at Athletic Park. Guided by wireless megaphones the crowd was dispersed slowly, but in an orderly way, and for more than an hour afterwards was streaming down various roads leading from the park.

BRITISH STYLE OF PLAY

Lessons From All Blacks
Change Since 1924 tour

By Telegraph — Athletic Reporter

WELLINGTON, SUNDAY

It was very apparent from the type of play adopted by the present British team that players in Britain had profited by the experiences gained from the visit of the All Blacks in Great Britain in 1924, said Mr S.S. Dean, chairman of the management committee of the New Zealand Rugby Union. The present combination played a type of football very different from that which was encountered by the 1924 team. During that tour the great strength of nearly every team the All Blacks played against lay in the forwards, whom they found hard and tight scrummagers and particularly good in the art of dribbling.

The present British team had developed an open style of play similar to that of New Zealand teams.

C.G. PORTER RETIRES

Noted All Black Captain
Last Game for New Zealand
'Happy End to My Career'

By Telegraph — Own Correspondent.

WELLINGTON, SUNDAY

The noted Rugby player C.G. Porter, captain of the All Blacks in the four test matches against Britain, has announced his retirement from representative football.

Speaking at the official dinner to the British team after the final test match yesterday, Porter said: 'This was my last game for New Zealand. I have had a long career in Rugby football, and this is a very happy end to my playing days.'

Porter has been an outstanding figure in New Zealand Rugby for many years. He is a brilliant wing-forward and a great general. He played a great game against Britain yesterday and scored two tries. He was captain of the victorious All Black team which toured Britain in 1924 and was recognised as one of the outstanding players of the tour. His generalship was the deciding factor in winning many matches. Since then he has led the New Zealand team on numerous occasions. Porter is now 30 years of age.

The desolate, littered terraces at Eden Park the day after the fourth test.

1950

27 May – Dunedin
10 June – Christchurch
1 July – Wellington
29 July – Auckland

26 April 1950

ITINERARY OF BRITISH ISLES TEAM

(O.C.)

ROTORUA, TUESDAY

A complaint that the New Zealand Rugby Union was 'after the big dollar' in arranging matches for the British Isles Rugby team in the main centres in preference to the country was made today by the secretary of the Rotorua Rugby Union, Mr C. Andrews. The tourists, he said, were to play three games in Wellington, but not one match had been arranged for the Rotorua or Bay of Plenty districts in spite of the fact that these contained about 60 per cent of the Maori Rugby players in the Dominion.

The decision to play the British Isles–New Zealand Maori match at Wellington was also criticised by Mr Andrews. It had been brought about, he said, because Bay of Plenty objected to the proposal to play it in Hamilton. As a result, the itinerary had been altered; but there was a feeling in the Rotorua district that the Maori advisory board of the New Zealand union had not made sufficiently strenuous endeavours to secure the match for a suitable centre of Maori Rugby activity.

Mr Andrews said that one other matter connected with the tour of the British team deserved ventilation. This was the proposal of the Auckland union to take upon itself the entertainment of the British team in Rotorua without reference either the Rotorua or Bay of Plenty Rugby authorities. 'I personally object most strongly to this' Mr Andrews said. 'I feel certain that the Maori people in Rotorua would be proud and happy to entertain the visitors in the friendly fashion with which they have entertained numerous sporting teams in the past.'

---

29 April 1950

TOUR WILL COST £47,000

British Rugby Team

(P.A.)

WELLINGTON, FRIDAY

The total cost of the British Rugby team's tour would be £47,000, or £13,000 more than the highest cost of any previous tour of this country. That was the reason for the increased admission charges. This advice was given by Mr A.St.C. Belcher, chairman of the council, when a remit from Manawatu asking for these reasons came before the annual meeting of delegates to the New Zealand Rugby Union today.

Costs had soared tremendously, said Mr Belcher, but the policy of the union was still to fix what was considered a fair ground charge for the average man. For the 1904 and 1908 British teams' tours the ground charge for ordinary games was 1s, for tests 2s, with stands at 4s and 5s. For the 1921 Springbok tour the prices were raised to 2s ground admission for ordinary games and 2s 6d for tests, stand charges varying from 7s 6d to 10s. In 1930 and 1937 ground charges for ordinary games were 2s 6d, and stands 10s. For tests the ground charges were 2s 6d and stands £1.

For the coming British team's tour, the stand charges for tests would be the same as in 1930 and 1937, but ground charges had been increased. These increases were considered justified in view of the tremendous advance in costs.

Mr Belcher listed the following tour costs:— 1930 British team: Steamer fares, £5325; cost in New Zealand, £28,948; total, £34,273. 1937 South African team: Steamer fares, £3991; cost in New Zealand, £19,600; total, £23,591. 1950 British team: Steamer fares, £12,000; cost in New Zealand, £35,000; total, £47,000. The increased charges were approved by the delegates. Another remit from Manawatu, that consideration be given to some permanent means of assisting unions which were financially handicapped through population or geographical circumstances, was replaced by an Auckland motion that the new council consider the overall financial position of backward unions.

---

2 May 1950

BRITISH TEAM ARRIVING THIS MORNING

From Our Staff Correspondent

WELLINGTON, MONDAY

Officials of the New Zealand Rugby Union had a busy time today completing the arrangements for the tour of the British Isles Rugby team, which is due to arrive in the *Ceramic* from Liverpool at 8.30a.m. tomorrow. There is great interest in Wellington in the arrival of the team.

It will be given an extremely warm welcome, but the official receptions at the start will be reduced to a minimum. The president of the New Zealand Union, Mr J.A. Finlayson, of Northland, and the chairman of the council of the union, Mr A.St.C. Belcher, will offer a formal welcome on the ship before berthing, and in the evening the members of the team will be the guests at a cocktail party to be given by the New Zealand Union.

Official photographs of the party will be taken in the afternoon. One group was taken at Twickenham before the team's departure from London, but for tomorrow's picture the team will probably be in the uniform of red jerseys and white shorts.

The Prime Minister, Mr Holland, will tender a State reception to the party on Wednesday morning, and the Mayor of Wellington, Mr W. Appleton, will give a civic welcome at midday. The visitors will then be free until their departure for Nelson on Wednesday evening.

For the first few days the New Zealand Rugby Union will be represented with the team by the immediate past-president, Mr D.S. Max, of Nelson, but on Friday the senior vice-president, Mr R.W.S. Botting, father of the All Black, will officially take over, and he will remain with the party until May 27.

Further appointments have not yet been made, but Mr L.V. Carmine, of the King Country, a member of the executive, and Mr W.A. Craddock, of Buller, a member of the council, are both available.

The most experienced man with the party will be the baggage man, 'Taff' Davies, of Auckland, who held this position with the 1930 British and 1937 South African teams. He has also been baggageman and masseur for League and soccer teams visiting New Zealand. Forty years ago Davies won a competition promoted by an American magazine as 'the world's most perfect specimen of manhood under 10st.' Today, at 60, he can still chin the bar and do handstands with the facility of a trained gymnast of half his years.

The masseur of the team is R. McQueen, of Dunedin, who has had this appointment with Otago Ranfurly Shield teams, and who toured New Zealand with the 1946 Australian team.

A representative of the Railway Department will travel throughout the Dominion with the team. Another member of the party will be a newspaper representative, Mr D.R. Gent, who played against the 1905 All Blacks for England.

---

29 May 1950

ALL BLACKS FORTUNATE TO AVERT DEFEAT

Draw With British Isles, 9 All, in First Rugby Test

From Our Staff Correspondent.

DUNEDIN, SUNDAY

New Zealand was fortunate to draw with British Isles at Carisbrook yesterday in the first international Rugby match of the season. Each side scored two tries and a penalty goal, nine points. British Isles led by nine points to three with 19 minutes of play remaining and New Zealand equalled the score seven minutes before the end.

The Lions team before the first test. From left: Back row: Evans, John, Preece, MacDonald, Cleaver, Jones, Kininmonth, Hayward. Front row: Clifford, McKay, Matthews, Black, Mullen, Kyle, Robins.

The crowd of about 35,000 became most excited and there were roars of cheering toward the finish. The performance of the British Isles team made the success of its tour appear certain.

The weather was perfect for Rugby — warm and dull, with a light breeze — when the game began. After a storm of cheering had marked their appearance on the ground, the teams were introduced to the Governor-General, Sir Bernard Freyberg, V.C.

British Isles won the toss and secured the first real advantage when Kyle put a long kick into touch. British Isles won the first scrum, but the All Blacks then won several in a row, until Hughes was penalised for not binding and from 35yds Robins kicked a penalty goal. There were triumphant chants of 'Red! Red!' from the crowd.

British Isles   3
All Blacks   0

Matthews tackled Elvidge very heavily in a rush into British Isles territory. Preece snapped up the ball and in a moment was clear, running toward the corner, with McKay and MacDonald moving up in support. As Preece moved into Scott's tackle he threw the ball high over McKay's head toward MacDonald, but the latter could not make the catch and a most promising movement broke down.

British Isles was awarded another penalty and

The Governor General, Sir Bernard Freyberg, meets K.D. Mullen, the British Isles captain.

Robins tried a shot from the ten-yard line without success. Johnstone burst through before kicking, and British Isles was in a serious plight until Kyle speculated the ball into touch. Preece changed the complexion of things when he snapped up an All Black pass and passed to Matthews, who dashed downfield, trying to work Jones into position. Finally, he elected to kick, and the movement ended 5yds from New Zealand's goal.

Robins tried another penalty shot from about 48yds, and the kick nearly succeeded. A minute later Robins aroused laugher by trying a kick at goal from inside his own half, about 63yds from the post. The kick was straight, but short.

Black figured prominently in two breaks from the scrum, and White was prominent in a burst from a line-out. Robins attempted another penalty goal from 35yds, and missed by only a yard.

For the first time in the match, Cherrington was sent away along the touchline. A good tackle by Cleaver stopped him. Several All Black rushes were stopped by severe tackling, Roper being brought down heavily on one occasion. Robins missed another attempt at a penalty goal from 46yds, and two minutes later, just on half-time, John nearly goaled from a mark.

The half-time score was:—

British Isles   3
All Blacks   0

Robins kicked down to goal-line to start the second half, and Scott promptly left-footed the ball into touch on the halfway mark. The All Black backs were showing some liveliness, but Elvidge's hands were uncertain. Scott came up into a passing rush, but his pass to Roper was not taken.

The All Black forwards were showing improvement, and they gave Bevan a quick heel, from which he gathered and started to run wide across on the open side. In an attempt to beat the British Isles defence, he gave the ball a tap with his foot. It bounced head high and Kyle had it. In a flash he was through the All Blacks, and racing for the line 25yds away. He swerved past Scott, and a shoulder-high tackle by Cherrington stopped him for only an instant before he was over the line. The crowd greeted the effort with great applause. Robins missed the goal.

British Isles   6
All Blacks   0

Roper made a strong dash, which crowded Meates out, but Evans tackled him well. A short punt by Beatty went to Cleaver, who kicked clear while held by a couple of All Blacks. Preece's dash up to a high centering kick misjudged the flight and accidentally headed the ball downfield toward Scott.

Kininmonth, Robins and Hayward broke away in a dribbling rush which looked extremely dangerous and then Roper began another of his fast runs. Beating Preece, he kicked into mid-field. Cleaver again was there with his expert hands, but a short time later Beatty received a pass from Bevan about the twenty-five. With the pace on he passed to Roper, who beat four men and scored a few yards from the corner. Scott missed the goal.

British Isles   6
All Blacks   3

The All Black forwards were now showing real zest, especially in the line-outs, but British Isles was fighting doggedly. In driving at Scott as the latter punted for touch, Evans was hurt in the face by a sprig and went off the field for a short time for attention.

The respite freshened Kyle. As Black gave him a long pass he jigged past Beatty and kicked long and low toward the corner. Jones pursued the rolling ball and was right upon Scott when the latter lost possession. Jones picked up and dived across for a try. Clifford's kick at goal swerved a yard outside the posts.

British Isles   9
All Blacks   3

There were cries of 'Send him back to the North Island' when Scott missed a dropkick at goal, but a moment later the fullback was a hero again. From 35yds he kicked a fine penalty goal.

British Isles   9
All Blacks   6

With a quarter of an hour left for play the excitement was great. Scott took a long time to make his mark for a kick at goal from 46yds and there were cries of disappointment when he missed.

With seven minutes left Scott came up into a rush and kicked high toward the British Isles goal. Clifford and John were both there to halt the rush

All Black captain, R.R. Elvidge scoring a try to tie the game, 9–9.

and a scrum was ordered not more than ten yards from the post. The All Blacks heeled and Bevan fed Elvidge on the blind side. Away went the All Black captain on an irresistible dash for the corner past at least three defenders. It was a great try. Scott missed the goal.

    British Isles   9
    All Blacks   9

Elvidge and Beatty figured in fierce assaults on the British Isles line, but Black, with a fine run on the blind-side, started a British Isles rally. Just at the end of the game Black made another run of about 30yds and Kyle jigged through. Then Roper made a run and John kicked into touch after a mark to end a most exciting game.

    British Isles   9
    All Blacks   9

Mr E.W. Tindall, of Wellington, gave a good exhibition as referee.

30 May 1950

BRITISH ISLES MAY ADOPT SPRINGBOK FORMATION

From Our Staff Correspondent

DUNEDIN, MONDAY

The British Isles Rugby team is almost certain to use the South African scrummage formation in the second test match with New Zealand at Christchurch on June 10. Since the drawn first test at Carisbrook on Saturday there has been considerable discussion in the touring party on the importance of securing the ball and in spite of the freely expressed dislike of the members of the party for the Springbok formation it is admitted that this is the only possible answer to the All Blacks' use of the style.

The British Isles players trained at the Otago Boys' High School ground today and, to the great delight of the schoolboys, apparently secured the promise of a half-holiday in celebration of the visit. It was the team's second appearance at a secondary school, the first having been made at Nelson College on May 5 on the day of the break-up for the term holidays.

The Otago High School boys greeted the team with several songs, two of which, 'Land of Hope and Glory' and 'Ye Mariners of England,' were particularly appreciated by the manager, Surgeon-Captain L.B. Osborne, R.N. Both Captain Osborne and the captain of the team, K.D. Mullen, made a plea for a half-holiday. Afterward, the boys appreciatively watched the British Isles players in training.

The Scottish wing-threequarter, D.W.C. Smith, this morning had his right arm re-encased in plaster because of a fracture suffered in a match several weeks before the departure of the team from Britain. The break had not been mending well. Smith's first appearance on the tour, accordingly, has been set back for several weeks. He is likely to have the arm in plaster for from three to four weeks. It had been expected that he would be available to play toward the end of June.

The team will leave for Timaru by rail tomorrow morning. After playing South Canterbury on Wednesday it will go to Christchurch and during a stay of about ten days will play Canterbury at Lancaster Park on Saturday and a combined Ashburton-North Otago side at Ashburton on June 6, four days before the second test match at Lancaster Park.

---

6 June 1950

V.C. WILL BE GUEST AT TEST MATCH

Honour for British Isles Team

From Our Staff Correspondent

CHRISTCHURCH, MONDAY

Captain Charles Upham, V.C. and bar, and Mrs Upham will be the guests of the British Isles

Rugby team at the second test match with New Zealand at Lancaster Park on Saturday. They will also lunch with the manager of the team, Surgeon-Captain L.B. Osborne, R.N., on Friday. 'We will feel greatly honoured to have Captain Upham with us,' said the manager.

Since his discharge from the Army Captain Upham has worked hard on his sheep farm at Hundalee, about 100 miles north of Christchurch. The week's holiday he is now taking is one of the first breaks he has had. The farm lies in an isolated area and until recently, when a generating plant was installed, the farmhouse lacked electric light.

Because of a kick on a knee received in the match with Canterbury on Saturday, W.B. Cleaver, fullback, is likely to stand down from the British Isles team which will meet Ashburton-North Otago at Ashburton tomorrow. His place is likely to be taken either by I.J. Preece, stand-off half, or by N.J. Henderson, a reserve centre. If Preece plays fullback G. Rimmer, a scrum half, will play at outside half.

The members of the team today had their first experience of trotting when they attended the second day of the Ashburton Trotting Club's meeting. They were delighted with the experience.

Eight members of the team, including K.D. Mullen, the captain, stayed behind in Christchurch and were guests of the Christchurch Golf Club at Shirley. After an indifferent start, Mullen did the last 12 holes in one over bogey.

The team practised for more than an hour. Smith trained particularly hard. Following the

Captain K.D. Mullen checks injured Lions, Stephens, Norton, Lane and Thomas.

application of plaster to his broken arm, it was thought he would not play in New Zealand. Since then the plaster has been removed and there is a strong possibility he will play at the end of this month, if not sooner.

12 June 1950

EXCITING INCIDENTS IN PLAY

Fast Moves Near End Of Match

From Our Staff Correspondent

CHRISTCHURCH, SUNDAY

The play in the second Rugby test match between British Isles and New Zealand at Lancaster Park was made memorable by a remarkable series of moves. Largely because of the individual brilliance of J.W. Kyle, there was an exciting British Isles run of 60 yards up the touchline and the All Blacks were hard pressed to save what seemed certain to be a try.

The moves originated with a run down the touchline by R.A. Roper about six minutes from no-side. He cross-kicked and the All Blacks heeled from a ruck. Roper cross-kicked again and when nearly to the goal-line the All Blacks heeled and the ball went away out to the other wing. Kyle tackled two men to save a try and then backed up M.C. Thomas when the latter caught a long kick on the other side of the field. Taking Thomas' pass, Kyle ran right up to W.A. Meates and by a change of pace beat him cleanly. With only Scott ahead, just outside the New Zealand twenty-five, Kyle cross-kicked and Thomas and P.W. Kininmonth made for the ball. Thomas was brought down several yards short of the goal-line. V.D. Bevan fielded the ball very finely and the All Blacks cleared. Perhaps there has never been a more exciting two minutes in Rugby.

When play began, the sun was shining brightly and a brisk south-west breeze was blowing. The ground was heavy and slippery and the backs of both teams were handicapped.

The teams were:—

BRITISH ISLES
Fullback: W.B. Cleaver.
Threequarters: K.J. Jones, B.L. Williams, J. Matthews, M.C. Thomas.
Halfbacks: J.W. Kyle, A.W. Black.
Front Row: T.L. Clifford, K.D. Mullen, J.D. Robins.
Middle Row: J.W. McKay, D.J. Hayward, E.R. John, R.T. Evans.
Back Row: P.W. Kininmonth.

NEW ZEALAND
Fullback: R.W.H. Scott.
Threequarters: P. Henderson, R.A. Roper, W.A. Meates.
Five-eighths: R.R. Elvidge, L.S. Haig.
Halfback: V.D. Bevan.
Front Row: J.G. Simpson, A.M. Hughes, K.L. Skinner.
Middle Row: P.J.B. Crowley, L.R. Harvey, R.A. White, J.R. McNab.
Back Row: P.A. Johnstone.

British Isles lost the toss and played with the wind and against the sun. Haig started a rush into the British Isles twenty-five and when Black missed a pass Crowley made a dangerous thrust. Bevan, too, missed a pass and Jones, Evans and McKay went away in a British rush of 30 yards. Scott took a penalty shot of 50 yards, but missed. Two minutes later Robins had a shot into the wind from 54 yards, but the ball fell short.

Scott tried dropkicks at goal first from one side and then the other, and Thomas slipped when he had passed Elvidge with a dummy. Scott had another penalty shot from the twenty-five yard line, but missed again. British Isles only just stopped a forward rush and a scrum on its goal-line resulted. Mullen heeled, and like a flash Crowley dived for a try. It was an excellent piece of quick thinking. Scott's attempt to convert the try was not good.

New Zealand   3
British Isles   0

Play had been in progress for 14 minutes, Henderson saved when Williams intercepted and

Prime Minister Holland shakes hands with D.J. Hayward. Next in line are J.D. Robins and T.L. Clifford.

kicked ahead. Williams then missed with a quick drop-kick at goal. Matthews slipped past Elvidge, but Haig was soon upon him. McKay was injured in colliding with a team-mate in trying to tackle Bevan and was carried off the field.

Henderson, from the blind-side wing, threw a pass to Haig, who saw a gap and clapped on the pace. He handed on to Elvidge, and the latter made a good pass to Roper, the winger scoring a splendid try. Haig kicked the goal.

New Zealand   8

British Isles   0

New Zealand continued to have much the better of the play and at the end of the half a fine run by Roper seemed certain to yield a try until Kyle, with a fast dash, overhauled him and made a tackle which caused a forward pass to Meates. The score at half-time was:

New Zealand   8

British Isles   0

After two minutes of play in the second half, Roper was away, but there was a forward pass.

All Black halfback V.D. Bevan holds up a British forward thrust. Others are (l to r) Johnstone, Hayward, Mullen, Kininmonth, Hughes and Robins.

Scott missed a 45-yard kick at goal, and John, having been awarded a free charge because of Harvey's over-eagerness, tried unsuccessfully to goal from a mark.

Meates dribbled skilfully down to Cleaver and was nearly through, and a moment or two later Cleaver saved another dangerous situation. Haig missed a 25-yard penalty kick, and three minutes later Scott also missed a rather easy one.

British Isles then had its best period of the match. Kyle burst through into the New Zealand twenty-five with two backs outside him, but Williams was not quite up for Matthews' pass and the latter's long delivery to Thomas was fumbled.

Meates and Johnstone nearly scored, and a promising situation ended when Roper fumbled. Seven minutes from no-side, Kininmonth cut out the All Black backs and ran for 30 yards. Supports were not handy and his kick ahead when challenged by Scott was not accurate.

The All Blacks came again, and Crowley and McNab both made attempts to score in the last three minutes. The game ended:

New Zealand   8
British Isles   0

Mr E.W. Tindall, of Wellington, did not referee with quite the same outstanding skill as he showed in the first test, but it was not an easy match to control. He awarded 19 penalties against New Zealand and seven against British Isles.

producing more of the spectacular touches which mark its play.

At one stage, especially after the defeats by Otago and Southland, there seemed a strong possibility that the British Isles team's tour would not be quite as successful as had been hoped. Subsequent displays, particularly those of the first test and the matches in the North Island, have removed this impression.

The reception of the team in Wellington has been remarkable. As an instance, I. Preece, who works for a gas corporation in Coventry, telephoned the Wellington Gas Company with a request that he might make an inspection of the company's plant. When he went this morning he was met by the board of directors, entertained at morning tea, and provided with every facility. Nor has Preece's experience been unusual.

Interest will increase from tomorrow with the assembly of the All Blacks, who will hold their first run in the afternoon. All the New Zealand players are understood to be fit and well, but the chairman of the selection committee, Mr T.C. Morrison, was in bed today with influenza. K.D. Mullen, captain of the British Isles team, is resting the thigh muscle which was torn in training yesterday. A decision on whether or not he will play will be made tomorrow.

J.W. McKay, the Irish wing-forward, who has been recuperating in Gisborne from the concussion he received in the second test, rejoined the British Isles party tonight, and will train tomorrow. A guest of the British Isles team at the test match will be Mr J.H. Phillipps, manager of New Zealand's successful cricket team in Britain last year.

28 June 1950

COMING RUGBY TEST

Interest in Wellington

From Our Staff Correspondent

WELLINGTON, TUESDAY

The topic of the hour in Wellington is the third Rugby test match between British Isles and the All Blacks at Athletic Park on Saturday. Many shops are carrying specially decorated windows.

The natural appeal of a test has been heightened, so far as Wellington people are concerned, by the exciting game between the tourists and Wellington last Saturday. This has been described on all sides as the finest game seen in Wellington for several years, and there is accordingly a general desire to see the British Isles

3 July 1950

POWER DEMAND DURING RUGBY TEST

There was a marked increase in power consumption between 2 and 4 p.m. on Saturday when the first Rugby test was broadcast from Athletic Park, Wellington. An official at the Penrose sub-station said last night that the increase during the two hours was about 10 per cent.

3 July 1950

ALL BLACKS AGAIN BEAT BRITISH ISLES

Six Forwards Battle Against Eight For 6–3 Victory

From Our Staff Correspondent

WELLINGTON, SUNDAY

The Rugby virtues of determination and courage in adversity were much in evidence when the All Blacks yesterday defeated British Isles by 6 points to 3 in the third of the four test matches of the season. The All Blacks lost their vice-captain, J.G. Simpson, because of an injury, after 20 minutes' play. Seven minutes before half-time their captain, R.R. Elvidge, was knocked out in a tackle, and four stitches were required for a cut above his right eye. He returned after

J.G. Simpson and G. Rimmer receive attention for injuries early in the first half.

Rugged up against the elements, three young ladies enjoy lunch before the rugby.

half-time, scored the only try of the match three minutes later, and gallantly remained on the field for the rest of the game. A crowd of about 45,000 was held in tense excitement from start to finish.

G. Rimmer, the British Isles scrum-half, was injured at the same time as Simpson, but played on. After the game he was sent to hospital, a broken arm being suspected, but the injury was found to be not quite so serious. Rimmer will be out of action for about ten days.

There were many technical failings in the play. The touch-finding was deplorable, the British Isles players appealed against decisions for offside when clearly the mistakes were theirs, and the All Black backs on attack were unimaginative and slow. Yet those failings seemed unimportant in a match which provided the stirring spectacle of six All Black forwards battling against eight, and a team of 13 physically effective players gaining the mastery of 15.

Crowd Cheers Elvidge

When Elvidge scored New Zealand's try the entire crowd in Athletic Park rose to cheer so noble an effort, and all through the game, as the play swung backward and forward, the roars of cheering were a just tribute to a magnificent battle.

New Zealand's victory could be ascribed almost entirely to its forwards. For some time British Isles had the initiative and the All Black pack was only just beginning to show its strength when Simpson was injured in a tackle. J.R. McNab

Sixteen minutes to go and the score is 3–3 at Athletic Park.

went from the side row to take Simpson's place and, with seven forwards against eight, New Zealand addressed itself more fiercely to the task.

When Elvidge retired, P.A. Johnstone went from the side of the scrum to the left wing, and he stayed efficiently there, even when Elvidge returned. The All Black pack thus was reduced to six men, packing 3–3, with P.J.B. Crowley usually on the open flank.

Fierce Play of Pack

From the moment Elvidge left the field there was in the All Black pack a fierceness and sting that was extraordinarily impressive to watch. Crowley played magnificently, quite above anyone else in the game, but obviously there were no failures to a six-man pack which, even in set scrummages, could gain the better of eight.

L.R. Harvey was scarcely less efficient than Crowley, and in the line-outs his play was powerful and effective. A.M. Hughes outhooked D.M. Davies by 20 to 11, and McNab, K.L. Skinner and R.A. White were worthy parts of the machine. The particular feature of the play of the pack was the forward drive from ruck and scrum through, round and over the British Isles defence. Crowley was wonderfully dashing in these moves, and he and McNab and the rest a great many times battered and crashed upfield.

Backs Lacked Combination

The All Black backline did not have quite the

inspiration of the pack and even before Elvidge's retirement and return to a 'seven-eighths' position between Scott and the backline proper there was a want of both penetration and combination. L.S. Haig at first five-eighths sought anxiously to help his forwards by kicking for touch. He failed to appreciate the possibilities of straightforward back attacks, especially in the second half, when Scott was constantly moving in to the rushes.

V.D. Bevan played splendidly behind the All Black pack, and W.A. Meates and R.A. Roper were particularly good with some severe tackling. For much of the game they played at centre and second five-eighths respectively. Elvidge, before his injury, was tackled too often in possession, but his courage afterward was like a shining light in the dull grey atmosphere.

P. Henderson, although once beaten by M.C. Thomas, made a fine impression with his energetic following up and his zeal. Scott had a singularly unhappy time with his line-kicking, which as often as not was deplorable. However, his wizardry in cool and clever defence was often displayed.

Mullen's Leadership Missed

Not without cause, the British Isles players were disappointed with their performance. They recognised the obvious fact that they ought to have won, and they were somewhat downcast, while paying the warmest of tributes to the All Blacks, that they should have lost the rubber with the odds so much in their favour.

Basically, the cause was in the forwards. The line-outs were won by 49 to 38 and the rucks were not won automatically by the All Blacks, as they had been in the second test. Nevertheless, the British Isles pack lacked the vigour, purpose and drive of the All Blacks, the following was not as fast and determined and the forwards did not smash ahead with anything like the controlled recklessness of their opponents. It seemed clear that K.D. Mullen's shrewdness in leadership was sadly missed.

Davies won much of the ball in the first half, but as the leader of the pack he was not equal to Mullen.

L.R. Harvey receives attention to an injured ankle at half-time in the third test in Wellington.

E.R. John again made splendid leaps in the line-out, although he too often used a one-handed knockback, and D.J. Hayward and T.L. Clifford were as tough in the tight stuff as R.T. Evans was vigorous in the loose. The efforts, however, were insufficiently concerted and in the last quarter of an hour, when the weakened All Black team should have been run off its feet, it was British Isles which defended.

Errors in Tactics

British Isles was also handicapped by some astonishing errors in tactics. Until almost the end of the game the line-outs were invariably short, thus playing into the hands of the reduced All Black pack.

Kyle was as graceful and elusive and dexterous as the crowd had hoped, and Rimmer, in spite of his injury, sent out many good passes, ran with pace and defended stoutly. The outer backline did not quite come up to expectations. Partly this was because of the very heavy state of the ground and partly because the injury to K.J. Jones deprived the team of a flying wing who might have capitalised some breaks in midfield. One of these was beautifully made by B.L. Williams, but McKay could not get up in support, and the pass back went to the ground.

Williams kicked rather too often in the second half and J. Matthews was so affected by the bump

8 July 1950

ALL-NIGHT WAIT FOR SEATS

Rugby Test Booking

Some 50 Rugby enthusiasts, many of whom had been there since the morning, had settled down at 10 o'clock last night outside the booking agent's building to await this morning's opening of the plan for the British Isles–All Black test match.

A miscellaneous collection of chairs and mattresses stretched in a single line which reached halfway up Swanson Street. The first of these began to appear at about 9 o'clock yesterday morning. In the forefront of the queue was a man who said that he had 'staked his claim' at about 8.30.

When fairly heavy rain fell during the morning and early afternoon bivouacs, hastily improvised from ground-sheets, blankets and umbrellas, were created close to the building.

Most of the people in the queue had made provision for passing away the hours of waiting.

Draught boards, dice, books and several card games were in evidence, and one person was absorbed in cooking a meal on a small spirit stove. An impromptu concert developed from the efforts of a man who regaled the assembly with a mouth-organ recital. Electric torches served as reading lamps for those who had taken books with them.

When asked his opinion of the all-night vigil, one man said: 'I thought I had finished with this sort of thing when I left the army, but I would gladly wait twice as long for the chance of a seat at this game.'

The first tickets will be sold at 8 o'clock this morning.

---

of heads which caused Elvidge's retirement that he suffered double vision. Thomas received few chances and N.J. Henderson, the substitute for Jones, was somewhat lacking in confidence. He and Williams might have had a try between them, but Henderson passed when Scott was still 20yds upfield, and by this slight error Williams was deprived of a good chance.

Cleaver, like Scott, miskicked a good deal, often with the good excuse that the All Black forwards gave him no peace. Although his kicking lacked Scott's length, he was safe and sure.

---

19 July 1950

WAITANGI VISIT

Outing for British Rugby Team
From Our Staff Correspondent

WHANGAREI, TUESDAY

What they described as the finest outing of their New Zealand tour was spent today by the touring British Isles Rugby team in a visit to the Bay of Islands. The trip, which was organised by the Northland Rugby Union, embraced a journey in private cars to Waitangi for golf, fishing and a visit to the national reserve.

'The finest place I have seen in New Zealand,' said the manager, Surgeon-Captain L.B. Osborne, R.N., in the visitors' book of the Waitangi Golf Club. The team captain, K.D. Mullen, in the same book remarked: 'My most enjoyable day in New Zealand.'

Speaking of the visit to the Treaty House, Captain Osborne said: 'The National Trust has done magnificent work in Britain in preserving areas of outstanding historical importance. It is gratifying to know that New Zealand has done the same with this magnificent reserve of the Treaty House and the adjacent area.'

A crowd of 10,000 is expected to attend the match at Rugby Park, Whangarei, tomorrow against North Auckland. The fine weather of the last three days has hardened the ground and, given good conditions, the game promises to be exceptionally fast. B.L. Williams and K.J. Jones of the British Isles backline, who were suffering from muscular strains, reported fit this evening, but a slight doubt

exists about J.W. McKay, who has been somewhat 'off colour' for two or three days. If the weather is fair, A.W. Black will appear at scrum half.

The North Auckland team had a training run this afternoon and both backs and forwards showed speed and good handling. The British Isles team last evening celebrated Captain Osborne's 21st wedding anniversary and sent a cablegram of congratulations to Mrs Osborne.

---

29 July 1950

KINDNESS TO BLIND CHILDREN

Teams Spare Time To Visit Institute

July 1950

SEATS FOR RUGBY TESTS

Union to Make Application

The Auckland Rugby Union decided last night to do its best to obtain 100 seats at Eden Park on July 29, the day of the Rugby test match between British Isles and New Zealand, for men of the British frigate *Veryan Bay*, which arrived at Auckland from the Mediterranean yesterday.

Keen to see the match, men of the frigate first wrote from Malta to the 'Lord Mayor,' Sir John Allum, asking him to secure 100 seats for the match. Sir John replied that it would be best to wait until the ship was nearer New Zealand waters. A second letter, addressed to the Rugby Union, was sent when the *Veryan Bay* reached Australia.

Sailors from the *Veryan Bay* attach a good luck charm to the crossbar just before the fourth test at Eden Park.

Many of the children at the New Zealand Institute for the Blind are now proud possessors of lion and silver fern badges from the lapels of British Isles and All Black Rugby players. The two teams visited the institute yesterday morning, and in an hour of speech, song and autograph-hunting, they and the children became firm friends.

All work was suspended as the children, adults and members of the staff of the institute gathered in the sunlit courtyard to greet the teams. A cheer marked their arrival, and throughout the gathering the blind people showed that they were not only keen football fans but equally avid followers of the British team's tour of New Zealand.

Singing Enjoyed

A delighted audience heard the team singing in its own inimitable way a Welsh song and the hymn 'All Hail the Power of Jesu's Name.' The blind children followed with 'The Empire is Marching,' the whole company joined in 'Now is the Hour,' and then the two teams combined in a comic song, 'Sons of the Sea.'

For the rest of the hour they were besieged by the children seeking autographs, some shyly, some eagerly. The youngsters had made their own autograph books especially for the occasion. The players mingled freely with the crowd and proved immensely popular. Dr K.D. Mullen, the British captain, had a particularly busy time.

A little Maori boy who answered to the name of Maurice clung silently to Dr Mullen while the latter talked to him and could hardly tear himself away after a few minutes' acquaintance. Maurice later became one of the lucky ones to have a New Zealander's silver fern badge pinned to his jersey. After the teams had chatted with the children and adults for some time, they were accorded three cheers.

'Wonderful Gesture'

Speeches of welcome were given by Mr Charles I. Nathan, chairman of directors of the institute, Mr J. Opie, president of the institute's Adventurers' Club, which arranged the function, Mr Julian Lee, on behalf of the blind, and Mr J.H.E. Papesch, the institute's musical director. Mr Nathan called the visit a wonderful gesture on the teams' part.

Dr Mullen and the New Zealand captain, Mr P.A. Johnstone, replied. Mr Johnstone said: 'We will be playing for all you people tomorrow as well as for ourselves.' Others present included Mr A.E. Cooke, a 1921 All Black, and Mr J.D. King, a member of the New Zealand Rugby Council.

31 July 1950

RECORD CROWD SEES TEST

58,000 at Eden Park

Big Job For Traffic Officers

Fifty-eight thousand people may not make a picnic under ordinary circumstances, but it was a picnic crowd of this size which jammed Eden Park for the fourth British Isles–New Zealand Rugby test match on Saturday. And on Saturday's official estimate, it was bigger by 2000 than the previous record New Zealand gathering which watched the final test between the All Blacks and South Africa in 1937.

Bright, warm sunshine and the principle of 'bring the family and your own lunch' gave the stadium and the multitude their picnic atmosphere. Although its tour was nearly over, the British team proved the greatest 'draw' ever seen in Auckland, and thousands of people came from all over the province, even at the expense of comfort, to watch what they expected to be, and was, exciting football.

Early Arrivals

To Whangarei must go the honour of providing the keenest spectators for this great occasion. Their enthusiasm aroused by the tourists' game with North Auckland a fortnight ago, two Whangarei Boys' High School pupils, Geoff Cook and Ivan Vitali, hitch-hiked to Auckland on Friday and took pride of place at the Cricket Avenue entrance of the park at 11 p.m.

Agile spectators climbed trees at Eden Park in order to secure a good view.

Shortly afterward an official let them into the ground. They pitched their tent inside the gate and snatched some sleep until 4.15, when they joined the queue, then four strong. By the time the gates opened just before 9 o'clock the queue was 150yds long and contained more than 500 people.

At the Sandringham Road entrance a party of four from Whangarei, complete with tent, was forestalled by a few minutes by Mr Horace Braithwaite, of Mount Albert, who came at 11 p.m. The Whangarei enthusiasts slung their shelter between the gate and the nearest power pole. When the gates opened the queue of nearly 1000 people was 250yds long.

Perched in Trees

The throng poured steadily on to the terraces after the first rush for strategic positions. By 10.30 the terraces looked full, but the fact that patrons were still arriving at 2 p.m. showed that Rugby followers have an elasticity all their own. Not content with seeing the game from ground level, several dozen men took to trees near the east end of the ground, and for long hours perched there precariously.

Orange peel, apple cores, bags of scraps and even bunches of leeks make effective but fairly harmless missiles, and barrages came frequently into action against groups who stood up and blocked others' view during preliminary matches. During the Mount Albert Grammar–Auckland Grammar game, outbursts of cheering usually meant success in local 'battles' rather than interest in the struggle on the field.

It was also a good-natured crowd which bantered an announcer giving out public notices. His habit of stridently interrupting play in the principal match was not so well received. A request for the crowd to sing 'Now is the Hour' after the game met with a half-hearted response.

Boys peddling tea, soft drinks and a variety of other delicacies did a busy trade in the heat, picking their way, as only small boys can, over and around the 40,000 pairs of feet on the terraces. The St. John ambulance brigade had one of its busiest days at the park. Many patrons who collapsed were carried from the terraces on stretchers.

Traffic Congestion

Litter left behind by the crowd made the terraces a sea of white. After the game the usual small boys with sacks went about collecting bottles, and yesterday morning a number of boys and at least two women were seen searching among the debris for spoils of the day.

Clearing the park and neighbouring streets of pedestrians and motor-cars after the match was the biggest traffic problem ever faced in Auckland. It was handled by traffic officers, police and the Legion of Frontiersmen. Some drivers were forced to park nearly a mile from the ground. Great South Road traffic on Saturday night was very heavy.

Special trains and trams which had brought people from all over Auckland to the match eventually took away the greatest number.

31 July 1950

NEW ZEALAND PACK TAKES CONTROL OF GAME

There have been many days of sunshine and good playing conditions during the tour of the British Isles' team, but Saturday's warm, windless weather was the finest of all. The one misfortune was that the sunlight handicapped the team playing from the Mount Eden end.

The Rt. Hon. P.C. Gordon-Walker, Secretary of State for Commonwealth Relations, was introduced to the two teams on the ground. When the National Anthem was played the great silent crowd made an unforgettable picture.

The teams were:—

British Isles: Fullback, B.L. Jones; threequarters, K.J. Jones, B.L. Williams (captain), J. Matthews, M.F. Lane; halfbacks, J.W. Kyle, W.R. Willis; back row, P.W. Kininmonth; middle row, J.W.

McKay, E.R. John, J.E. Nelson, R.T. Evans; front row, G.M. Budge, D.M. Davies, C. Davies.

New Zealand: Fullback, R.W.H. Scott; threequarters, W.A. Meates, R.A. Roper, P. Henderson; five-eighths, J.M. Tanner, L.S. Haig; halfback, V.D. Bevan; back row, G.G. Mexted; middle row, P.A. Johnstone (captain), L.R. Harvey, R.A. White, P.J.B. Crowley; front row, K.L. Skinner, A.M. Hughes, H.W. Wilson.

British Isles won the toss and played with the sun behind it. The All Black forwards began vigorously and it was five minutes before British Isles crossed the halfway line. Meantime, Tanner had been caught in one rush and had given a bad pass in another.

All Blacks Open Scoring

Bevan shot through a gap and Mexted carried on almost to the British Isles goal-line. K.J. Jones cut off his pass, and a subsequent penalty saved British Isles.

Willis fumbled the ball at the base of a scrum and Crowley dribbled fiercely on. Wilson was there as the ball was kicked over the line and he scored. E.R. John conceded a free kick by charging too soon and Scott kicked the goal.

New Zealand	5
British Isles	0

K.J. Jones (with ball) intercepts a pass from G.G. Mexted (on ground).

The first British Isles rush got out to K.J. Jones, whom Henderson tackled hard. Kyle beat three men before kicking ahead. He caught Scott in possession and the ball went into touch. Haig gave away a penalty by standing offside and from 30 yards B.L. Jones kicked a fine goal.

New Zealand   5
British Isles   3

White led a good movement and the British Isles' line was close at hand when Bevan ran from a scrum, only to be swamped. Crowley conceded a penalty and British Isles cleared.

Back came the All Blacks and John made a fair catch to stem a rush. He failed to find touch with his high kick and Scott had ample time to catch, aim and drop-kick a goal from 45 yards. The ball cleared the bar by no more than a foot. However, it was a glorious kick.

The half-time score was:—

New Zealand   8
British Isles   3

The second half had only been under way a minute when Williams tried a drop at goal from a mark 45 yards out. The ball fell short. Crowley threw Willis very hard and the halfback had to go to the touchline for about three minutes for attention.

Spectacular Break

Kininmonth 'dummied' the All Black inside backs. He had no support and elected to kick, the ball bouncing into touch. It was a spectacular run.

Meates had no one in front of him when he took a pass in his own half. B.L. Jones, however, overhauled him and tackled him into touch after a fine run of about 70 yards. Kyle and K.J. Jones replied with a dash of about 60 yards and when Crowley conceded yet another penalty B.L. Jones had an easy kick from 40 yards. He missed, as did Kininmonth when he tried a dropped goal from a mark. B.L. Jones had an even easier chance from 35 yards, but the ball went a yard outside the left-hand post.

Meates was tackled at the corner by B.L. Jones after good work by Tanner and the crowd roared that Haig had gone over close to the posts, but Mr Sullivan ordered a scrum five yards out. The All Black backs were now hammering hard and Lane had to make a brilliant save on his goal-line. Matthews went through a gap and the situation looked favourable for British Isles until Roper tackled Williams.

Then, after 27 minutes, Roper kicked toward the touchline during a back attack. The ball

B.L. Williams is tackled by R.A. White as the ball goes into touch in goal during the last minute of the game.

bounced into Henderson's arms as the winger at great speed ran for the line and dived for a capital try. Scott missed the conversion.

    New Zealand   11
    British Isles   3

Bevan sparkled with two dashing breaks and Meates almost scored from the second. B.L. Jones took a pass on his own goal-line, broke through to Scott and the flying K.J. Jones completed a magnificent piece of work with his try. B.L. Jones converted from in front.

    New Zealand   11
    British Isles   8

With three minutes to go, Scott almost scored. John dummied through and Willis had a clear field ahead when he received the pass. Henderson's tackle saved the situation, but Williams, from the ensuing ruck, almost scored, grounding the ball as he struck the corner flag.

The excitement was at full pitch when the match ended with the score:—

    New Zealand   11
    British Isles   8

Mr Sullivan awarded British Isles eight penalties and New Zealand one.

31 July 1950

'THE BEST TEAM WON'

'I will never forget the last 20 minutes of the test match at Auckland,' said Mr P.C. Gordon-Walker, British Secretary of State for Commonwealth Relations, in a national broadcast last night. 'It was as good Rugger as I ever hope to see, with a picture-book try scored by each side. The best side won — but only just the best.'

4 August 1950

RICH ADVENTURE FOR PLAYERS

British Isles Team Sails

(S.R.) WELLINGTON, THURSDAY
A crowd of several hundred enthusiasts turned out this afternoon to bid farewell to the British Isles Rugby team on its departure in the *Wanganella* for Sydney.

'It is with sad hearts that we go,' said the captain, Dr Karl Mullen. 'This tour of New Zealand has been a wonderful experience. We have made hundreds of friends. We have been privileged to see this beautiful country from end to end, and from start to finish we have had enjoyable football. I speak for my team mates in saying that it is a wrench to leave. However, we have had the experience of the tour and for all of us this has been unforgettable. May I thank all New Zealanders for their very great kindness to all of us.'

'What more can I say than that this has been a rich adventure for myself and every member of the party and that words could never adequately express our gratitude for the kindness with which we have been treated,' said Surgeon-Caption L.B. Osborne, manager of the team. 'The tour has been, I think, of benefit to the whole of Rugby and has enriched the game. Our backs, with their open style of play, have shown qualities which have pleased the New Zealand public. By the same token, your forwards have never failed to impress us by their drive, their fitness and their courage. I am sure that the influence of the tour will be just as strong in the British Isles as it will be in New Zealand.'

The crowd joined in singing 'Now is the Hour' and 'Auld Lang Syne.' The British players sang two of their hymns and cheered the crowd heartily several times.

W.B. Cleaver dons a Maori skirt to entertain onlookers with a dance.

A procession through the streets of New Plymouth on the morning of the Lions match against Taranaki

1959

18 July — Dunedin
15 August — Wellington
29 August — Christchurch
19 September — Auckland

9 April 1959

PARTIAL BAN MADE ON AUTOGRAPHS

From our Rugby Correspondent

A genuine effort is to be made by the New Zealand Rugby Union to protect the British Lions touring players this year from the horrors of autograph hunters.

The council of the union yesterday unanimously passed a series of recommendations from the executive on the subject.

These provide that applications for autographs must be submitted through the responsible local union of the district in which the players for the time being are residing. They also provide that where autograph books are submitted directly to the team's hotels they will be left there at the owner's risk. Furthermore they will not be dealt with by the team.

'Some decisive steps will have to be taken to curtail the time spent by players in signing autographs,' said the chairman, Mr C.S. Hogg. The burden imposed on the Springboks had been, he said, unfairly heavy. Players had had to spend hours a day signing their names. The New Zealand union must protect the Lions from this strain.

---

30 May 1959

2000 LIONS' NAMES ARE READY

N.Z. Autograph Hunters

From Our Rugby Correspondent
On tour with the Lions

SYDNEY

Invitations to attend pig-hunts, hunting expeditions, farmers' days and the like are beginning to pour in upon the British Rugby Lions from New Zealand.

The putting-off of these invitations, at least for the time being, is only one of the many activities of Mr O.B. Glasgow, the genial Northern Irishman who is honorary secretary of the touring party.

During the war, Mr Glasgow was exposed for a time to the secretarial practices of an equally genial Southern Irishman while the two were serving in an Army transport organisation.

Without fail, the Southern Irishman used to fire all incoming correspondence into the waste-paper basket. His theory was that if a matter were of real importance, the writer would certainly put pen to paper a second time.

Mr Glasgow, on the other hand, likes, if possible, to answer all incoming letters on the same day.

One of Mr Glasgow's chores has been to supervise the production of sheets bearing the autographs of the team.

At the time of assembly in Eastbourne, it was made known that the New Zealand Council intended to apply restrictions designed to reduce for the Lions, at least to some extent, the enormous burden of autographing which was borne by the 1956 Springboks in New Zealand.

As a prudent business man, however — he is head of a family concern connected with the dyeing and finishing of textiles and has many business connections in New Zealand — Mr Glasgow decided to forestall the possibility of some woebegone but fanatic New Zealand boy bursting into tears at being deprived of the autographs of the players.

Each day since assembly, therefore, players have stuck their names down on sheets which are likely to get into the hands of these and other enthusiasts.

So far, about 2000 sheets have been produced. Mr Glasgow hopes there will be more by the time of arrival of the team in New Zealand.

---

11 June 1959

SHOULDER-PADS ARE OPPOSED

Touring Manager Wants Law 5 Enforced

From Our Rugby Correspondent

TAMWORTH

The manager of the British Isles touring Rugby team, Mr A.W. Wilson, intends to insist that New Zealand players appearing against his men will not wear shoulder-pads.

The only exceptions he will allow will be for men who are physically impaired, or for whom medical certificates are available.

Mr Wilson made the stipulation that the Australian fifteen which played the Lions at Brisbane last Saturday should take the field without shoulder-pads.

Although shoulder-pads are worn almost as extensively in Australian Rugby as in New Zealand, his request was carried out.

'So far as New Zealand is concerned,' Mr Wilson said, 'I have no intention of being unpleasant about the matter.

Law 5 quoted

'But Law 5 of the laws of the game specifically states that protective devices may not be worn by players.

'For this reason, I could not countenance any breach of the laws.

'So far as I am concerned, shoulder-pads will not be allowed.'

Mr Wilson's statement — and he was very firm indeed in his remarks — is likely to cause some consternation among New Zealanders who are chosen to play against the Lions.

The International Rugby Board, at its meeting in London a couple of years ago, directed that the wearing of shoulder-pads should cease.

Opinion Hardening

British opinion against these protective devices had been hardening ever since the appearance of the 1947–48 Wallabies team, the members of which appeared to be as heavily accoutred as American football players.

Mr C.S. Haig, the New Zealand delegate to the board, tried manfully on his return to persuade the New Zealand Council to implement the board's direction.

For various reasons councillors failed to insist upon this.

After some hesitation players began to wear the pads as freely as before.

It is evident that Mr Wilson, as at Brisbane, intends to stand pat on the relevant law.

---

23 June 1959

CUPS OF TEA IN WITH COST OF SEAT

Scotsmen's Stands At Eden Park

'Scotsmen's grandstands' in backyards overlooking Eden Park are receiving last-minute touches in preparation for the three big Rugby matches in Auckland this season.

Although many survive from past seasons, the inevitable 'new' stand is appearing on the scene this year to tempt the fan who may have been unable to get seats in the park.

Some of the stands hold up to 70 people, while other more intimate affairs are obviously for the exclusive use of the householder, his family and friends.

As well as being able to cope with bigger crowds — hundreds of people are expected to watch the three Lions matches from 'Scotsmen's grandstands' — prices of seats are reported to be higher than in former years.

During previous Rugby series, fans have paid anything from 5s to £2 to sit on the home-made structures, although for the Springbok games in 1956 one householder was rumoured to have asked £3 a seat. From investigations this week, £2, £3 and even more is being paid for seats this year.

24 June 1959

BAN ON BOXES AND BEER IN BULK AT EDEN PARK

There will be more thirsty spectators watching the Lions play Auckland at Eden Park on Saturday than there were during the Springbok games. This year, the police have the authority to stop anyone going into the park with a carton or sack of beer and also those carrying boxes to stand on while on the embankment.

The chairman of the Eden Park Board of Control, Mr S.C. Hay, said yesterday that trust board bylaws have just been gazetted which cover these two points. In the past the police have been unable to prevent anyone taking a large amount of liquor into the park although they could intervene when a disturbance occurred.

'These are two important matters,' said Mr Hay. 'With the help of the police, we are going to try to control the amount of liquor taken in and also the carrying of boxes which are a cause of annoyance to people on the embankment.'

Boxes might have been banned at Eden Park, but these four fans at Carisbrook used more than a couple of crates to get a good view.

'The fellow who goes along and has a bottle of beer with his lunch while waiting for the game is not the worry,' added Mr Hay. 'But we are determined to stamp out any drunkenness.'

As an added attraction, some entrepreneurs have indicated that cups of tea will be provided for customers.

With the first Lions match in Auckland less than a week away, bookings on the 'Scotsmen's grandstands' are reported to be heavy. And at least one householder in Walters Road has sold out for the test match in September.

26 June 1959

OUTSIDERS LOSE VIEW

High Eden Park Seating 'No Longer a Paddock'

None of the private stands behind the Eden Park terraces is likely to give an unobstructed view of the Auckland–Lions match tomorrow.

Although the temporary stands erected by the Auckland Rugby Union will not affect three 'Scotsmen's stands', these will be masked by a special stand to be erected today by D.B. Waite, Ltd.

The contracting firm which built the new main grandstand at the park, D.B. Waite, Ltd, intends to erect a 1000-seat stand at the scoreboard end of the terraces.

'We have the permission of the union to do this,' said Mr D.B. Waite, principal of the firm yesterday. 'Most of the seats will be taken by men who have worked on the main stand project. The residue will be given to the Rugby Union to dispose of.'

Mr Waite thought there would be no trouble in erecting the stand in the time available. It would be of tubular steel scaffolding, similar to the official Rugby Union stands. Residents of Cricket Avenue, whose properties back on to the portion which will be affected by the contractor's stand, had not expected the new move, and yesterday they were finishing off their own scaffolding stands.

No Obligation

The two temporary stands of the Rugby Union were about half completed yesterday afternoon. Each will extend about 40 yards on either side of the main terrace exit, and will rise about eight to 10 feet above the back fence.

'The reason we have gone so high is not to block out the private stand owners,' said Mr T.H. Pearce, chairman of the Auckland Rugby Union. 'It is simply that we have contracted to sell advertising on the back fence and that must not be obscured.'

Mr Pearce said it was unfortunate that the owners of private stands had to suffer, but he felt the Rugby Union was under no obligation to notify the owners of its intention of erecting the temporary stands.

Fair Profit

'All received a fair profit out of the Springbok games,' he said, 'and that should cover losses for this match. These residents must realise that Eden Park has progressed beyond a cow paddock and is now an international ground.'

Most of the private-stand owners accepted the Rugby Union's decision to block out their view philosophically. All agreed that little could be done.

A deputation from the owners was received by the Rugby Union yesterday morning.

Moral Right

Speaking for the deputation, Mr D. Coates, one of the stand-owners' solicitors, said the owners thought they had a certain moral right in the issue and that arrangements in many cases had been made for people who were travelling long distances to see the match. He said that the union's action was a little belated and that people from the South Island were already on their way.

'We have a duty to our patrons,' said Mr Pearce in reply. 'We have had to make additional reservable accommodation at Eden Park as the present accommodation is insufficient.'

To try to help the private-stand owners accommodate any patrons who may have travelled long distances, Mr Pearce said the union would allot 50 seats on the temporary stand to the private owners. These have been left in the hands of the owners' solicitors.

Heavy Demand

Proof of the heavy demand for seats was evident at the union's office yesterday morning. When the secretary, Mr L.F. Warren, arrived at the office there were some 50 to 60 people waiting for him and a large pile of mail was on his desk. The telephone was ringing continuously and continued to do so for the rest of the morning.

Private-stand owners also had a fairly continuous stream of visitors yesterday, as well as numerous telephone calls. Most of the patrons who have bought tickets in the stand have elected to wait until Saturday to 'see how the land lies.'

The Canterbury Rugby Union is unlikely to follow the Auckland lead in blocking out private stands, states a Press Association message from Christchurch.

'We have not considered any action and it is unlikely that we will do the same as Auckland,' said the president of the Canterbury Union, Mr H.C. Blazey, yesterday. A stand has already been erected on private land adjoining Lancaster Park for the three Lions matches to be played there.

Fans climb billboards to get a good vantage point for the first test at Carisbrook.

27 June 1959

SOME SAD FACES AFTER DAY AT RACES

Although there were sad faces among the British Lions after some of them had failed to 'break the bank' at the Avondale races yesterday, one face last evening began to glow with a pleasure which is likely to last for days.

The face belonged to N.H. Brophy, the injured Irish winger, who had just received word from home that he had passed the intermediate examination of the Chartered Accountants' Institute of Ireland. Brophy sat the examination within a few days of arrival in Melbourne at the beginning of the Lions' tour about six weeks ago.

Less success attended the punting activities of Mr A.W. Wilson, the manager, and Mr O.B. Glasgow, the secretary, at Avondale. A joke among the team members last evening was that the two officials had lost a fortnight of expenses' reimbursement money by speculations which they had made not wisely but too well.

Most of the team had a quiet day. J. Butterfield and M.C. Thomas went to Auckland Grammar School and a number of players dined in Auckland homes last evening.

J.R.C. Young, the English sprinter, and B.C. Robinson, the New Zealand hurdler, renewed an association they formed at the Empire Games at Cardiff. And 'Ned' Ashcroft looked pleased. Timely backing of the last two race winners had shown him £7 profit.

---

15 July 1959

BEST WISHES AND SUMMONS

Own Correspondent

NEW PLYMOUTH

Rugby has warmed the frigid formality of the Justice Department. Ross Brown, Taranaki and All Black first five-eighths, has just received a summons to answer a charge of exceeding 30 miles an hour in a restricted area while at Wellington for the inter-island match last month. Attached to the summons is a note signed 'Magistrate's Court, Wellington,' and reading: 'Best of luck for Saturday.'

---

20 July 1959

SADDEST VICTORY FOR N.Z. RUGBY

Six Penalties from Clarke Beat Lions by One Point

From Our Rugby Correspondent

DUNEDIN
New Zealand, 18 points; British Isles, 17.
Not even the most enthusiastic supporters of New Zealand Rugby were able to leave the scene of the first test between New Zealand and the British Isles at Carisbrook in Dunedin on Saturday with a feeling of contentment.

As the records will show, New Zealand won by one point — but only by scoring six penalty goals by D.B. Clarke, the last of them within two minutes of the final whistle. Against this the Lions scored four brilliant tries, one of which was converted, and a penalty goal.

One cannot evade the issue. The Lions left the field with hard feelings — as hard, and for much the same reasons, as New Zealand have always felt since A. Geffin kicked South Africa to victory over the All Blacks at Cape Town in 1949. Except in dominance of ground, in which the All Blacks held an advantage, the Lions were decidedly the superior in seizing scoring opportunities.

Even before two of the New Zealand loose forwards, B.E. Finlay and P.F. Jones, became partly crippled with leg injuries, the British forwards were destroying the legend of All Black invincibility.

Such experienced New Zealand forwards as R.C. Hemi and I.J. Clarke said later the Lions, as

A Welsh supporter proudly waves a leek at the first test at Carisbrook.

scrummagers, were very little inferior to the Springboks of 1956 — high praise indeed. Yet the Lions lost.

From the 35 to 40 penalties awarded by the referee, Mr A.L. Fleury, Clarke took 10 shots at goal and each of the six he converted was like a hammer blow of fate for the touring team.

Perhaps the surest index of the average reaction to the All Blacks' penalty parade was seen in the final two minutes following Clarke's last goal.

As one man the thousands of spectators took up a chant of 'Red! Red!' as the Lions surged down the field in a tremendous rush.

All Blacks were pushed out of the way and to roar upon roar of cheering the Lions at last reached

to within a few feet of the goal.

N.A. Murphy went down but W.R. Evans took his place and, grabbing at the ball, prepared himself for the irresistible dive which would surely have meant winning the game.

At this fateful moment, Mr Fleury sounded his whistle yet again. He ruled Evans had handled in the scrum — to most observers it appeared to be still a loose rush — and with this final penalty the game came to an end.

New Zealand had won a victory no New Zealander could possibly glory in. In fact it looked the saddest victory in all New Zealand Rugby history. What a pity it was that so exciting a match should have had so unfortunate an end.

Because the future could not be foreseen, all loyal enthusiasts for the All Blacks greeted Clarke's two opening penalty goals warmly enough and the cheers were compellingly enthusiastic when the Lions replied with a penalty goal and two beautifully constructed tries to take the lead at 9–6 just before half-time.

Figure of Doom

Another lovely try to the Lions, which emphasised their splendid opportunism, was answered about 10 minutes later by Clarke's third goal and then the Lions, with yet another superb try, went into what looked to be an unassailable lead of 17 points to 9 with only 15 minutes to play.

It was then that Mr Fleury, an industrious whistler from the start, turned into a figure of doom for the Lions. Two penalties spaced five minutes apart permitted Clarke to demonstrate his gigantic powers — one kick was from 48 yards and the other from 45. This made the score 17 to 15 with eight or nine minutes to play.

Thus was the stage set for the final penalty from 30 yards and as the ball flew over the bar Clarke established a test match record in the number of penalty goals scored.

No doubt Mr Fleury penalised each infringement as he saw it and he was exceptionally vigilant.

Even the Lions, who so bitterly disputed two of the awards which Clarke turned into goals, admitted that four of the penalties they conceded were properly called.

The Lions captain A.R. Dawson, followed by S. Millar, leads the team onto the field.

Better Scoring Team

Even in losing the Lions were so plainly the better scoring team that they not only disposed of all of the disparagements their recent performances had provoked but they also aroused doubts about the All Blacks' chances of winning the remaining matches.

The first great contribution to a grand performance was made by the forwards.

Will Evans in outstanding form in the line-out and A.R. Dawson striking even more swiftly than Hemi in the scrummages, the Lions soon were able to show that the vaunted power of the All Black pack was an illusion built upon the unsound foundation of virile training runs.

As the second half began, G.K. Smith succeeded in stopping R.J. Urbahn's effective passing of the first half while those sturdy players of the tight game, B.G.M. Wood, H.F. McLeod and R.H. Williams, worked as effectively as any All Black.

As might have been expected, R.E.G. Jeeps soon proved courageous and effective at scrum half and played a big part in checking the All Black forward rushes by constantly claiming marks under the noses of the biggest and most formidable of the onrushing New Zealanders.

If A.B.W. Risman was still not at his best, he was nevertheless a fit companion for Jeeps and two particularly astute kicks ahead and a masterly break of a yard or so past R.H. Brown led to three of the tries scored by the Lions.

M.J. Price and D. Hewitt proved to be resolute defenders and P.B. Jackson, with his dazzling sidesteps and dummies, fooled the All Blacks as convincingly as he had fooled lesser teams.

D.B. Clarke in action.

Faults Appear

For 10 minutes or so the All Blacks looked the men of their reputation. Then the faults started to appear. Until I.N. MacEwan began jumping finely in the second half the New Zealand line-out play was untidy. Of the loose forwards, only E.A.R. Pickering measured up to expectations.

The spirited attacks of the All Black backline, especially for several hectic minutes late in the second half, could not conceal some of its weaknesses.

Brown too often resorted to tactical punting, even at one important part of the second half, when he looked to be breaking past Risman. T.R. Lineen was fit to be in the best company and R.F. McMullen, too, looked very effective.

Foolish Mistake

However, McMullen was decidedly at fault in not playing P.T. Walsh and B.E. McPhail into position and appeared to be responsible for the loss of a try in the first half when he tried to go it alone and was nailed from behind.

Neither Walsh nor McPhail made a great impression, and the latter contributed to a Lions try with a foolish mistake. But he had real pace and looked worthy of encouragement.

Clarke's goalkicking was, of course, wonderful, but his general play — even his touch-finding — was less authoritative.

He began the game by failing with a kick from 30 yards, but after 24 minutes he placed one from 40 yards, and two minutes later followed it with another when J. Faull got offside.

Within four minutes the Lions — who for most of the time had been defending — reached close to the All Black twenty-five, and when W.J. Whineray and Brown stopped Murphy from chasing after Urbahn, Mr Fleury awarded a penalty, which Hewitt turned into a goal.

From a set scrum Jeeps sent Risman off and later bumped and shouldered out of Brown's tackle. Price compelled McPhail to desert A.J.F. O'Reilly, who tore away from D.B. Clarke to score brilliantly in the corner.

Smart Move

Risman and Jeeps were next associated in a smart move which Risman made dangerous with a raking punt ahead. Jackson drew clear of All Black defenders to bundle the ball ahead to the goal line, and Price put a scoring hand on the ball as it lay in the goal area.

Scotland failed with the attempt at the

conversion of O'Reilly's try and Hewitt rather badly sliced the attempt following Price's try.

Eight minutes after the start of the second half Evans cut off Urban's pass to Finlay. At halfway, Smith carried on the run to the twenty-five, where Jackson took over for a thrilling chase down the touchline to the corner.

Risman failed with this conversion, but he placed a lovely goal after Price had kicked the ball ahead for 50 or 60 yards, where K.J.F. Scotland picked it up, fooled Walsh and put Price in for the try.

Meanwhile, Clarke had laced a goal from only 10 yards, and he followed Price's try with the two long goals and the final one from 30 yards.

It was great goal-kicking — but what New Zealander could believe in a New Zealand victory by such means?

The selectors' solutions to the many problems they now face will be eagerly awaited.

---

21 July 1959

SYMPATHY FOR TOURISTS

Sign Greets Team

Press Assn

GREYMOUTH

'Deepest Sympathy,' read the sign. There was no doubting who the condolences were for or why. There was a football boot below it to remove any doubts.

This was the sign that greeted the British Rugby team in a Reefton tearooms yesterday afternoon when the players stopped for afternoon tea en route to Greymouth by bus from Christchurch.

Travelling in bright sunshine for most of the way, apart from a belt of rain on the summit of the Lewis Pass, the Lions saw some spectacular mountain scenery which was recorded by dozens of cameras — movie and still.

Later, the Lions' buses had to break streamers held across the road by enthusiastic children.

The team for tomorrow's match against the Combined West Coast-Buller side will train today on Rugby Park where the match is to be played.

---

7 August 1959

ALL BLACKS WIN THRILLING TEST

Gallant Lions Narrowly Beaten 11–8 Last-Minute Try by D.B. Clarke

From Our Rugby Correspondent, Wellington

New Zealand 11 points; British Isles 8.

It will be a long time before the last minutes of the second Rugby test between New Zealand and the British Isles at Athletic Park on Saturday are forgotten. Lagging by two points, the All Blacks summoned all their strength in the final stages to overpower the Lions by a goal and two tries to a goal and a penalty goal.

The dramatic change of fortunes began from a scrum in front of the British goal when the ball was skilfully heeled to K.C. Briscoe, the halfback, who sent it to J.F. McCullough at five-eighths.

As the record crowd cheered their heads off, D.B. Clarke surged through a gap to take McCullough's pass.

It was inevitable that Clarke must score but to make sure he hurled himself over the line with a tremendous dive for the winning try.

No Recriminations

So for the second time in two tests the gallant Lions were beaten at the very moment when their hands were reaching for the laurels of victory.

Fortunately, for the good of Rugby, there was no cause for recriminations over the merits of the second victory by New Zealand.

There were blemishes in the All Black performance and an unfortunate obstruction by D.B. Clarke left a taste it was not easy to forget or forgive.

In all honesty, too, it was possible to quibble with the decision of the referee, Mr C.R. Gillies, of Waikato, that T.E. Davies, the Lions' fullback, had knocked the ball forward and so caused the vital scrum only three minutes from the end.

But when all depended upon the response of every member of the All Black team, not one man failed. The attack was pressed home with a faultless precision which fairly reflected the finest qualities of New Zealand Rugby.

Early Penalties

When the teams took the field, the Lions were greeted by a cheer which was half sympathy with them in their many troubles and half an appeal to play with the speed and skill of their finest displays in the provinces.

Right from the start Mr Gillies made it plain he was going to stand for no nonsense by penalising C.E. Meads in one line-out and I.J. Clarke in another.

From the second of these infringements Davies' kick at goal from 50 yards was fine and long but not quite good enough.

Now it was seen that the lethargy of the All Black pack of the first test had been overcome by the transfusions of new blood and it was with great vigour that it entered scrummages and line-outs.

D.B. Clarke was unable to place a penalty from 50 yards. A few minutes later the excitement of the crowd turned faintly hysterical when T.R. Lineen slashed through but J.R.C. Young was too fast for the attackers.

This for the time being was New Zealand's game and when Lineen kicked most accurately behind the British backs, the entire crowd seemed to rise in concert with the swiftly running All Blacks.

Davies was slow getting across. Young was outflanked and the young wing R.W. Caulton, playing his first test, beat them both as the ball rose to his hand.

So New Zealand was ahead after 14 minutes of play and if D.B. Clarke could not place the goal from a yard from the touchline, no one seemed to care.

Fine Spirit

The Lions still looked somewhat ill assorted but their fine spirit showed when M.J. Price picked up a bouncing ball and with a step and a swerve, went past the first line of defence.

A kick ahead threatened New Zealand but Briscoe, though new to the test atmosphere, was playing well, and saved a dangerous situation.

Then came one of the great moments of the game when Lineen, with a superb burst of speed, made a complete break past W.M. Patterson and kicked ahead. From a five-yard scrum, New Zealand heeled. McCullough was caught in possession but he wriggled clear enough to pass.

Caulton was on the ball in an instant and the ground rang with the cheers of Wellingtonians saluting one of their own as he went across for the try. Six points to New Zealand, none to the British Isles.

From the kick-off the Lions surged relentlessly into the attack and when an All Black infringed practically on the goal-line, Davies took a penalty from only 23 yards.

By now his injured leg seemed to be distressing him and perhaps this was the cause of his failure — an important failure which later was to have its effect upon the game.

The Lions forwards now were in command of the All Black pack and they were soon again only a yard or two from the New Zealand goal. However, R.E.G. Jeeps, once more a tower of strength for the tourists, put the ball into touch in-goal.

A six-point lead was a help but it did not seem enough when the second half began with the Lions attacking dangerously.

Jeeps made a superb break which would almost certainly have yielded a try had not N.A. Murphy let the ball roll forward as he was tackled only a yard short of the line.

Then came the bad moment of the game when A.J.F. O'Reilly lobbed a punt over D.B. Clarke toward the goal-line and sped ahead.

Without the least hesitation, Clarke dropped his shoulder and knocked O'Reilly to the ground. Had not the ball ultimately gone dead, Mr Gillies must have awarded a penalty try for this grave breach.

As it was, Davies easily placed the resultant penalty to warm cheers which assured the Lions that no one in the audience condoned the offence.

After threatening the All Black line several times the Lions finally got across when Price,

A huge crows filled Athletic Park to capacity. Thousands were turned away when the gates closed well before midday.

getting the ball from a tight-head scrum, sent Young racing for the flag with a high pass. Davies placed the goal to put the Lions two points ahead.

Until now, much of the advantage of the second half had been with the Lions and it remained so for the next few minutes during which Clarke tried unsuccessfully to goal from 50 yards.

Desperate Resolve

But the All Black forwards were stirring with desperate resolve into their last and most thrilling effort which led finally to Clarke's glorious try, an effort which he had no difficulty in improving with his finest kick of the day.

The Lions responded with a tremendous effort and with only a little bit of luck Patterson and Young might have broken clean through.

But time, the great enemy, was against the Lions and New Zealand kept its slender lead until the end of the game.

17 August 1959

RECORD CROWD SMASHES PARK ENTRANCES
Press Assn.

WELLINGTON

Estimates of the crowd at Athletic Park on Saturday varied between 58,000 and 65,000 but only 43,000 passed through the turnstiles — a record in itself.

The crowd turned away when the gates were shut at 11 a.m. were estimated at between 10,000 and 15,000. They saw nothing of the test.

When the gates were closed, assaults were made on the entrance at both Rintoul Street and Adelaide Road. Thousands poured in over fences and through gates lifted off their hinges.

17 August 1959

LIONS ROCK PARLIAMENT HOUSE WITH HAKA

From Our Rugby Correspondent

WELLINGTON

The British Lions easily topped the popularity poll at the State reception they were given at Parliament Buildings last evening.

After a speech of welcome by the Prime Minister, Mr Nash, a choir from the Ngati Poneke Concert Party offered the hand of friendship in song.

The associate to the Minister of Maori Affairs, Mr Tirikatene, representing the Maori people, spoke, and the Leader of the Opposition, Mr Holyoake, went as far back as the 12th century to adorn a tale of football.

Mr A.W. Wilson, the manager, expressed his thanks for the reception the team had received in New Zealand, and A.R. Dawson, the captain, used the phrase 'in the interests of Rugby' in pledging that his players would maintain the open attacking game, which has won them so much popularity in New Zealand. To the unconcealed delight of the concert party and to the satisfaction of the audience as a whole, A. Ashcroft, the choirmaster, then put his team through 'Haeremai,' the song which, sung by a schoolgirl choir, so affected the tourists at their first reception in Napier.

Then the team sang their version of 'He Puuru,' and then the Maori party, now thoroughly worked up, replied with a mixture of a song and a haka.

Ashcroft and his men completely captivated everyone with a rough but extremely forceful haka.

It was the most effective and spontaneous contribution one can remember a football team having made in these hallowed surroundings.

26 August 1959

BED AND SEAT FOR £30

Staff Reporter, Hamilton

Seats on the stand for the third Rugby test at Christchurch are being offered privately in Hamilton. The price is £30 for a seat and a night's accommodation.

31 August 1959

ALL BLACK PACK HUMBLES LIONS

Forwards Smash Way to 22–8 Victory
Dr Craven Not So Confident Now

From Our Rugby Correspondent

New Zealand 22 points; British Isles 8.
CHRISTCHURCH

Some of the greatest days of New Zealand Rugby were vividly recalled when the All Blacks smashed the British Lions into defeat by two goals, two tries, a dropped goal and a penalty goal to a goal and a penalty goal in the third test at Lancaster Park on Saturday.

The New Zealand forward play was superb, D.B. Clarke's famous boot struck with merciless accuracy. R.J. Urbahn played as clever and resourceful a halfback game as could be wished.

And in an age of supposedly indifferent backs, R.W. Caulton not only played brilliantly but also proved himself to be decisively the back of the match in a game which was almost completely memorable.

No wonder that eminent man of South African Rugby, Dr D.H. Craven, should decide to sidestep round his recent confident predictions that the Springboks would certainly win back the world championship from New Zealand next year.

'South Africa,' said Dr Craven, 'will have to

take fresh stock. The All Black forwards were impressive.'

Criticism of Backs

However, some of the 60,000 spectators were not completely delighted. Many of them, it was perfectly plain, would have preferred the Lions to win.

Sentiment apart, they had cause to criticise both the New Zealand tries in the second half, specially one that began from what appeared to be a knock-on.

Almost silence greeted this try, and this phenomenon suggested that the crowd was most anxious that justice should not only be done to the Lions but also that it should appear to be done.

Finally, the inability of the All Blacks to clinch the advantages of the first half, when the score was 14 to 8 in their favour, aroused the criticism that the backs were unwilling to put everything into the attack.

Great Performance

But no matter how deep might be the sympathy for the Lions, or how critical the examination of the All Black attack in the second half, this was still unreservedly a great performance by the New Zealand team.

The forwards played as well as R.C. Stuart's team against England in 1954 and as well, too, as R.H. Duff's men against the Springboks in the third test of 1956 — one finds it impossible to believe there could be higher praise.

The lethargy and bumblings of the first two tests were no more. The onslaught was sustained and furious. The Lions' superiorities in the line-out were made completely negative by the jumping and catching of I.N. MacEwan, S.F. Hill and C.E. Meads.

R.J. Conway entered rucks or made tackles with a tigerish ferocity, and once he tackled first one Lion and then another and then picked up the ball and ran with it.

W.J. Whineray had his finest game as the New Zealand leader, and R.C. Hemi confounded his critics by winning no fewer than five tight-head scrums. K.R. Tremain, though a mere youngster, sturdily assisted his fellows.

Wonderful Vitality

Best of all was the newcomer M.W. Irwin, who on all counts, and in spite of fierce competition from MacEwan, Conway and one or two others, looked the forward of the match.

The vitality of all these men was wonderful. It was a warm afternoon, yet these forwards kept to the task like highly trained Olympic athletes.

To criticise the backs, who by the scoring record so notably assisted their forwards, is probably unjust. Yet one did have the feeling that J.F. McCullough somehow lacked some essential quality — perhaps it was all a matter of speed — to transfigure the attacks which Urbahn so often very cleverly began.

Not to mention McCullough's services on cover defence would be a disservice to a gifted young player, but what thrust the All Black backline might have developed if A.H. Clarke had been there at his best.

Superb Kicking

T.R. Lineen ran dangerously and R.H. Brown performed most valuable service, especially on defence. So, too, did R.F. McMullen who was inferior only in pace to the celebrated A.J.F. O'Reilly.

Clarke's kicking for touch was inferior to his goalkicking. This was not surprising, as his set kicks were superb. And his cat-like judgment enabled him to stop D. Hewitt in what could have been the critical run of the game.

There remains only Caulton, with his lithe quickness, insatiable ambition to do the right thing and football intelligence — the main characteristics of a singularly promising young player who might follow in the footsteps of R.A. Jarden. Need more be said?

The Lions, to their credit, were generous in defeat. 'We were well beaten,' said their captain, A.R. Dawson. 'We got hammered today,' said the manager, Mr A.W. Wilson.

Dawson himself, H.F. McLeod, that great lock forward, R.H. Williams and, to a certain extent, W.R. Evans, fought on level terms with the All Black forwards. But the rest of the pack was more than contained. For all his tallness, J. Faull could make no capital of the long throw-in. G.K. Smith, too, was outpointed (even in their one brief open-air fight) by Meads. And both Smith and H.J. Morgan were inefficient in discharging the normal tasks of tackling inside backs.

Effective Runs

Smith, for instance, was nowhere to be seen when Caulton went in at the corner for the simplest of blind-side tries and Morgan was quite unable to control Urbahn's brisk and most effective runs on the open side.

The problems of the forwards were aggravated by the difficulties of the backs.

No one could possibly have done more for his side than R.E.G. Jeeps at scrumhalf but some terrible misadventures befell such players of talent as K.J. Scotland, Hewitt and M.J. Price.

Hewitt's try — as a demonstration of speed and elusive running — was undoubtedly one of the great events of the tour. But even so it was eclipsed by the misfortunes attending his decision in the 19th minute to move infield when only Clarke lay ahead and O'Reilly was in close support.

Ghastly Blunder

By some incredible means, Clarke reached out a staying hand and what should certainly have been five points at a time when the scores were 3–all, turned instead into a ghastly blunder.

There were numerous other blunders, two at least of try-scoring possibilities, and by committing them the Lions lost whatever hope they might have had of controlling the game.

'Alas, poor Horrocks!' murmured a local wit in talking of the newcomer at fly-half, J.P. Horrocks-Taylor. The implied criticism was over-harsh.

For a man so out of touch with match play, Horrocks-Taylor performed remarkably well, but when sharpness was wanted he could not summon it.

Yet the feeling remained that even with A.B.W. Risman in his finest form, the Lions would still have been overpowered because this truly was a magnificent All Black pack.

In a first half in which the advantage lay often with the Lions, a sudden attack put the All Blacks down into the left-hand corner and when Hemi won the scrum against the tight head, Urbahn sent Caulton in at the corner.

Faull soon replied with a penalty goal but Clarke struck death-dealing blows to the Lions' hopes with two marvellous goals — one a place-kicked penalty from 50 yards and the other a dropkick from the field with the left foot.

Hewitt whizzed past Clarke to score a try made by Horrocks-Taylor and Faull goaled but before halftime both Jeeps and Scotland were swamped by an All Black forward rush which ended with Meads scoring and Clarke converting with a superb kick from the touchline. When Caulton — after what looked like a knock-on — ran back a loose kick, a rush developed which Urban finished with a try in the corner.

Finally Caulton skidded through the defence and as he bounced over the goal-line, he seemed to score while lying on his back. Clarke easily placed the goal.

Mr C.R. Gillies, of Waikato, was the referee.

———

15 September 1959

AUTOGRAPHS RULING

——

Flood of Requests

——

Because the demand has at times got out of hand, seekers of autographs from the British Lions will be strictly disciplined in the last week of the tour.

The only books which the players will sign will be those which have been put through the Auckland Rugby Union in the manner prescribed by the New Zealand union at the beginning of the tour.

A variation in this procedure in recent weeks has caused the Lions to be inundated with books, so much so that the players now compute that each of them has spent three full days signing his name since arriving in New Zealand.

'Until now, the Lions have been signing every book that has come to them,' the New Zealand Rugby Union representative, Mr G.A. Brown, said yesterday.

'They still do not wish to disappoint Rugby followers, but the position has got out of hand. The Lions have even had to pay a good deal of postage on books which have been sent to them without reply-paid envelopes.

'From now on only books which have come through the unions will be signed. None will be accepted at the team's hotel.'

18 September 1959

'EXPERIENCE OF LIFETIME' FOR LIONS TEAM

Touring Manager Reviews Great Rugby Event

Admiration and astonishment — these have been the principal reactions of the manager of the British Lions, Mr A.W. Wilson, to the most successful Rugby tour in the history of the game in New Zealand.

His admiration has been aroused, Mr Wilson confesses, both by the quality of New Zealand forward play and also by the extent and depth of the passion for Rugby felt by the people of the country.

He has felt astonished at the tendency to neglect the possibilities of attacking Rugby.

'With forwards as great as yours,' says Mr Wilson, 'I would have thought that your back play would have had no difficulty in reaching the same level.

'In actual fact, both the Lions' players and I have been astonished at how little your centres are brought into the game.

'I should have thought that your national attacking policy would have been to run the ball out to the wings and then to run — but not kick — it infield again.

Luck of Bounce

'But for your own good reasons, you do not do that. If you aim to bring the forwards into the attack, it is usually by kicking to them — and that, of course, means depending on the luck of the bounce.

'The 1951 Springboks, who were so successful in the British Isles and who gave poor old Scotland such a terrible hammering, were masters at making play to the forwards.

'One of their plans would be very well suited to New Zealand. The scrumhalf used to run wide on the diagonal and at the right moment snap the ball in a reverse-pass to the inside centre, who by going against the direction of the attack would bring the forwards into position to carry the ball on in mass formation.

'This is a terribly difficult form of attack to stop. It would be ideally suited to the great players you have in New Zealand forward packs.'

One feature of the New Zealand game which has greatly impressed Mr Wilson is the ability of scrum halves to make quick kicks to open ground.

'I have never seen this better done,' he says.

'I am going to make a big point of it when I return to Scotland and once more become involved with advising club or national teams.

'Our Scottish halfback, Stan Coughtrie, who was a very much better player than New Zealanders ever had the chance to appreciate, was also an extremely good kicker — but I don't think I have ever seen the idea better exploited than by New Zealanders.

'You people talk an awful lot about how few good backs you have.

'Believe me, you have a number of very good scrumhalves indeed. They all know their onions and some of them are remarkably promising.

'If I seem critical about some aspects of New Zealand's back play, I am certainly anything but critical about some New Zealand players in the backs.

'Young Caulton as a wing is a rare discovery.

'Robin Archer impressed me greatly as a splendidly sound fly-half.

'And I liked very much the cut of young Bayly, the Taranaki fullback. There was a boy who was as cool as could be, and very well clued up in all aspects of the game.

'Best of all was the Maori Bill Gray, who played against us at Rotorua.

'What impressed me so much about his game was the few balls he wasted. Everything was done with constructive purpose. He was looking to attack rather than looking to the touchline.

'I would unhesitatingly say that Gray was the best midfield back we have played against.'

In surveying the tour of the Lions, Mr Wilson had no doubt at all that it had come up to expectation.

'We have been sorely troubled by injuries, especially by injuries to key players,' he said.

'As only one example, the loss of Risman for the month which included the second and third tests was of tremendous significance to the results of matches in that time.

'Against that, I feel that some of our younger players — and we have a good many who would qualify by age for the Junior All Blacks — have come off outstandingly well.

'Our speedy and youthful centres have been tremendously helpful.

Cause of Injuries

'A good deal of speculating has been done about the causes of all our injuries.

'Some people have told me that our players are not robust enough and others have said they are too lightly framed.

'It has also been suggested that the light weight of our boots, and especially their cutting below the ankle, have been a direct cause of all these wretched muscular injuries our players have suffered.

'I wish I could make up my mind as to the principal cause. Frankly, I cannot come to any certain conclusion.

'It looks to me as if these injuries might have happened even if our players had been put into riding boots. This is one case where you never can tell.'

Mr Wilson's enthusiasm for the efforts of his team, especially their efforts in adversity, did not deter him from criticising some aspects of the Lions' play.

'I feel that our defeats were mostly of our own making because in suffering them we neglected to carry out the policy of a free-running attack which we all endorsed at the beginning of the tour,' he said.

'Speed was always our strong point, and our principal hope for success against the All Blacks.

'When we neglected to use it by playing a defensive type of game, we were losing our main weapon of winning.'

Mr Wilson also thought that the Lions' forward play had suffered for want of a sufficient sternness in the defensive play of the loose forwards.

Inaccurate Catching

He also blamed inaccurate catching in the line-outs as a particular cause of difficulties or defeats sometimes suffered by the Lions.

But he has no doubt that great good will be done to Rugby by the tour.

'It was of tremendous importance to these tours that members of the International Rugby Board should see one of them at first hand,' Mr Wilson said.

'To some of us, it sometimes seems that these tours go on for too long and contain too many matches.

'Purely as a personal thought, too, I feel that there should be a rest of a week before each of the test matches.

'The International Board members were able to see things for themselves and I should think that this fact will have great influence on later developments of the world government of the game.

'It has been a long tour. Most of us are now fairly tired. We will all, I am sure, be glad to see our kinfolk.

'But none of us would have missed the experience for worlds.

'To a Rugger man, a visit to New Zealand is the experience of a lifetime.

'How lucky we have all been to have had this.'

September 21 1959

LIONS CLOSE TOUR WITH FINAL TEST WIN

All Black Pack Beaten by Fitter Team

By Our Rugby Correspondent

British Isles, 9 points; New Zealand, 6.

Even if only three points separated the teams and even though D.B. Clarke could have levelled the scores with a short-range penalty only five minutes from the end, none of the 60,000 spectators at Eden Park on Saturday had the least doubt as to which was the more deserving side.

The All Blacks scored two penalty goals and several near-misses, also from penalties. The Lions replied with three tries, two of which were so superbly executed that even the patrons of the 30-shilling seats stood up so that they might get a better view. Three tries to none. Need more be said?

Although the All Black forwards began with a vim which suggested that they were going to take up where they had left off in the third test, it took half an hour for the game to come alive. Only after halftime had passed with the score at 3–3 and later when it was 6–3 to the Lions, 6–6 and finally 9–6, did the atmosphere become supercharged with test match emotion.

It was then that one heard the cry, sweeping from end to end of the terraces of 'Red! Red!' to urge the Lions onward. It was then, too, that an utter silence was felt rather than heard as D.B. Clarke came forward to attempt the goal which could draw the game.

Was Clarke once more to play a leading part in the high drama of modern test match rugby? No man could have been better fitted by nature and experience to face the difficulties of a heavy ball, a

E.A.R. Pickering awaits with outstretched arms as P.B. Jackson fields a kick.

A.B.W. Risman racing through the All Blacks defence to score the third try of the match.

narrow angle and the issue of the match.

Then Clarke kicked. Within a second cries—some sad, most glad—broke out. The ball was bearing off to the left, far away from goal. It would, of course, be gross over-simplification to even suggest that there was only one team in the game, but there are merits to the contention that the All Blacks, notwithstanding some excellent forward play of the first half, played for most of the game like a beaten side.

Perhaps the chief point of difference between the victors and the losers was that while the Lions were frequently willing to treat attacking rugby as a game for 15 men, the All Blacks appeared more concerned in keeping it as the preserve of no more than 10.

Often the number was as low as nine because R.J. Urbahn, for his own good reasons, made much use of a kick over the scrum into touch and this tactic, of course, further limited the opportunities of his companions in the backline.

Few Chances

For all the chances that he got, A.H. Clarke, as an example, might just as well have watched the game from the grandstand. A statistician computed that T.R. Lineen had to wait 25 minutes to receive the ball. R.W. Caulton and B.E. McPhail on the wings performed duty as throwers-in from touch and defensive work excepted, had little more to do.

What a pity it all seemed. New Zealand, after all, had won the rubber. Its reputation was safe and most of the 60,000 spectators would have been willing to share, if need be, in its glorious death. But there was no glory. It is right to presume that New Zealand cannot play attacking Rugby because it lacks the capacity to do so?

Whatever the criticisms, the two particular features of the match were that the Lions' backs had far more initiative than the New Zealand line and that the Lions forwards lasted the game better than the All Blacks. This latter point was of tremendous significance.

Active Chase

Throughout the first half, S.F. Hill, C.E. Meads and M.W. Irwin were much more adept catchers of the ball than the Lions. In the second half, even though the statisticians declared that the All Blacks won the greater number of lineouts, it was R.H. Williams, W.A. Mulcahy and J. Faull who became the catchers-in-chief.

The All Black loose forwards especially K.R.

Contesting possession in a lineout are T.R. Prosser, R.H. Williams, S.F. Hill (obscured) and W.A. Mulchahy.

Tremain, E.A.R. Pickering and R.J. Conway, with a good deal of help from Meads, most actively chased all Lions for the first 50 minutes.

Their efforts were destructive, as intended, but unproductive and it was A.B.W. Risman's masterly coolness of the last half-hour, during which the All Blacks could not get near him, which played so important a part in the issue.

Risman was one of the Lions' attack. Even if he kicked a little too much, his raking punts were so expertly judged that the ball remained a good deal of the time in play. This compelled the All Blacks, back and forward, to keep running and played a decisive part in the wearing and tearing of the All Blacks' physical resources.

The second king-pin was the right wing, P.B. Jackson. The Lions had intended from the beginning to run the ball, but in the harsh atmosphere of a test the initial resolution tended to falter and both Risman and K.J. Scotland in the centre kicked too often in the first half-hour.

It was in this period, and later, that Jackson so strongly proclaimed his intention not to be bound by the atmosphere, or the state of the game, that his teammates were emboldened to imitate his freakish elusiveness and his unconquerable determination. It was Jackson's try, shortly before half-time, which in effect gave the Lions the heart to go on. Of this try, one would go so far as to say that no other wing-threequarter in the world could have scored it. Could there be a higher tribute?

A.J.F. O'Reilly on the other wing was also tremendously effective while T.J. Davies fielded with immaculate skill. At times his enterprise reflected the finest qualities of Welsh rugby.

Risman was a beautifully effective player whose try was a gem of purest ray serene. A.A. Mulligan's early tentativeness soon disappeared and his display outmatched Urbahn's at every point.

What a tribute it was too, to the Lions that they should field forwards who could outlast the All Blacks! A.R. Dawson was not of the quality of R.C. Hemi as a hooker, but he most nobly looked after the front of the lineout and led his team with distinction.

W.A. Mulcahy and Williams were wonderfully vigourous in the forwards. T.R. Prosser, a hard man, gave them full assistance and N.A. Murphy for the first half hour and H.J. Morgan for the last half hour were loose forwards of first-rate quality.

Nothing of the Lions' rushing to the ball and packing round it matched the best moments of the All Blacks. Perhaps, too, none of the Lions was harder or more durable than S.F. Hill, whose last international season has been easily his finest.

But the inspirational fire of the third test which burned brightest in Irwin, Conway and Meads was reduced now to a slow burn. Even Whineray, try as he might, could not lead the pack to the quality it had so recently reached.

As for the backs, the least said the better. D.B. Clarke had to bumble around chasing loose balls and he missed the most vital goal of all. But, as always, he was a much finer player than he looked and without him New Zealand would have been sorely distressed.

First Goal

D.B. Clarke had several shots at goal, mostly from about 38 yards, before he landed his first goal.

The Lions replied before halftime with Jackson's try, to which O'Reilly contributed a material hand by venturing on to the open side from the blindside flank.

A one-handed pass left Jackson with three or four men to beat. The last, Urbahn, seemed to have him covered, but, with a magnificent, masterly sidestep, Jackson broke clear to score in the corner.

Soon after halftime the Lions attacked in the left-hand corner and at a heel Mulligan made enough of the play to bring McPhail hurtling upon him. A deft pass transformed O'Reilly into a ball of fur, who scored in the corner while the All Black forward defence was still gathering its wits.

Mulcahy was too fast round the scrum and D.B. Clarke duly landed the penalty from a short distance.

Then came the movement for which this match will be longest remembered and which yielded one of the great tries of test match history.

O'Reilly meaningly appeared on the open field when a scrum was formed close to the Lions' left-hand touchline. As Mulligan received the heel he began sprinting to the open side, and the All Blacks, divining his intention to create an initial thrust before putting O'Reilly clear, went hotfooting after him.

Sheer Perfection

The development of the situation was sheer perfection. As Risman crossed behind Mulligan he received a reverse pass of fine quality. A sharp sprint put him past the remnants of the All Black scrum and, as he slowed to approach McPhail, one could sense that New Zealand was in trouble.

A sidestep as wide as a barn door left McPhail floundering. As he made it Risman instantly gathered speed. D.B. Clarke, who had been elsewhere, hurtled along in dismay and amazement, but nothing and, more important, no one could reach Risman as he hurried the last 15 yards or so to goal.

As D.B. Clarke missed the goal which would have drawn the game a man in the grandstand said as penetratingly as he could: 'Hooray'.

That was the general feeling.

In a convivial mood before their departure from Whenuapai are J. Butterfield, A. Mulligan, A. Ashcroft and P.B. Jackson.

The Lions singing a farewell song before their plane left for Fiji.

Lions captain, M.J. Campbell-Lamerton trying his hand at the bagpipes. Assisting him is R.J. Conway, captain of Bay of Plenty.

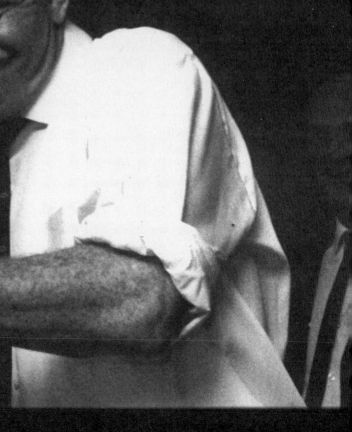

1966

16 July – Dunedin
6 August – Wellington
27 August – Christchurch
10 September – Auckland

The 1966 Lions squad.

2 March 1966

AUTOGRAPH BOOKS TABOO IN HOTELS DURING LIONS TOUR
By T.P. McLean

CHRISTCHURCH

Former All Blacks will be entitled to buy two seats for any match played in New Zealand by the British Lions but, by an odd distinction, the New Zealand selectors — who are likely to be present at a large number of the tourists' games — may only buy tickets for the test matches.

This is one of the recommendations approved by the New Zealand Rugby Council for the domestic arrangements of the Lions' tour.

Of greater general interest and foreseeably of greater embarrassment to the touring team is the stipulation that autograph books will not be accepted at hotels during the tour.

This decision follows a recommendation of the New Zealand councillors who acted as liaison officers with the Springboks last year and who experienced at first hand the chaos developing from a splurge of autograph books, dumped in hotel lounges and signed by the conscientious and spurned by the lazy among touring players.

Though the Springboks last year never suffered a tenth of the plague of autograph books which descended upon their predecessors in 1956 (who discharged a dreadful burden more conscientiously and graciously than any team I have ever seen) there was no doubt the books at some places more than others represented a confounded nuisance.

Of Importance

But whether it likes them or not the New Zealand Rugby Union must accept the fact that autograph hunters, be they genuine seekers or merely creatures of impulse, are important figures on any tour and the union must also accept that many of the hunters, especially the young, are actually or potentially lifetime enthusiasts for and among the most devoted servants of the game.

It is foreseeable, therefore, that the ban on books in hotels may lead to the pestering of players on the streets or at grounds and to some hard thoughts and words about Rugby players in general and the New Zealand union in particular if the response from the Lions is unsympathetic.

The decision to allow old All Blacks to buy two seats for any match through the offices of the various unions staging games will be welcomed.

It took the New Zealand union a good many years to wake to its obligations towards past representatives and as recently as last year I encountered one All Black who was on the point of giving away the game forever because of the extremely ungracious way his very proper application for seats for a test match had been spurned by a provincial union located some hundreds of miles south of Auckland. Another of the arrangements has an interest and importance beyond the domestic. This is the decision not to appoint any one referee to more than one provincial or non-test fixture without the approval of the Lions manager.

This is a drastic and radical variation of the system of last year under which the union chose only a few referees and by and large placed them on a roster for appointment in regular rotation.

Some of the referees, about whom the Springboks had doubts, soon disappeared, but others like Mr J.P. Murphy, of North Auckland, and Mr D.H. Millar, of Otago, kept appearing and giving satisfaction to both sides.

Career Plums

Naturally enough, referees look upon appointments to matches played by visiting teams as the plums of their careers and the system of last year in its restrictiveness denied a number of them the opportunity they would have liked.

Was it, one wonders, because of pressure from the New Zealand Referees' Association that the restrictive system, in spite of its comparative success, was dropped? Or have the Lions already conveyed that they would prefer the devil they don't know to the one they do?

There is just one other item in the list which is of special interest. The New Zealand council has made a grant of £400 for entertainment at test matches, of £200 for other special matches and of £100 for provincial games. Of recent years there has been much covert criticism of the union's excessively generous hospitality and this, it seems, is the answer.

---

7 June 1966

BIG NEW ZEALAND WELCOME FOR TOURING LIONS

Press Association

INVERCARGILL

The British Lions touring Rugby side raced through Australia but chugged into Invercargill — the setting of their first New Zealand game — last night in a 1924 Garrett steam-wagon and a fleet of vintage cars.

As their manager, Mr D.J. O'Brien, stepped from the aircraft he was greeted by two City of Invercargill pipers — Sgt C.E. Hays and Cpl N. McMillan.

Next off the aircraft was the captain, M.J. Campbell-Lamerton. As he and the manager entered the foyer of the airways building they were challenged by Manu Tamaka, leader of the Murihaiku (sic) Maori Concert Party.

The Lions stood fascinated as the Maori party performed the haka and sang an action song.

Manu Tamaka then laid a gift — a hand-carved mere — at the feet of Mr O'Brien.

Song in Maori

In accepting it the manager rubbed noses with the Maori leader and the captain led his side in return songs — one of them a Maori number.

It was all greatly appreciated by the huge crowd which packed the foyer.

Hundreds followed the Lions to their vintage transport and a long line of traffic followed them into Invercargill. They were besieged at their hotel door and before they went in to dinner they waved to the crowd from a second-storey balcony.

Earlier in Christchurch a crowd of 3000 welcomed the team.

The party, at full strength after the arrival of C.H. Gibson and B. Bresnehan, was met by Mr H.C. Blazey, president of the New Zealand Rugby Union, and Mr T.C. Morrison, chairman of its council.

The team sang two songs on the tarmac before leaving for Invercargill. The captain officially opened the New Zealand tour with an address in Maori.

Mr O'Brien said the side looked forward to the New Zealand section of the tour. Asked if he considered the tour too long he said: 'I love it.

'I think the team will agree with me that this is a wonderful experience. I think big tours happen to a player only once in a lifetime and are here to stay.'

'Bit Flattering'

The margin of 31–0 in the second test in Australia was a little bit flattering, he said. 'Things just went right for us in the last 20 minutes.

'Big factors in our win were very good running with the ball and good switches of play and direction. But we are not overflattered.

'I do not think a new replacement rule for international matches is strictly necessary.

'One of the most interesting things in Rugby is to see who is injured after 10 minutes and then see which team has the guts. I think the law is satisfactory as it stands.'

Mr O'Brien said K. Savage was the only unfit member of the party and Gibson and Bresnehan would be ready to play in about 10 days. Savage had an injured back but M. Weston had not been as badly hurt in the test as was supposed.

'The emphasis in our training,' said Campbell-Lamerton, 'will be on soft-ground forward tactics.

'In your climatic conditions the ball bounces as it does in Scotland and our training will be directed toward meeting this.

'The immense forward skill of your teams will make us look closer at how our own forwards are going. We are not satisfied with our forward standard.

'We have got to learn the art of running with the ball on your heavy grounds.'

---

2 July 1966

MIDDLE-AGED WOMAN KNEW ALL THE ANSWERS

Lions 'Frightened' By Rugby Fervour

By T.P. McLean

NEW PLYMOUTH

It is becoming a common experience to hear members of the British Lions touring Rugby team — and very uncommon with any other team I have travelled with — talk of things about New Zealand Rugby which are, and this is a very strange word in international company, 'frightening' to them.

I make haste to say that these things are not the body contact encounters inseparable from first-class Rugby. What's bugging them, if I may use a mod but non-Rugby word, is the intensity, the white-hot intensity of New Zealand's Rugby enthusiasts and their passionate wish to put the Lions right on all the failings, large and small, which have appeared in their play in various matches.

Confrontation

After the defeat by Otago two of the Irish Lions, N.A. Murphy and R. McLoughlin were strolling along the corridor of their hotel doing no harm to anybody when they were confronted by a New Zealand woman, who, if not middle-aged, was certainly at the least too matronly of appearance to look more than a past player of vigorous female hockey or basketball.

In the words of 'The Ancient Mariner,' she fixed them with a glittering eye.

'Young men,' quoth she — or words to that effect — 'your play today was not good. It offended against the best canons of the game.'

'Madam,' they replied, 'we couldn't agree more. But what are we to do about it?'

The good lady's eye flashed.

'This,' she said firmly. According to the Irishmen she then proceeded to give a dissertation on tactical Rugby which was not only remarkable for its breadth, but to McLoughlin, who is a pretty profound student of Rugby, was expert, really expert, in its points.

Expert Skill

The British Isles, even the Irish part of them, does not, so one gathers, contain matrons who can dissect with expert skill the failings of a touring Rugby team. Which is but one reason why, so the Irishmen say, the British Isles, even the Irish part of them, are less 'frightening' in Rugby than New Zealand.

Nervous Smoker?

When the manager of the Lions, Mr D.J. O'Brien, appeared before the press at a conference in New Plymouth on Thursday night, he was not smoking his pipe. This was remarkable. These days Mr O'Brien is practically always smoking his pipe.

Within the span of his lifetime this, too, is remarkable — and psychologists might see in it a most interesting commentary on the severe pressures of management of a Rugby team, especially one which is not having the happiest of experiences.

Pipe Not Used

When Mr O'Brien set out on the expedition he was a smoker of perhaps 10, or as many as 15 cigarettes — a week. There would be weeks in which he would not smoke at all. He had never smoked a pipe. Somewhere along the road in Australia — and it was a pretty hard road too, notwithstanding the current belief in New Zealand that the Aussies must have been a pushover — he took up a pipe and he took up many more cigarettes than he was accustomed to smoking.

These days he smokes a good deal, especially on the pipe. His expression with it in his mouth is benign in the manner of all pipe-smokers and very often he wears a detached, contemplative sort of look.

But the mere fact that this man who smoked so little is now smoking more than he ever used to is surely interesting. It must also surely be significant.

Film Fan

During their stay in Nelson the Lions held a picture evening and the many players who have shot hundreds of feet of coloured film of their expedition through Australia and the early part of New Zealand displayed their products.

Naturally enough, the Sydney Harbour Bridge figured pretty prominently and some of Denzil Williams 'pan' shots, in the course of which he attempted to depict the bridge from end to end, were remarkable for the kind of high speed blur which resulted. The undisputed champion was, without any doubt at all, Alun Pask.

His films were clearcut, the subjects were well chosen and extremely interesting, and practically nothing was wasted. This came as no surprise to admirers of Pask, the cameraman. Moviemaking has long been his favourite hobby and he has acquired a great reputation in Wales because of it.

Most Popular

During the tour of the Lions in South Africa in 1962 he shot a good many feet and on return home sliced this down to a film of 40 minutes' duration. Taken about from one Welsh Rugby club to another, with a superior running commentary from this highly intelligent man attached, this was immensely popular.

Out of the present tour he will produce some similar form of memorial and because of the affinity in Rugby between Wales and New Zealand it is possible that this may prove even more popular than the South African edition.

Pig Escaped

A number of the Lions had a great day out when they went pig-hunting in Nelson on Tuesday. The reaction of Denzil Williams to his slaying, with the aid of a couple of dogs, one beast which cleaned out at 50 pounds was a volley of words which could have been English or Welsh or even heathen Chinese, but which all expressed the ultimate in delight.

When the local hunter in charge of one of the parties disappeared down a bank, rifle and all, to see what the dogs were up to Don Rutherford, the English fullback, casually happened to turn about to look down the track. There at a range of about 100 yards, trotting blithely, and before Rutherford or anyone else in the group could do anything about it, the pig trotted off through the bush.

Lions they might have been — but they couldn't catch a pig.

18 July 1966

ALL BLACKS WERE SUPERIOR IN EVERY PHASE

Heavy First Test Loss By Lions in Dunedin

From T.P. McLean

DUNEDIN

The All Blacks justified their reputation as the finest international Rugby team in the world by defeating the British Lions by 20 points to 3 at Carisbrook on Saturday.

The All Blacks scored with a goal, two penalty goals, a dropped goal and two tries. The Lions scored their points from a penalty goal.

In almost everything that they did the All Blacks were superior. Their exhibition of forward power was quite frightening to behold. Their halfback, C.R. Laidlaw, spun out glorious passes. Their young second five-eighths, I.R. MacRae, made the boldest sort of entry into test match play.

The team bent to the policy of attack with a spirit which argued that no one was so glad as the players to see the end of 55-yard Rugby.

Because this was only the first test of the series there had to be a blemish on the performance.

M.A. Herewini, notwithstanding much excellent play, including a dropped goal, which had a devastating effect upon the Lions, had to be the instrument of this. He punted in the second half at least half a dozen times too often. These tactics were followed at the cost of a running attack, which almost certainly would have yielded two or three tries.

The crowd of 43,500, which paid £23,400 to watch the match — both figures were records for Carisbrook — took unkindly to this kicking.

The spectators were otherwise warmed on this bitingly cold day with the thermometer at only 48 degrees [9°C] by the magnificence of the All Black spectacle.

Lions Harassed

Within the first couple of minutes R.M. Young and D. Watkins were harassed on their own goal line.

Two or three minutes later E.J. Hazlett, the new cap in the pack, appeared to score.

Then Herewini, as of old, was dummying about on tiptoe and nipping to the goal line for a try, which Mr J.P. Pring could not allow because MacRae had been accidentally offside.

So heavy was the pressure that the Lions could not hope to cope, and in only the fifth minute B.E. McLeod was across for the first try.

This followed from a pass by W.J. Nathan, who had shrugged off a tackle or two. Not long afterwards the All Blacks were thrown back to their own line, and when C.E. Meads conceded a penalty at the 25 yards dropout, S. Wilson carefully placed a fine goal across the north-east wind from about 35 yards range.

The goal seemed a promise of better things from the Lions. But only once more during the game did they look like scoring.

This was from the penalty attempt by Wilson who, however, from about 27 yards, slightly sliced the ball outside the righthand upright.

The rest of the match was indisputably with New Zealand. M.W. Williment's first splendid kick at goal to convert McLeod's try suggested that he was on target. But his three attempts at penalties in the first half hour from about 26 yards, 42 yards and only 20 yards all went astray.

There was thus no profit from the relentless plundering by the All Black forwards.

Twice, very cleverly, the Lions saved themselves at throws-in from touch on their goal line by peeling men away until there were only two catchers in the line.

Fine Tackling

More often, they saved themselves by lion-hearted tackling, especially by the midfield backs.

C.W. McFadyean, the Lions wing, stemmed many varied and enterprising runs by such as B.J. Lochore, MacRae, R.E. Rangi and A.G. Steel.

In the 32nd minute Herewini artistically wheeled away from a tackler, steadied and drop-kicked a beautiful goal from more than 30 yards.

M. Williment dives over the line for his try as C.M.H. Gibson makes the tackle.

In effect, the effort announced the end of the Lions. Though the All Blacks before half-time, at which stage they still led by 8 points to 3, and again in the second half missed several opportunities, their dominance of ground was practically complete. One of the most spectacular efforts was the tremendous run of C.E. Meads. He sold two or three perfect dummies and failed by only a couple of feet in his long lunge at the goal line.

The All Black forwards, though sometimes defeated in the line-out by B. Price and thrice at the scrummage by K.W. Kennedy — McLeod almost levelled the score of heels against the head by winning two himself — stirred the pride of their countrymen.

Superb Try

There was pride in their discipline, their physical fitness, their sensible grasp of tactical possibilities and, most of all, in their enormous output of combined strength.

The Lions' defence shuddered at the impact, and bit by bit the points came along.

First there was a superb try on the blind-side when Williment came up outside I.S.T. Smith and stretched himself for the goalline in a magnificent dive.

McFadyean ran very fast to save a try looming for MacRae after Herewini had checked in flight a tactical kick ahead by Watkins.

MacRae soon afterwards almost weaved his way to the goal line.

MacRae was prominent again when he made a breakthrough, which was supported by a thundering phalanx of forwards. The move ended in Lochore scoring a splendid try.

Then, as the Lions' defence grew ragged and spasmodic, Williment, twice in the last 20 minutes, placed comfortable penalty goals from as close as 20 and 10 yards respectively.

All this represented a great day for the All Blacks. One could not say enough about the forwards. Nathan, reputedly not at his best, shrugged and shook off tacklers by spirit and strength. Each of the Meads brothers was indomitable.

Lochore headed deliberately into tackles, and the forwards dutifully swarmed behind him, driving over the ball with superb technical skill.

K.F. Gray held the short end of the line-out under command. Even Price, with all his roaming up and down, could never be sure of possession from S.T.

Laidlaw clears Young on the ground as Nathan, Lochore and Meads look on.

Meads, K.R. Tremain and Lochore at the field.

It was to be expected that the effort of the backline would not quite match the technical standard set by the battle-hardened and experienced pack. But it was pleasing to see the backs going to the attack.

And how sad it seemed that Herewini should have persuaded himself, notwithstanding the look of both the scoreboard and the Lions, that punts were the most prudent investment.

Laidlaw committed two or three blunders. The most expensive was his failure to be at the heels of a ruck near the Lions goal-line immediately after kick-off for the second half.

His play otherwise was magnificent, especially in the speed, accuracy and length of his passing.

Herewini's hands and feet were as tidy as ever. He lost nothing in comparison with Watkins.

MacRae was 'just the job.'

Rangi, two or three times, passed before he needed, at the cost of probable tries to the All Blacks, but redeemed himself by his toughness and eagerness. Steel, more enterprising and safer of hand than Smith on the other wing, made a couple of fine runs without quite revealing the speed of a sprint champion. Williment's goal kicking was below the Williment standard, but in other respects he played extremely well.

It was a pity that several of his attempts to slice the defence by joining in back attacks were forestalled by those Herewini punts.

Out of charity one must pass quietly over many aspects of the Lions.

Wilson was admirably courageous and steady at fullback, D.I. Bebb and McFadyean on the wings worked like trojans. C.M. Gibson made splendid tackles, and Watkins used his speed and nip to get in touch-finders to stem attacks.

Young was as ever a brave man in the face of the stream of All Black forwards.

Responded Little

But the forwards responded little, if at all, as a combined force to the pleading and urgings of

M.J. Campbell-Lamerton. Only the captain himself, Price, R.A. Lamont and, occasionally, A.I. Pask commended themselves as of international class.

The defects were numerous and alarming. If, as may be expected, the All Blacks turn out to be even more efficient in the second test, the strain upon the tourists will be greatly increased.

'We come from a proud heritage,' Campbell-Lamerton said later.

True enough. Now is the time to prove it.

18 July 1966

GATE REMOVED AT TEST

Press Association

DUNEDIN

A mob of about 200 people removed a gate and poured into Carisbrook shortly after the start of the first test on Saturday.

The gate, standing 12 feet high and made of steel piping and wire mesh, was lifted off its hinges by the crowd, who then poured into the ground.

The secretary of the Otago Rugby Football Union, Mr J.N. Keenan, said it was a waste of time trying to stop them and get them out of the ground.

25 July 1966

QUEUE MOSTLY FEMININE

Women outnumbered men two to one in a queue of people who waited several hours at Eden Park on Saturday to obtain tickets for the Lions vs Auckland game.

The women were well prepared for their wait. Most had brought books and newspapers, sandwiches, hot drinks, radios, knitting and warm clothes. The men seemed less well-equipped, but quite content with a cigarette or pipe and the sunshine.

Officials said a limited number of tickets was available for seats inside the ground and for standing room in the No. 3 stand enclosure.

They were priced at 7s 6d, 10s and 12s 6d and were rationed to four a person.

First in the queue was Mrs G.W. Symmans, of Remuera, who had left home for Eden Park at 9a.m. and had to wait three hours.

8 August 1966

LIONS IMPROVE, BUT N.Z. WIN 16–12

All Blacks Took Their Chances in Mud

From T.P. McLean

WELLINGTON

Three chances taken, three chances missed — in essence this was the story of the Rugby test match at Athletic Park on Saturday.

The All Blacks became two up with two to play in the series by defeating the touring British Lions by 16 points from two goals, a penalty goal and a try to 12 points from three penalty goals and a dropped goal.

K.R. Tremain in the 15th minute, C.E. Meads in the 43rd and A.G. Steel in the 75th scored tries for the All Blacks, and M.W. Williment improved two of these efforts into goals while also placing a penalty goal.

By contrast the Lions three times in the first half lost scoring chances — once when C.W. McFadyean passed forward to D.I. Bebb; another time when A.J. Hinshelwood dropped a ball; and the third time when Hinshelwood passed forward to C.M. Gibson.

They were restricted to penalty goals by S. Wilson in the 9th, 28th and 78th minutes and to a dropped goal after a heel against the head by D. Watkins in the 17th minute.

In the 12th minute, incidentally, Wilson from 27 yards struck the right-hand upright with yet another of his superbly accurate kicks at goal.

K.R. Tremain takes the ball, with K.F. Grey behind him. I.S.T. Smith has beaten B.E. McLeod to tackle D. Bebb.

Win Deserved

The All Blacks by their performance deserved the victory. Yet the effort of the Lions was the best by far of the tour, Australia included.

The contribution made for one of the nobler test matches which afforded the greatest pleasure to most of the 44,425 spectators.

The contribution of the Lions was such, in fact, that New Zealand's status as the leader of world Rugby was imperilled.

It may endlessly be debated what unfortunate influence was exerted when the referee Mr J.P. Murphy in the 68th minute ruled a penalty kick for the Lions at the cost of a try which the threequarters McFadyean and Hinshelwood seemed to have in their grasp some 70 yards downfield.

Williment had dropkicked at goal and the ball slithered from his left foot far across the field.

'Red, Red'

As McFadyean picked up and began a run spectators who had been chanting 'Red, Red' watched in silent agony. Steel dashed forward from an offside position and made — and missed — his tackle.

Mr Murphy instinctively blew his whistle for off side and in immediate dismay at his failure to apply the advantage rule apologised to the Lions for his mistake. To their credit the Lions accepted this one human blemish in a splendid display of refereeing without a show of criticism or irritation and plunged forthwith into further attempts to force back the All Blacks from their quarter.

Despite the predominance of the All Blacks in the fight for possession the Lions, even after this misfortune, could still have won the game had they taken their chances.

There was an immense improvement in their spirit and techniques upon their play in the first test at Dunedin.

C.R. Laidlaw getting the ball away during the second test at Athletic Park.

Bad Conditions

The day served to sustain the unfortunate reputation of Athletic Park as a place for test matches. After all-night rain, the morning was calm, warm and not discouraging. An hour before kick-off, however, a small breeze began to whisper out of the south and by the time the game began it had stiffened and was fresh and cool.

The combination of the wind and an extremely heavy and fatiguing pitch meant that the dice were going to be loaded for the team winning the toss.

B.J. Lochore, having won the call, elected to play the first half into the wind. It was a more than sensible gamble because of the nervous tensions which grip even the best-drilled teams in the first quarter of a test. The gamble paid off.

The Lions missed their chances and when they turned into the wind with a lead of only nine points to eight it was inevitable that they were going to lose. But what a fight they made. How glorious was their defence and how soundly they played under the extremely heavy pressure the All Blacks exerted for so much of the second half.

This was the real point of contrast between the two teams. The All Blacks were magnificent when they scored their tries; they were equally magnificent in their covering defence, especially by Lochore and S. Meads.

Pushed Back

At the scrummage that mattered they were able to contain the ball and with remorseless tread push the Lions back and back through the mud.

But the All Blacks, despite these virtues, were not sound — not at least by the highest standards.

C.R. Laidlaw began the game with curious little flick passes which blooped the ball somewhere out into the backline.

M.A. Herewini naturally had no great idea of where the passes were going and when later something like a proper rhythm was established Herewini's kicks for his outer backs or ahead of the forwards were by no means well judged.

It was extraordinary, in fact, how many of the so-called tactical kicks of the All Blacks went to the hands of Lions or were charged down.

The element of unsoundness persisted into the threequarters on the All Black side. On a dismaying number of times when they were running the ball downwind in the second half man and ball were taken in the tackle.

There were two shining exceptions to this general want of sturdiness.

I.R. MacRae was almost certainly the finest back in the game and whether he was running at full speed with the ball, turning and swerving at every stride or crashing into the tackle, his display was impeccable.

He made the first try by picking up one of Laidlaw's more curious passes on the half-volley, ducking under the arms of Watkins and Gibson as they rushed forward and running his forwards into perfect position.

The move which followed involved Tremain, Laidlaw, B.E. McLeod and finally Tremain again for the scoring of a magnificent try over 40 yards of ground. Williment was the other star of the hour. He was admirably sound in most things and brilliant in others.

Startling Effort

Once when he gathered a kick on the half-volley, slithered about on the treacherous ground and still managed to find touch down the field, the effort was startling in its quality.

Despite their dominance in many phases the All Black forwards were not quite so massively effective as in their first test.

This was a left-handed tribute to the Lions who had improved so much.

Nevertheless C.E. Meads made three or four runs of his inimitable brilliance; W.J. Nathan surged upon Watkins through the second half; S.T. Meads roamed all over the field; Lochore if not so spectacular as in the first test covered acres of ground; and the pack as a whole wanted nothing in spirit.

Perhaps because of the conditions the Willie-Away was not well played and a certain amount of jumbling at the back of the line-out was unexpected.

Tremain made his try and set C.E. Meads up for another, but Tremain also gave away three points by trudging along the base of the line-out in breach of the law requiring a single line until the ball is in the air.

M.A. Herewini clearing as R.A. Lamont dives to tackle and B.J. Lochore ducks.

Squandered

Statistics can be tiresome things, but a study of the play of the halfbacks demonstrates how the superior possession of the All Blacks was so often squandered from one cause or another.

Such squandering provided an unsatisfactory undercurrent to the dominance of the All Blacks in the second half.

Laidlaw got what the statistician described as 'useable' ball 45 times.

He kicked 12 times and passed 33. Herewini got useable ball 27 times and translated this into 13 kicks, one run and 13 passes.

A.R. Lewis, on the other hand, received only 25 balls, kicked five of these and passed the other 20, all of which Watkins received.

Five Passes

Watkins, in turn, kicked 14 times, ran once, and passed only five times. It was tempting to suggest that Watkins must have been the superior player in the exchanges because his outside backs were evidently so much the superior set.

In fact one has to ask why the possibilities of the backline were not better appreciated.

Gibson's one failure with the tackle of MacRae was his only mistake. McFadyean made one lovely run. Bebb was the next best back to MacRae in the game. Hinshelwood survived the experience well.

Wilson glided into the attacks of the first half as dangerously as J.W. Kelly of old.

This is surely a want of understanding by the Lions themselves of their potentialities in running plays. Despite the greatness of C.E. Meads in his smashing runs he could not be put ahead of the young Welshman W.D. Thomas in point of value to his side.

Thomas had an extraordinarily fine first international and may one of these days become a great forward.

W.J. McBride was scarcely less physically strong and dynamic. The back row of N.A. Murphy and J.W. Telfer and R.A. Lamont performed prodigies in defensive work.

They could not hope to equal the All Blacks' back row in skill at moving almost by numbers to exactly the right places when, of a sudden, counterattacks were set up and runners began looking for supports.

Irish Lament

Mr D.J. O'Brien, the manager of the Lions, lamented in the Irish way the failure of his team to bring off the victory.

He thought it a shame that so rich a chance was not seized. Yet he had cause to admire the very remarkable improvement in the look, quality and performance of his players and if the improvement can be maintained the third test at Christchurch on August 27 will perhaps imperil the All Blacks' standing even further.

Suffice to say of the match as a whole that though there were inevitably in the conditions a great many scrummages and line-outs the play otherwise was vitally alive.

A couple of explosive gestures involving C.E. Meads, some early trouble with the props K.F. Gray and C.H. Norris until Mr Murphy intervened, and one late tackle were the only disturbances of the peace.

For this relief, after the effort of Eden Park, one could only murmur 'much thanks.'

24 August 1966

BIZARRE LESSON FOR PROP

From T.P. McLean

CHRISTCHURCH

It was bizarre certainly, but it really was not part of the Goon Show at Lancaster Park yesterday afternoon.

It was merely an attempt by the British Lions, on the eve of their critically important third test with the All Blacks, to turn into a tighthead prop forward their 23-year-old Welsh lock W.D. Thomas, who had never played in the position before.

Many hands bent to the task of preparing Thomas, in three anything but easy lessons, with

the pressure-cooker course he must complete by the time of final training tomorrow afternoon.

Two highly experienced props in R.J. McLoughlin and D. Williams were there, the captain, M.J. Campbell-Lamerton was there, even the manager of the Lions, Mr D.J. O'Brien, was lurking around in football togs to lend a pound when any pushing was required.

It only added to the atmosphere of fantasy that the coach, Mr J.D. Robins, was not there — at least not closer than the touchline and as silent as stout Cortez on a peak in Darien.

Yet Mr Robins, one seems to remember, played 11 times for Wales and goodness knows how many times for the 1950 British Lions in Australia and New Zealand — always as a prop forward.

29 August 1966

LIONS TEAM DESERTED BY LUCK IN TEST

All Blacks Win 19–6

From T.P. McLean

CHRISTCHURCH

Although the margin was 13 points and the score was three tries to two, there was a certain unreal, almost a Ripleyan aura, to the victory of the All Blacks in their third test with the British Lions on Saturday by 19 points (two goals, two penalty goals and a try) to 6 points (two tries).

After an extremely strenuous first half in which the All Blacks were discovered to be deficient at the line-out and not at all efficient behind the scrummage the two teams were level at six points each.

M.W. Williment had placed two penalty goals for New Zealand and R.A. Lamont and D. Watkins scored tries for the Lions to the rapturous pleasure of the crowd of 50,000.

For the first 10 minutes of the second half the Lions, with a freshening breeze at their backs, were

A.G. Steel scoring the All Blacks' first try.

arrestingly superior, and in this phase the All Blacks began to wear almost a hangdog look.

A breakaway which yielded a simple try to A.G. Steel on the All Blacks' left wing was helpful to the New Zealand cause, but within 10 minutes S. Wilson floated with perfect judgment into a run by the Lions backs.

Nothing, absolutely nothing, could, so it seemed, stop a try by D.I. Bebb which in that state and stage of the game could have meant the winning of the match.

Try Lost

Almost incomprehensibly, Wilson chopped infield and after he was tackled by the cover defence the thrilling movement collapsed.

Subsequently W.J. Nathan scored two tries which Williment improved into goals.

The second of these, from a superb thrust on the blind-side by I.R. MacRae and perfect support from three dreadnoughts in K.R. Tremain, K.F. Gray and W.J. Nathan put the game with only 10 minutes remaining out of reach of the Lions.

No fewer than four times in the second half in the fifth, 18th, 24th and 25th minutes, the Lions mostly because of the superior quality of their back play slashed the New Zealand defence and put men into positions to score tries no one could have stopped.

Each time an error of commission prevented the fulfilment of the brilliant promise of the movement.

In the first movement A.R. Lewis, D. Watkins and C.M. Gibson repeated their brilliant dummy scissors of the New Zealand Maori match at Auckland.

Gibson, thrusting through the defence, placed C.W. McFadyean and on the right S.J. Watkins into perfect positions for the try.

The last-mentioned was actually scoring it as the whistle of Mr J.P. Murphy very rightly sounded in punishment of the McFadyean's massive fumble of the pass from Gibson.

In the next movement, Wilson suddenly was visible outside R.E. Rangi with the ball in his arms and Bebb haring alongside with Williment almost certainly committed to the tackle of the ball carrier.

Was it a wish to traverse some ghostly corridor

A bloody-nosed Lions flanker R.A. Lamont is surrounded by All Blacks after scoring a try.

which caused Wilson to turn inside? There seemed no human reasonable explanation for the fault.

In the third of these princely pieces of work McFadyean was the thruster-in-chief and Bebb was again intended to be the man of fulfilment.

This time McFadyean threw a hard, high pass between neck and ear which Bebb could not hope to catch — the pass was forward, too.

Finally and only a minute later Wilson made a magnificent save when Rangi and Steel were rushing the ball upfield and all was confusion as the Lions counter-attacked.

They brought the ball into the clear behind the mass of All Blacks and put it into the arms of Gibson.

The defence was gone, Gibson must have scored behind the posts — and a fiery blast from Mr Murphy announced all too rightly that Lamont, the man who made the pass to Gibson, had fumbled the ball.

Because these were all errors of commission by the Lions they would seem not material to the case that the All Blacks in winning by so heavy a margin of points were flattered or fortunate or both.

Perhaps so. Nevertheless they emphasised not only the fragility of the All Blacks' defence close to the scrum, but also the superior enterprise and attacking qualities of the Lions' backs.

It was another aspect of the Ripleyan atmosphere that the All Blacks' backline at no stage looked capable of mounting a try-scoring attack by planned rather than fortuitous means.

There is a strain of melancholy to the thought, too, that while New Zealand's score included 10 points from place-kicks at goal by Williment the Lions were unable to score a point from kicks.

All things considered, therefore, the All Blacks

C.M. Gibson being tackled , ball and all, by W. Nathan.

were aided and abetted by the goddess of games, Lady Luck, while the Lions vainly reached supplicating hands for her favours.

What grandeur, what magnificence, what a demonstration of the value of experience there was in the display of the All Black forwards.

New Spirit

They with Williment and the one outstanding New Zealand back of the attacking line, MacRae, were undoubtedly the architects of a victory which placed the All Blacks three up with only one more test to play.

The Lions' forwards made splendid efforts in the first half.

W.D. Thomas, who emerged from his severe test as a prop forward with augmented reputation, especially at the line-out, and W.J. McBride and A.E. Pask, either won the ball from line-outs of the first half

or prevented the All Blacks from winning it quickly.

M.J. Campbell-Lamerton, contained in the strenuous contest of the tight-forward play, was actually next to Lamont when the latter scored.

In the first ten minutes of the second half the turning of the game and the winning of a notable victory seemed to be within the grasp of the Lions.

It was at this critical stage that the All Black forwards roused themselves to display the fire, control, passion, technical skill and enormous physical vigour which makes this surely one of the great New Zealand packs.

Almost as if a clarion had sounded the forwards responded to the emergency. When M.A. Herewini had placed a superbly accurate grubber-kick across the Lions' goal-mouth the All Blacks' forwards were twice called upon.

When they won the ball at a scrum Herewini, after a criss-cross sort of move, all but reached the

D.I. Bebb being restrained by C.E. Meads and I.S.T. Smith.

goal-line with link and nip and dodge.

When he went down in a tackle the forwards went over the top of him, and back came the ball.

As Laidlaw gathering it felt the hot breath of S.J. Watkins dashing at him from the blind-side wing and only a yard or two from the corner he was able to flip a pass to Steel so quickly that the latter was able to run unopposed into the in-goal area.

This was a forward effort. And they were forward efforts, too, which produced the next two tries.

First, MacRae, running the blind, kicked ahead so accurately that Bebb and Murphy were unable to make the catch. On the instant the forwards were at the ball they crashed, bundled and hurdled it down the touchline. When they passed it to Nathan with Wilson gallantly offering a standing-up sort of tackle nothing could have stopped the Black Panther going in at the corner.

Next time MacRae ran the blind, weaved out and weaved in and at the inevitable tackle looked for support.

From out of and probably from under a great heap of bodies, first Gray, then Tremain and finally Nathan had extracted themselves to range alongside MacRae to take his pass. By putting it from one man to the other to Nathan he had the simplest of tries behind the posts.

Meads Great

And all of the time between these great efforts the great C.E. Meads, by subterfuge, cunning and strength, was winning the ball at the lineout.

S.T. Meads was crashing at the defence, and Gray was spearheading drives at the short end of the line-out. What a pity, therefore, that the back effort, MacRae and Williment honourably excepted, so seldom measured to the forward standard.

If they want to be acclaimed undisputedly as world champions the All Blacks will have to do better next time.

---

12 September 1966

ALL BLACKS SET NEW RECORD

Clean Sweep in Home Four-Match Series

By T.P. McLean

In farewell, celebration and, not least, lamentation, thousands of spectators of the Rugby test match at Eden Park on Saturday sang 'Now Is the Hour' after the All Blacks had defeated the British Lions by 24 points (from three conversions, a penalty goal, a dropped goal and four tries) to 11 points (from a goal, a penalty goal and a try).

For all their indifferent records of eight matches lost and two drawn in 25 games in New Zealand and a brand of Rugby which never consistently expressed the classic quality of previous British teams in this country, the Lions were more than entitled to a song of farewell.

Match by match, in sun, rain or wind — and sometimes all three within the one match — they had held the attention of a huge number of New Zealanders.

Even when they had no possible hope on Saturday of winning or squaring the test series, their popularity was such that 300 had to be locked out of the ground after 58,000 had paid the record and enormous sum of £43,000 to get in.

Fair cause this, surely, for a tribute in song. Perhaps even for another one, at the special request of the New Zealand Rugby Union, 'Will Ye No' Come Back Again?'

Took Toss

All too sadly, there was cause for lamentation. In the 27th minute, A.E. Pask at the field end of the line-out was cartwheeled in a tackle on to the point of his shoulder.

There was a doubt that he had the ball in his hands when he took the toss.

Dismay about this turned to grief at the sight of him being strapped up and carried by stretcher from the field. His left collar-bone was broken.

Magnificent as was the gallantry of the Lions after he had gone, and stirred as all were by the heroic defiance and bristling counter-attacks of the straitened team, with Pask's departure the match was as good as lost.

This was lamentable. Worse, it was a tragedy for a team which has been more plagued by misfortune than any other team to visit New Zealand, the 1956 Springboks alone excepted.

It was not the only cause of lamentation. Midway through the second half, D. Watkins, the Lions' captain, dropped like a stone from a punch by C.E. Meads.

Malcolm Dick scoring a try in the fourth test at Eden Park.

It was said later in Meads' defence that Watkins had flared up and offered a punch after hurriedly putting in a kick to touch.

It may have been so. The accusing fingers of the Lions' players pointing out Meads to Mr J.P. Murphy were the visible expression of a general attitude of amazement, dismay and regret.

History Made

There was every cause for celebration. This was the first All Black team in history ever to sweep through a four-match home series — a signal achievement expressive of the concentrated purpose, energy and power of the side.

They produced in the best phases not only of Saturday but also of all the tests a wondrous capacity for dreadnought charges at the enemy goal line.

Except for the last effort, the try by A.G. Steel, which appeared to result from two forward passes, the scoring movements of the All Blacks bespoke power, strength and intelligence.

All warranted celebration and the best effort among them, the surging stride of M.J. Dick past three defenders, was greeted with one of the great shouts of Eden Park history.

But the All Blacks took no more than part of the glory. When the Lions, devastated by the loss of Pask, reacted by running in two classic tries, the crowd erupted with pleasure and admiration.

It is impossible, so the experts say, to score from set-piece plays, especially in test matches.

Impossible? B. Price leaped like a gazelle at a line-out just inside the All Blacks' twenty-five and, coming down, handed A.R. Lewis a copybook pass.

The ball sped from Lewis to Watkins to C.M.H. Gibson to S. Wilson and finally to A.J. Hinshelwood, far out on the right.

M. Williment, the All Black fullback, was across there — Steel was already well outflanked — but being on the dead run, he could not hope to check as Hinshelwood stepped inside, cut out and set sail for the goal line near the corner flag.

As he dived, only M.A. Herewini was near. It was a try to treasure — and it came from a set-piece play.

The next effort, only four minutes later, was even more spectacular. Lewis, swooping onward, grabbed the ball and broke clear. Gibson appeared inside him. At the pass, Gibson, wrongly, so one supposed, cut back infield.

Wrongly? Not one of three men could touch him as he sidestepped and skedaddled toward midfield. When Steel blocked his path, he threw a long, hard pass.

Tearing along at Olympic speed, C.W. McFadyean took the ball and ran at least 30 yards to the goalposts. When Wilson placed the goal, the Lions were 8, the All Blacks were 10, the sun was coming out to shine blindly into the faces of the New Zealanders for the second half and anything, so it seemed, could happen.

The anything, up to and including victory for the Lions, almost certainly turned upon the frantic moments of the 15th minute of the second half when I.R. MacRae, cornered, slammed hard into a dropkick at goal.

The ball rebounded immediately to Gibson. Williment had already gone up into the backline. There was no one in front. Gibson had an advantage of at least three yards as he footed the ball ahead. Reaching into the All Black twenty-five, still with an advantage, still with no one in front, Gibson appeared to make a dab at catching the ball as it bounced.

He swore afterwards — and he is a truthful man — that his knee, not his hand, touched the ball. Mr Murphy reacted as did most of the crowd. He ruled a knock-on. The movement died. The All Blacks counter-attacked. The Lions later, through Gibson with a dropkick and D.I. Bebb with a couple of runs, made strong efforts to score.

Critical Point

But this was the critical point. In the 24th minute of the half, when Gibson mishandled with Wilson up, K.R. Tremain and MacRae swooped upon the ball, kicking it ahead to the goal line where MacRae, with powerful assistance from Dick, made the try. Williment, with an easy conversion, turned it into a goal.

Instead of 10 to 8, the All Blacks were now 15–8. All of a sudden, in the most human and forgivable sort of way, the resistance of the Lions vanished. Steel ran in his disputable try and Herewini corkscrewed around to dropkick a glorious goal. And at the end, after Wilson had placed a 30-yard penalty, Williment replied with another to which many of the crowd objected because they would have preferred the All Blacks to chance their arm at a run.

And that was the end of the Lions, the tour and the series. But not of the debates about tries and incidents and misfortunes and even such things as tight-heads. Despite the dazzling brilliance of the Lions' trics, one had the feeling, even before the departure of Pask, that the All Blacks were going to win. Their possession from the line out, aided by obstructive tactics, and from rucks was such that C.R. Laidlaw handled the ball 39 times to Lewis' 18.

As in previous tests, their seizure of opportunities was extraordinarily quick.

When D.I. Bebb, dangerously unsteady on an uncertain turf, managed to put the ball into touch only a couple of feet from the corner flag, C.E. Meads among the five All Blacks who had run 50 yards or so to harry him, instantly seized it, threw it underarm to W.J. Nathan and Nathan,

The incident that led to the All Blacks first try.

unhindered, hurled across for a try which Williment turned into a goal.

Encouragement

This was a startling encouragement for the All Blacks. The next try was not less a fine example of instant reaction and perfect recoil. When Herewini's dropkick at goal skewered off a Lion 30 yards across the field, Dick flashed upon the bouncing ball. With the thrust and speed of his great days he sped past three defenders to a try which Williment also turned into a goal.

These 10 points in the first 24 minutes won the game. As the play wore on, B.J. Lochore secured winning efforts — 31 to 20 all told — from such as the Meads brothers and K.F. Gray at the line-out.

At the rucks and after them, Gray, Lochore, Nathan and the fabulous flanker, K.R. Tremain, won the ball and made strenuous progress with it.

Unhappily, the All Black back effort failed for the fourth time to reach an estimable international level. C.R. Laidlaw, though much improved on his last test, was not as of old in quality and placement of passing. His breakaways were too tentative by far to bring the outer backs or the forwards forcefully into the attack.

Herewini, who took a hard crack on the head at a ruck which developed when he all but splintered the defence, thereafter tended to kick too much and not always with profit. MacRae went for the barge, which yielded little, too.

R.E. Rangi scarcely saw the ball, Steel for a sprinter was slow off the mark and only Dick of the backline proper had a completely satisfying game.

Williment wrenched his side so painfully in trying to stop Gibson that he had to spend some minutes off the field. Whatever he did, before and after, was commendably sound, however.

Price at the line-out, R.A. Lamont at the loose, K.W. Kennedy for quite magnificent hooking with a reduced scrum and W.J. McBride for general services were all valiant contributors to the Lions' forward effort. In one feature, pressure upon the halfback to five-eighths, this, for all its gallantry, was decidedly inferior to the All Black standard.

The inability of the Lions to win the ball consistently was, too, a serious burden for the backs to carry.

Battled Staunchly

Lewis, though under heavy pressure, battled staunchly. Watkins could not manage breakaways and Gibson was able to produce only a few of his

LEFT: Lions captain M.J. Campbell-Lamerton riding a Timor pony in Westport.

RIGHT: D. Grant watches S.Wilson line up for a drive with S. Hinshelwood on the ground with ball during a relaxing game of golf for the Lions.

touches of uncommon brilliance.

Both he and Watkins had handling lapses and these increased the New Zealand pressure.

McFadyean on defence or attack was magnificent, perhaps the back of the game. Hinshelwood, with one chance, took it superbly.

Bebb was caught once by Dick, outsped him another time but had on his conscience that unfortunate mulling which yielded the first try.

Wilson, hitherto the Admirable Crichton of the tour, for once turned human. The turf in the twenty-fives looked soft and uncertain and perhaps this explained his misfortunes.

Thousands streamed across the field to listen to the speeches at the end and 'Now Is the Hour' and 'Auld Lang Syne' were sung. And so the tour has ended. Perhaps the appropriate token for the Lions was: Better luck next time.

12 September 1966

LIONS TOUR TAKINGS RECORD £400,000

The British Lions tour which finished in Auckland on Saturday grossed about £400,000 — a record for teams touring New Zealand.

Although no official figures were available from the New Zealand Rugby Union last night it is estimated that total paid attendances for the matches were well over 700,000.

Gate takings at Eden Park on Saturday were £43,000 — £2750 more than the previous record gate takings in New Zealand, set at the final Springbok test in Auckland last year.

George Earney, the Lions baggage master, organises the team's luggage at the St George Hotel in Wellington.

1971

26 June – Dunedin
10 July – Christchurch
31 July – Wellington
14 August – Auckland

13 February 1971

HAURAKI WILL DEFY BAN

Radio Hauraki says it will broadcast some of the British Lions Rugby matches in New Zealand this year in defiance of the Rugby Union's rejection of its application for broadcasting rights.

During in-committee discussions in Wellington yesterday the council of the New Zealand Rugby Union rejected the bid by Radio Hauraki to secure broadcasting rights for six of the Lions' matches.

At the same time, it granted exclusive broadcasting rights for the year to the NZBC.

'Our application was rejected without explanation,' the chairman and managing director of Radio Hauraki, Mr D.J. Gapes, said last night.

'Our intention is to proceed with live broadcasts anyway, certainly the Auckland matches, with or without the union's approval,' he said.

'I don't think we can broadcast outside Auckland, but we will certainly do so in Auckland.'

'Reasonable Fee'

'We have already engaged Winston McCarthy to cover the matches.'

Mr Gapes said Radio Hauraki had made a straightforward request to the union and had said it was prepared to pay a reasonable fee for the broadcasting rights.

He said he considered the situation ridiculous.

'We wrote to the union only because we considered it a mere formality. Nevertheless we were refused without explanation and an opportunity to discuss fees.'

Reluctant

Mr Gapes did not say how the matches would be covered.

The chairman of the council of the New Zealand Rugby Union, Mr J.L. Sullivan, was reluctant last night to discuss details of the union decision.

When asked why Radio Hauraki was offered no explanation for the union's decision, Mr Sullivan said: 'This is their business. The issue is very simple, we have made our decision and that's where it rests.'

After being told that Radio Hauraki intended to broadcast in spite of the union's ban, Mr Sullivan again added: 'That is their business.'

Early 'Pirates'

In the early days of broadcasting in New Zealand there were occasions when commentators flouted official refusal and broadcast sports matches from vantage points outside the grounds.

Football, horse racing and cricket were all involved.

In January 1940, the chairman of the Wellington Cricket Association voiced strong exception to the action of the then National Broadcasting Service in broadcasting Plunket Shield commentaries from a house overlooking the Basin Reserve. He thought the association should record its amazement that a State department should adopt tactics which 'could only be compared to a small boy climbing over a fence to see a match for nothing.'

In the immediate postwar years, Australian racing clubs, believing a fall-off in attendances was due to punters staying at home to listen to radio broadcasters, banned commentators from Randwick racecourse.

Radio retaliated by renting a house adjoining the course and broadcasting from the top floor, which overlooked the track.

The radio stations won their point and are now allowed to broadcast from the track.

---

25 May 1971

ROUSED FROM SLUMBER BY LOUD AND CLEAR CALL
T.P. McLean

WANGANUI

Men of Harlech and other places who are members of the British Lions touring Rugby team were roused from slumber yesterday morning — but not because the foe in growing

number were threatening this fair land.

It was because a receptionist in their hotel grew exasperated that at 8.10 the only member of the team in the dining room was the manager, Dr Douglas Smith.

Over the hotel loudspeaker at a force of many decibels came the announcement, crisply stated by a woman who evidently knew her own mind: 'Members of the British Lions Rugby team will kindly assemble in the hotel dining room for breakfast.'

Sensational

The effect was sensational. Within 20 minutes at least half of the team, many of them shaven, were at table tossing up whether to have eggs, loin chops or kidneys.

By 9 o'clock at least two-thirds of the team had gone through the menu.

For the Lions, who to a man — with the exception of Dr Smith, who has strong views about rising early — believe that it's nice to get up in the morning but nicer to lie in bed, this was a remarkable achievement.

But they were grateful when at training later their coach, Mr Carwyn James, put them through some fairly stiff tasks which still did not seem more than passing rugged by comparison with the tasks which, for example, Mr F.R. Allen used to set his Auckland and All Black teams.

---

26 May 1971

UP RIVER WITHOUT A PADDLE

T.P. McLean

WANGANUI

In light-hearted preparation for their important match at Wanganui today, members of the Lions tour party sizzled up the Wanganui River yesterday by jet boat.

The jet boat expedition was not entirely comic for two boats ran out of gas a mile or two above the city and came back to town slowly and painfully.

But when the team manager, Dr Smith,

interestedly inquired about the difficulties the results were quite sensational.

He was told that a jet was just like a car. What was more, he was invited to see for himself. Dr Smith is a big man. He has a heavy hand on the throttle.

Within seconds his craft was screeching at 50 miles an hour. It passed over a sandbank, according to one allegation, rather like a Boeing 737 lifting off Auckland International Airport.

More or less coincidentally, Mr Carwyn James, the coach, in association with the New Zealand Rugby Union's liaison officer, Mr F.D. Kilby, the baggage master of the tour, Mr G. Earney, and a Welsh newspaperman, Mr Tudor James (no relation to Carwyn by the way), was slowly and delightedly trundling bowls up and down the St Johns club's green.

The green was slowish by New Zealand standards but the pace of it was a killer for the Welshmen.

They were too heavy with every bowl and at the end, until someone of charitable mind inserted the figure one, they were heavily beaten by 13 to 4. The Lions show a great capacity for getting on well with each other. It could be a strength of their tour.

---

28 June 1971

MEMORABLE RUGBY WIN FOR LIONS TEAM

Promise of Exciting Series of Tests
T.P. McLean

DUNEDIN

One perhaps can be too sentimental. Perhaps the Rugby test match at Carisbrook on Saturday in which the British Lions became exalted by defeating the All Blacks, 9–3, was not as enthralling and exciting a game as it seemed.

Perhaps too much sentiment was taken from a game in which there was only one tasteless incident of men striking each other, and at the end of which the Lions gathered to salute the All Blacks from the field.

It was no small thing either in these days of tense and often bitter rivalry in international sport that the first man into the Lions' dressing room to salute them was the captain of the All Blacks, C.E. Meads.

There might even have been a tendency to suppose that the game was better than it actually was so that one could gloss over the utter misery of W.F. McCormick, not only for failing to place two goals from penalties within the Lions twenty-five, but also for playing a game completely out of character.

It might not have been a good game. The score might have flattered the Lions who so often were penned back to their quarter.

There might have been weaknesses in the All Black forward play for a significant period of the first half when the Lions, despite having to play into the glaring sun and a cool, fresh breeze, kept three points in the lead until the very last minute.

At that stage a strange decision by Mr J.P. Pring permitted McCormick to place his only goal.

Strong Defence

Overall, however, the match did have truly memorable qualities. To start with the defence by both teams, but especially by the Lions, was incredibly strong.

Secondly, the All Blacks used their backs as regularly and confidently as if they were halfway through a successful tour.

Thirdly, the spirit within the teams was quite dauntless.

And lastly, the 30 players, not forgetting the unfortunate McCormick, committed themselves so totally to the struggle that every man was spent to the point of exhaustion of body and mind by the end.

From all these factors one forms the opinion that the series seems certain to become the keenest and best fought since the matches between the All Blacks and the Lions of 1959.

Mental Block

The Lions might not care to admit this, but it is true that they went into the match inhibited by a mental block. They wanted most desperately to win, and when they did so they felt an overwhelming joy.

But they did not think in their hearts that they could win.

No one, they shivered among themselves, ever beats the All Blacks in New Zealand.

Because of the block their play on attack fell below the standard they had been aiming for and often achieving.

Apart from the fortuitous moment of scoring when the tiny J. McLauchlan charged down a clearing kick, so low slung that it could not even clear him, the Lions only thrice looked likely to score in the threequarters.

Superbly Done

The threequarter run of finest quality was a kick and a follow by Gerald Davies. Everything was superbly done.

He had the legs of three or four All Blacks, and the ball pitched perfectly to run into the in-goal.

A cranky little bounce, which carried the ball into touch in goal, however, defeated Davies in the instant that he dived and pressed the ball down.

The All Blacks had no mental block, only an intense ambition. Whether by the instruction of the coach, Mr I.M.H. Vodanovich, or C.E. Meads, or both, the team set out to gratify the ambition by hitting the Lions at every point.

The speed and power of the opening few minutes were magnificent. Again and again throughout the game, and especially in the second half, the All Blacks renewed their dynamic assaults.

Twice or thrice Hunter seemed certain to go over.

Big Threat

Meads headed for the goalposts with such a charge that if he had hit them he would have knocked them down. I.A. Kirkpatrick and A.R. Sutherland were electrified. S.M. Going's amazing strength carried him free of men who seemed to hold him securely.

And every so often the ball went into the threequarters: to B.G. Williams, who always looked dangerous, to Hunter who was, and too seldom to K.C. Carrington, who made a lasting impression with his side-stepping, fearless running.

But there was an impediment. R.E. Burgess and W.D. Cottrell in the five-eighths both kicked a

B. John taking a shot at goal during the first test at Carisbrook.

little too much. The fault was understandable.

Burgess was a 'new boy' and theirs was a new partnership. But Burgess was swift, his hands were exceptional and his positional play was excellent.

On the basis of their play one feels sure that the All Blacks will materially improve.

There is already talk that McCormick will have to go and that competitors for his place will be L.W. Mains, of Otago, and R.D. Whatman, of Auckland.

But it would be a pity if the selectors dabbled too much with the rest of the team. By and large the 'new boys' all came off.

R.A. Guy and B.L. Muller were not well matched to prop for R.W. Norton and perhaps this accounted for the latter's defeat by J.V. Pullin in two especially vital heels on his own head.

Nor did P.J. Whiting make as much impression at the line-out as had been hoped for. This was not by any means his fault.

Mr Pring either neglected or did not notice the quite fiendish amount of obstructing which went on most of the time from five to eight in the line-outs, and at which the All Blacks were by a small margin, a little more expert.

Thus Whiting and W.D. Thomas, acknowledged as expert jumpers, were anchored.

More Fluid

This was a pity. The game would have become the more fluid, and hence the more interesting, if the play at the line-out had been precise and proficient.

From a critical point of view Meads probably did too much on his own. Certainly that run at the goalposts would have been better if he had thought of the three backs streaming along to the left.

But no doubt the great man was desperate to set his men an example. As it was he did.

Of the newcomers among the forwards, A.N. McNaughton made a good impression for speed and chasing, and marred this by a couple of penalties including the late tackle of B. John. From this penalty John sewed up the match with his second goal.

Sutherland and Kirkpatrick, if less often involved than Meads, had much of his dynamic strength. Muller too showed the value of experience by the way he caught and ran with the ball, a Sherman tank in All Black clothing.

Best Back

Of the backs Going was undoubtedly the best. His passing was good and his running and dodging sharp. And so to the Lions and their hopes of producing an improvement good enough to give them the series.

They did not field a forward of the quality of Meads, but they did field eight men who were uncommonly gifted at getting back to the checked ball. And their techniques in rucking have improved amazingly in the last two or three weeks of experience in the South Island.

Mervyn Davies grew exhausted toward the end, but before he did so his contribution was astounding

in a man who had not played for three weeks.

J. Taylor and P.J. Dixon, on the flanks, were great gatherers to the ball and, perhaps of all the forwards in the game, Pullin ranked next best to Meads.

The 'tiny' front row performed prodigies too, McLauchlan haring around (once or twice offside) like a three-quarter.

From their back play the Lions drew the comfort that their man John was the greatest player in the game, and one of the greatest seen in the country.

Not Dismayed

He was not dismayed by the loss after only five minutes of his halfback partner, G.O. Edwards.

This was partly because R. Hopkins, as a substitute, was magnificent for coolness and reliability. By and large John set himself to the task of playing ten-man Rugby as efficiently as it has ever been done. His powerful punts increased the heavy strain McCormick had to bear.

On firmer footing John would have perhaps had a go or two on his own.

And then there was C.M.H. Gibson, the perfect technician, especially in tackling, and J.P.R. Williams, the fullback of the heart the size of Everest. McLaughlan's try and John's two goals were not only the means to victory, but they were an encouragement to the Lions, not only to remove the mental block but to transfer it to the minds of the All Blacks.

It was a great day for the Irish yes, and the Welsh, English and Scots as well.

———

28 June 1971

MEADS: 'LIONS THE BETTER SIDE'

Press Association

———

DUNEDIN

The All Black captain C.E. Meads was one of the first men into the Lions' dressing room after their 9–3 win on Saturday.

After congratulating the Lions, Meads told reporters 'The better side won. We had more chances to score than they did, but just failed to take them.

'I congratulate the Lions on their performance.'

The All Black coach, Mr I.M.H. Vodanovich, said the All Blacks missed two easy penalties and had other scoring chances they did not take. He heaped praise on the Lions' defence. 'It was outstanding.'

The Lions' manager, Dr D.W. Smith, summed up the win in two words: 'Bloody marvellous.'

He told guests at the after-match function an hour afterwards: 'I am still speechless. I am so thrilled.

'The All Blacks played very well and at times were unfortunate, as we were. I think my two–one to the Lions prediction for the test series will be fulfilled.'

'They could be a truly great pack.' This was Lion's coach Mr C. James' tribute to the New Zealand forwards.

Mr James said it was obvious the Lions would have to work on their line-out play and rucking. But he said the way the Lions' forwards, conceding seven stone all round, moved the New Zealand pack in the scrums was 'a joy to the eyes and music to the ears.'

The best kept secret before the test was the injury to the Lions' halfback G.O. Edwards.

Edwards went into the game with a hamstring injury. It went on him after ten minutes and he was replaced by another Welshman, R. Hopkins.

Edwards suffered the injury in training on Thursday, but the Lions said nothing about it.

It was decided he should go into the game in the hope the injury would stand up to it. In fact, there was really little chance of him seeing out the match.

---

29 June 1971

PIPE DOWN YOU . . . !

QUEENSTOWN

One of the unpublished stories to illustrate the good feeling which permeated the Rugby test between the British Lions and the All Blacks at Carisbrook on Saturday:—

In one passing rush by the Lions C.M.H. Gibson, in the centre, fumbled the ball.

It looked to be a knock-on. No whistle sounded. He kept on going. He was tackled. He went down.

Four or five inches from him lay the New Zealand captain, C.E. Meads, also trapped in the bottom of the ruck.

Spoke up Meads: 'What about the knock-on, ref?'

Spoke up Gibson: 'I quite agree with you, Colin.'

Said Meads, with a big grin on his face: 'I wasn't talking to you.'

---

29 June 1971

TEST SEAT WAS 5000FT UP
Press Association

DUNEDIN

An Otago Gliding Club instructor, Mr J. Shanks, literally had a bird's eye view of the Rugby test on Saturday.

With a transistor in his lap he watched the whole match from his Slingsby-Dart glider at between 4000 and 5000 feet above Carisbrook.

The fact that he happened to strike just the right kind of 'wavelift' — air bouncing back off a hill — to maintain him in the air at the same spot for about two hours, was quite unusual for this particular part of Dunedin.

12 July 1971

THE GAME OF THE PENALTY TRY

All Blacks Make Return To Best Form

T.P. McLean

CHRISTCHURCH

Only the kitchen sink was missing from the second Rugby test match at Lancaster Park on Saturday in which the All Blacks defeated the touring British Lions by 22 points to 12.

Everything else was thrown into a magnificent game which pulsated with excitement from the first minutes when R.E. Burgess scored a glorious blind-side try to the last movement or so when the Lions' fly-half, B. John, steadied and dropkicked a goal.

In the short term, the match is likely to be principally remembered for the extraordinary moment nine minutes into the second half when the referee, Mr J.P. Pring, checked a stinging movement down the blind-side by S.M. Going and B.G. Williams.

He spoke briefly to the Lions' right wing, T.G.R. Davies, and then ran 30 yards along the goal-line with his arm upraised to signal a penalty try to the All Blacks.

In the long term, this decision, which was right and proper, but which is likely to promote, without any disparagement of Mr Pring's ability, the movement for the appointment of neutral referees for test matches, will be superseded by other considerations of capital importance.

Were the All Blacks, for example, as good as they looked while they were building a lead of 22 points to 6 with five minutes remaining?

Did their display justify the feeling that New Zealand Rugby has been restored to its greatness of the 60s?

Did the Lions invite destruction by hewing to an inferior tactical plan, by incompetent back-row play on both attack and defence, by back play, especially at scrumhalf, which would be regarded with horror by the coach of a schoolboys' team?

Much Better

There is no doubt whatever that the All Blacks, forgetting all about the penalty try, were much the better team.

Though they won the line-outs only by 19 to 17, their possession from these was much the cleaner. They were pushed back yards in many scrums, but even so R.W. Norton won two heels against the head.

In that majestic part of the game which is unified forward rucking for the checked ball, the All Blacks were decisively superior. Their advantage here was 15 to 5, an enormous disparity at international level, and their play, thanks in good part to the outstanding leadership of C.E. Meads, was overwhelmingly better than it had been in the first test.

So it was the combined work of the pack and the decisive superiority of the loose forwards which turned the trick.

Those loose forwards will forever be personified by I.A. Kirkpatrick because of the try he scored late in the game when he broke from a ruck at leat 45 yards from the try-line.

Boring to the right, he kept dodging tacklers here, fending others there, instantly accelerating after every check. And when he went in at the right corner, after a run of probably 70 yards, the entire crowd of 57,501 stood to him and brought down the roof of heaven.

But the try, for all its brilliance, was no more than the cream on the coffee. The devastation was wrought throughout the game by five winging forwards.

There were, not necessarily in order of importance, S.M. Going, the halfback, R.A. Guy, the loose-head prop, Kirkpatrick on one flank, A. McNaughton on the other, and A.J. Wyllie at the back.

Heavy Crack

From early moments, these men struck at the nerve-centre of the Lions — the famous Welsh halfbacks, G.O. Edwards and John.

As was to be seen in the last few minutes of play, when the Lions scored a glorious try from a scrum with five backs handling and John dropped his goal, the Lions' backs with the ball in hand could be menacingly dangerous.

More so than they were prepared to appreciate, in fact, because there were three occasions when they had four runners against three defenders or three against two but each time chose to kick.

One supplementary statistic is explanatory, too. John ran on his own twice, to little or no profit. Burgess ran three times and from two of these scored tries.

The tries, especially the first in only the third minute, conclusively demonstrated the incompetence of the Lions' back row, not one of whom defended as adequately as any of the All Blacks' wing-forwards proper.

They also established Burgess as one of the three truly memorable players of the game.

The others were Going and the Lions' fullback, J.P.R. Williams.

Going was great, simply great. He demolished Edwards. Burgess was not noticeably the inferior.

He did not drop one ball, he played shrewdly, his tackling was decisive, and in those two moments when the try-line beckoned, he established himself as a player of extraordinary competence, cool, long-headed and sharp all in one.

Williams, too, was outstandingly fine. He remembered little or nothing of the match. In fielding an early high punt by Going, he was engulfed by All Blacks and presumably took a heavy crack on the head.

Not too long afterwards, he fielded a bad kick by Going into the Lions' twenty-five and began to run. Soon he was with C.M.H. Gibson, with T.G.R. Davies in support. When Gibson committed Mains, McNaughton, who had run a prodigious distance at prodigious speed, just touched Davies' heel. The later recovered and went on to a wonderful try.

And now one comes to the nub of the question — were the All Blacks as great as they looked in the great game which generated such constant excitement and in which the movements were so often thrilling and exhilarating?

The answer is: not quite. Outside of Burgess, the backline did not bristle with the danger of the Lions.

W.D. Cottrell has become a quiet man, H.T. Joseph gave service adequate to a new cap without unfolding promise of a greater quality. B.A. Hunter perforce was a cover-defender, Williams three times kicked where in South Africa last year he would have run and beaten his man.

Mains had an excellent match, full of soundness.

The forward play, too, justified some small but not serious criticisms. For an inexperienced test pack, the quality was high.

But there was a want of drive at the line-out, some of the tackling was indecisive, and the pressure which Meads extracted from his players lacked that last touch of grinding power which would have made impossible the late recovery of the Lions.

Fine Force

Nevertheless, Meads, who was slowed down by a nasty crack on the lower leg, stoutly led a fine force in which McNaughton was a man of distinction because of his diligent chase of man and ball.

Norton heeled with celerity and looked after the short end of the line-out like a Dutch uncle. A.J. Wyllie most ably served in the tight-loose, especially at the line-out, and P.J. Whiting made excellent deflections at the line-out.

B.L. Muller served well in the lineout, too. Guy covered ground like a hare, and Kirkpatrick entered Valhalla with that try which will now become one of the legends of the field of Lancaster.

Forward, the Lions were largely anonymous. W.J. McBride took a black mark for a late tackle of Joseph which cost three points but was otherwise a powerful worker.

Great Pity

For the Lions, the great pity was the breakdown of their halfbacks. To say that Gibson was magnificent was to say the usual. So, too, was Dawes. The quickness of the man's reaction was fascinating, never more so than when he made no attempt to field a pass he was receiving as he was being tackled but instead knocked it with his arm instantly to D.J. Duckham.

Duckham, like John, had a chance to stop the Kirkpatrick try and for failing to do so deserved criticism. He had no chances of consequence.

T.G.R. Davies most brilliantly capitalised his two chances. But there was no doubt whatever that he clasped B.G. Williams while the latter was almost at the goal line and before Going attempted the pass which seemed to a great many observers to go forward, thus justifying the suggestion that Mr Pring was precipitate in awarding the penalty try.

For making the early tackle of a man who might otherwise have scored, Davies jeopardised, if not destroyed, the chances of his team scoring their second victory of the series.

The final factor in the destruction of the Lions was Barry John, the goalkicker failed with two conversions and two penalties.

His approach looked unusual, he seemed to expect the ball to go over the bar.

But every great goalkicker there ever was has had a day like this; and John's disasters were not the last or the loudest of the warnings the test conveyed to the Lions as to the steps they must now take if they wish to win the third test at Wellington in three weeks' time.

Burgess with two tries and Going and Kirkpatrick with one each, Mains with two conversions and a penalty goal were the scorers for the All Blacks. T.G.R. Davies with two tries and John with a penalty of 45 yards and a drop goal of 30 yards were the scorers for the Lions.

---

13 July 1971

PROMISED CURE BY NEPIA

Press Association

MASTERTON

R. Hopkins, the Lions halfback, consulted the legendary All Black fullback George Nepia last night over his leg injury.

The burst blood vessel in his left thigh is causing Hopkins increasing concern.

Nepia vowed to have it cured before Hopkins leaves Masterton. But the great Maori was keeping the treatment for the injury secret.

Nepia told Hopkins, 'I will have it cured before you leave or I will go he.'

Nepia suffered similar injuries during his illustrious career. Hopkins paled a little when Nepia told how one such injury was treated by immersing in a hot bath and then pierced in several positions. But Hopkins was assured there would be no such blood-letting in his case.

Hopkins was not required to train at all yesterday and has been excluded from the team and reserves for the match against Wairarapa-Bush tomorrow.

---

19 July 1971

KEL TREMAIN PAYS TRIBUTE TO MEADS

Because this was the first test match I was to watch since giving up playing Rugby, I wondered how I would feel. Would my hankering to be in there with the boys make the match pretty well unbearable to look at? The answer is that I felt the hankering all right. I would have loved to have been on Lancaster Park with 'Pinetree' and his team. I suppose it will be a year or two before I conquer the feeling.

But the joy of being a New Zealander and seeing my own side play so well and win so decisively when their backs were to the wall, soon superseded my regrets. I got tremendous pleasure out of many aspects of the game. For example the gesture of Colin Meads in calling the team together while Laurie Mains was taking a kick at goal was tremendously significant.

This must be one of the youngest teams New Zealand has fielded and you can be sure that the lads in it hang on everything 'Piney' says. They regard him with reverence. The significance of his calling the players together was that he was telling them as plain as a pikestaff not to sit back; not to relax; not to think that their lead of a few points was good enough. He was demanding more pressure; more points; more tries.

This was tremendously important to the run of

Colin 'Pinetree' Meads being consoled by Lions captain, W.J. McBride.

the game and to the confidence of the players. I am sure it made youngsters like Rob Burgess want to go on and on with the job of beating the Lions.

What a player Burgess is. I would say unhesitatingly that he is the best first five-eighths produced in New Zealand in my time. There is no doubt that Barry John is a great player in this position. But look at the difference between these two in their methods and consider the value to their teams of their different techniques.

John is the most flat-footed five-eighths I have seen. He makes up his mind after he has received the ball. He does not move his threequarters.

Burgess, on the other hand, was always moving. He had the line swinging with him and, when he made his best moves with his two tries, he was actually splitting the defence as he was taking the ball. But John was trying to split the defence after he had taken the ball. The difference was all in New Zealand's favour.

As a more or less free agent on the morning of the match I had talks with players of both teams. The result was that I felt the All Blacks were going to win.

I must congratulate Ivan Vodanovich, Pat Walsh and Bob Duff on sticking to their old pack. I got the impression they knew they were going to play better.

Also, I had the feeling that the Lions, in their hearts, believed they were lucky to win the first test and that, because of this, they thought the second test might be the one which was going to cost them their unbeaten record.

I would say this was the poorest game the Lions have played — and in saying this I am not disparaging the All Blacks and their great effort.

The delivery of the ball by the Lions was not good; their passing was often frantic and I was badly shaken to see them throwing the ball about behind their own forward pack — play which really amazed me.

Perhaps we, as a nation, are not game enough to try this sort of thing. But, from my experience, I would say that no team at the top level can afford to do it.

Had Waka Nathan been playing for the All Blacks, I am sure he would have scored at least one try from the ridiculous sort of stuff the Lions dished out among themselves. The technique would have been even more disastrous had the All Blacks been as good as teams of a few years ago at driving play in the line-out through numbers, 3, 5, or 7.

A person like myself, educated on the basic demands of forward play, finds it hard to believe that our forwards now are not using these techniques. Were they to do so, I don't think the Lions would see which way the All Blacks were going.

Let me make a couple of other points:

What a joy it was to see Meads playing so well and controlling his team so expertly. Our youthful players need him; he gives them a confidence nobody else of the moment can impart.

Also, I would like to congratulate young Bruce Hunter and Sid Going — the one for fantastic cover defence, the other for all-round brilliance. I think that Sid is the best half in the world.

Then there were others — like Burgess who played so brilliantly.

Finally, I have been interested — as probably all New Zealanders have been — in the remarks of the Lions' manager, Dr Douglas Smith, about the weakness in the All Black team.

After seeing the second test, I am sure Dr Smith is now looking ever more closely at his own team.

---

24 July 1971

VISITORS SAVED GIFT WORRY

T.P. McLean

The chances of the British Lions beating the All Blacks in the fourth Rugby test at Eden Park on August 14 were probably enhanced by a brisk hour or two yesterday which suggested the British still rank high as a nation of shopkeepers.

Players were offered samples of sheepskin rugs, jade and paua brooches and cufflinks, table mats with Maori motifs, Maori records, dictionaries and the like. They responded by ordering, as only one item, no fewer than 83 rugs. Their reaction, in fact, was totally enthusiastic.

Now will come the work of putting the orders through the various firms and the parcelling and/or despatch of the goods to Britain.

One effect will be that players will be spared the usual hectic last few days of shopping before the end of the tour — and before the start of the fourth test, which in Rugby terms is the more important issue.

The famous Springbok centre John Gainsford remarked before the 1965 South Africans played their last match that they had lost it on the floors of Auckland shops.

Many other managers and players of touring teams have felt as deeply as Gainsford.

Hence the welcome given by the manager of the Lions, Dr D.W.C. Smith, to the suggestion of a Wellington newspaperman, Mr G.R. David at the start of the tour, that a pre-test shopping scheme should be arranged.

A fair amount of sweat and toil — but no tears — were involved by the organisers.

But the drinks — for them — will be on the Lions if the test turns out to be a repetition of the famous match of 1959 when 60,000 Aucklanders prayed that D.B. Clarke would not land the first penalty which would have drawn the game.

---

2 August 1971

GREAT MILESTONE FOR BRITISH RUGBY

Test Victory Confirms Trend Toward Coaching

T.P. McLean

WELLINGTON

It is unlikely that any event in international Rugby history has exceeded in importance the third test at Athletic Park on Saturday in which the touring British Lions defeated the All Blacks by 13 points to 3.

They thus placed themselves in a most favourable position to win the series by three rubbers to one.

In terms of actualities and potentialities this was the most significant event of British Rugby history since Lions teams were formed.

In terms of the impact upon New Zealand Rugby from top to bottom and with a greater emphasis upon the top than the bottom, the event was no less important.

Fabric Weakens

There have been other sensational Rugby efforts in the last generation, but Saturday's victory was peculiarly important.

It represented so decisive an encouragement of the trend toward coaching which was reluctantly accepted in the British Isles only a few years ago, and it so comprehensively displayed, too, the weakening and rending of the fabric of New Zealand Rugby.

Not since the 1949 All Blacks suffered defeat in their four tests in South Africa has New Zealand Rugby been so deeply acquainted with such bleakness.

British Rugby is now sailing with eased sheets. The team of Saturday was imperfect in some particulars. The forwards, for example, were inferior to the All Blacks in winning possession, though in pluck, resilience and stamina they were most certainly superior.

New Zealand Rugby, however, is in the wars. The All Blacks, inspired by C.E. Meads, who tried to do the work of at least 10 men, hewed valiantly.

Some of the charges to the Lions goalline in the second half were as furious as any of old and, with a little precision, especially in control, they must have yielded tries.

But there were many impurities in the display.

Surely not even the oldest old-timer who was there could recall an All Black line-out with so many holes.

Surely, too, it was an aberration on the part of someone which turned the brilliant R.E. Burgess from a running into a kicking five-eighths, who punted no fewer than 10 times in the first half alone.

The want of attacking competence in the backline was dismaying, putting things mildly.

A grim catalogue of the faults of the All Blacks could be compiled starting from the point that within the team there was wanting that capacity to control a situation which, in the past, had so often made so many All Black teams dominant and victorious.

One could surmise that this weakness originated in selections of players who were unable, for various reasons, to form a harmonious partnership of the old sort.

Grave Mistake

It was certainly a grave mistake which brought B.J. Lochore back to the colours for he was evidently not attuned as of old to test match play.

But Lochore was less blameworthy than other forwards, notably I.A. Kirkpatrick, in allowing Lions forwards to pour through the line and to scrag S.M. Going.

This gravely affected the latter's control of static situations as well as reducing his opportunities to tear around the flanks in the attacking runs he performs better than any other halfback in the world.

First Praise

However, first praise must go to the victors. The Lions, gambling that the wind would not increase and having sufficient confidence in themselves as a seasoned

Lister and McBride exchanging blows early in the game.

team, decided on winning the toss to take first use of the fresh north-wester blowing down the field.

One supposed that they would need to take 15 points from this advantage to ensure victory, and, when at the half, their lead was 13 to nil, it seemed possible that they had not done quite as well as they ought to have.

Of a surety they had neglected at least two scoring chances, which would have removed all possible chances of the All Blacks recovering ground and winning the match.

As things turned out the All Blacks did not have the finishing qualities to round off their many attacking moves of the second half.

Meantime the great opening phase of 18 minutes in which the Lions scored all their points, the first a drop goal by B. John, decided the match.

Not for the first time the build up to the first point established the profound difference in the psychological approach of the two teams.

The Lions backs began passing in their own 25, and when T.G. Davies, on the right, received the ball he moved past K.R. Carrington before putting in a kick.

When B.A. Hunter fielded this he was brilliantly tackled by J. Taylor, and from the ruck C.M.H. Gibson gave John a chance to steady and crack over a goal.

On the Lions went, superbly well. By the time the All Blacks began to exert control, which they did well enough in the last 20 minutes of the half to deny John the ball on all except five occasions, the visitors were well steadied when their opponents kicked or ran.

The clock moved remorselessly onward while the All Blacks plundered useless ground.

All Black forward I.A. Kirkpatrick is in for a hard landing as he misses this tackle on Lions fullback J.P.R. Williams.

L.W. Mains diving over unopposed to score the All Blacks' only points in the test match.

Heroic Defence

It is just to applaud the Lions' opening phase; to shout the praises of G.O. Edwards, John, T.G. Davies and the back row forwards Taylor, D.L. Quinnell and T.M. Davies, who so earnestly and effectively chased and backed up.

But it is not less just to say of the team in the second half that the 15 men frequently took on the cloak of heroism as they rebuffed the All Black attacks. Heavy indeed were many of these. Meads, on the right, and then again on the left, ran furiously with the ball in is hand.

Kirkpatrick, a number of times, broke and began to run. A.J. Wyllie, the outstanding All Black forward, at one stage, according to his comrades, actually did score and was denied the try only because Mr J.P. Pring was too quick with his whistle.

But the Lions withstood the heavy brigade assaults and, by doing so, brought glory to British Rugby. So for the Lions there was nobility both in their attack and defence. What more could be asked?

W.J. McBride, powerfully and vehemently, led the forwards. And thanks to the back row, among whom Taylor was brilliant, and also to the tight core work of S. Lynch, J.V. Pullin, I. McLauchlan and the new cap G.L. Brown, the response, if not quite so effective overall as by the All Black forwards, was consistent, fine and courageous.

A perfectionist might say, while offering the warmest of praise to Edwards, John and T.G. Davies, and a sufficiency of praise to S.J. Dawes, Gibson, D.J. Duckham and J.P.R. Williams, that the Lions' backline might have devastated the All Blacks if they had chanced their arm a little more.

Did Enough

A pragmatist on the contrary would assert that the Lions' backs, Edwards, John and Gibson in particular, did enough under the heavy pressure of the second half to establish their outstanding qualities of coolness and sound judgment.

It was extraordinary how many times the All Blacks scrummed and rucked five yards from the Lions' goal line and lost the ball.

And it was a commentary on the quality of the All Blacks' lineout at 7 and 8 that the long throws in by Carrington in these situations did not yield the powerhouse drives of old for the sufficient reason that the ball was either lost or not controlled.

Under heavy pressure Going played well. Burgess was off key from the start.

W.D. Cottrell braked back inside too often, H.J. Joseph displayed no real flair and B.A. Hunter tended to slow down his run.

Carrington was impressive even though he was beaten. But there must be better deeds by New Zealand if the country's remarkable reputation in world Rugby is to be sustained.

AS KEL TREMAIN SAW IT

Changed Tactics Spelled Disaster

Well done the Lions. That is my first reaction to their win in the third test. Well done, particularly for taking from the All Blacks the most successful tactics the New Zealanders had used to win the second test.

That is the thing that puzzles me. Why did the All Blacks change their tactics? Why did Alan McNaughton switch from chasing out on to and containing Barry John to chasing on to Gareth Edwards? Why did the All Blacks line-out loosen up so much that Mervyn Davies and other Lions' forwards were tearing through the holes?

Why did Bob Burgess do so much aimless kicking, especially in the first half, instead of running in his brilliant way of the Lancaster Park match? And, finally, why was no one taking the right steps to relieve the pressure on Sid Going?

I had great hopes for the All Blacks after the second test. That was a good win. The team played well. The All Blacks were on top again after suffering defeat in four tests out of five. We could look forward, so I thought, to a resumption of the fine standards New Zealand had preserved over so many years.

And then Bingo — we throw the whole lot away. I do not want to sound uncharitable about the Lions because theirs was a great effort. But I think it fair to say they were not so greatly improved on

Christchurch. The difference was that the All Blacks were such a hell of a lot worse.

It was unbelievable. The forward drive was not there. The ideas, the plan, the pattern were not there either. I had the feeling the All Blacks had wrapped themselves in complacency. They gave me the idea that they thought they only had to step out to play as well as they had done.

Things don't work out that way in test matches. You've got to take and exercise control. This time there was no control.

I am not blaming the backs. The line at Athletic Park was no worse than it was, say, five years ago. But the difference was that five years ago Freddie Allen was demanding that the backs do something. He was making them get the ball through their hands. At Athletic Park, however, I counted three times when the line had a two-man overlap and tossed the chance away.

Test Rugby is thinking Rugby — you've got to be on the ball all the time. Why, therefore, the cuts back infield of Wayne Cottrell, much too good a player to do such foolish things? When the cut back was wanted, which was one time when Bruce Hunter tearing down the right wing had the chance to wrong-foot three defenders by nipping back inside, he didn't take it.

I am sure it was because of McBride that the Lions' forwards patched up their line-out holes at Christchurch so well. I am sure, too, it was he who saw to it that Gareth Edwards got the kind of armchair ride Going had had in the second test. It was the best game I have ever seen Edwards play in the last six weeks. He did everything right, especially in passing.

And with Edwards playing so well, that uncanny Barry John had time to pick his teeth, read a chapter of a good book and still pot a goal that set the Lions going. Under the old tactics, McNaughton, of course, would have been setting his sights on John and maybe he would have had to have a go too quickly to get on balance.

As it was, the change in the forward pattern presented this brilliant Welshman with what he wanted — time and space. I must give the Lions every credit. John, with Mike Gibson not far

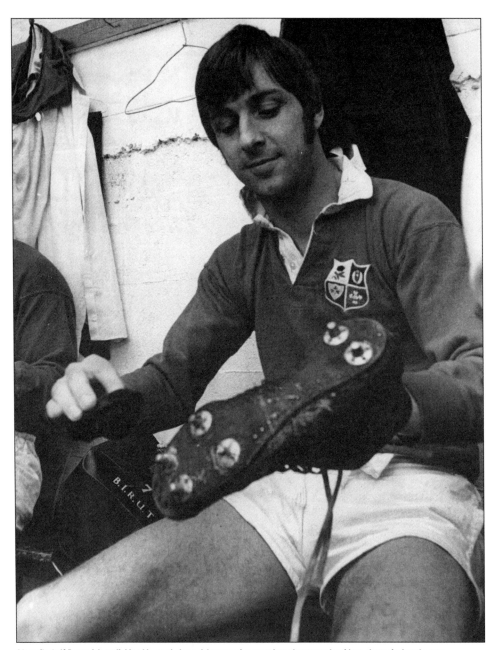

Lions fly-half Barry John polishing his magic boot. John scored more points than any other Lions player during the tour.

behind, demonstrated a great weakness in New Zealand Rugby — backing up. John, Gibson and most of the other Lions got back to check the rush and stiffen the defence. Not so the All Blacks. They didn't seem to get there.

Well, there is plenty for our selectors to work on now. I wonder what they will do to meet the tremendous challenge the Lions are going to offer in the final test. The Lions, so I reckon, will really chuck everything at the All Blacks. They will be very hard to beat. I hope we can produce the stuff to meet their challenge.

The Lions have convinced me that the touchline is not our final refuge. Their willingness to run the ball from what we would call defensive situations and which we would always resolve with a kick has enlightened me as to the possibilities.

For one, they may find the defence stretched. For another they are able, if they do find themselves in the cart, to widen the angles to the touchline for defensive kicking. That was how Barry John peeled off such distances, whereas our blokes, using our old method of charging on the blind side, reduced the angle and, consequently, very severely limited the possibilities of efficiently gaining stretches of ground.

Moreover, the willingness to run from the defensive line gives the Lions another option — with players like Mike Gibson, John Dawes and Gerald Davies, not forgetting John Williams, there is always the chance of an unstoppable thrust up the field.

---

16 August 1971

EXCITEMENT THERE, BUT NOT A GREAT TEST GAME

T.P. McLean

It was the luck of the game which made the fourth and final Rugby test between the British Lions and the All Blacks at Eden Park on Saturday the least momentous and memorable of a series which the Lions won by two rubbers to one, with one drawn.

Naturally, drama and excitement were inevitable in a contest which finished in a draw, 14 points a side, with each team scoring a goal, to which the Lions added two penalty goals and a drop goal and the All Blacks two penalty goals and a try.

Very likely, the start and the finish of the match will be remembered when much else, especially the mistakes and mishandlings, the want of rhythmical back play in the Lions, the absence of the old forward drive in the All Blacks, descends to the bottom of the subconscious.

The finish was made very lively indeed because the All Blacks, after leading by 8 points to nil in the first 11 or 12 minutes, forfeited their advantage and were lagging by 11 to 14 with only a few minutes to play.

Then S.M. Going lured P.J. Dixon off the side of the Lions' scrum by feinting to run the blind while the ball was still in the scrum.

After L.W. Mains' penalty levelled the scores amid a tremendous roar from the 56,000 spectators, the Lions attacked and at a scrum no distance from the goalposts, the champion goalkicker, B. John, positioned himself for a drop goal.

By John standards, it was a simple chip shot and a piece of cake. But the pass from G.O. Edwards came at him rather high, he fumbled the ball into his hands and with All Blacks bearing down upon him he had to move too quickly to hit the ball on balance.

So the game blazed to the excitement of the draw and a ceremonial farewell of the Lions which would have been a great deal more moving had not 'Now Is the Hour' been sung at varying speeds by the crowd.

The start was truly tempestuous and for several minutes the game trembled between a sporting contest and an exhibition of unseemly mayhem.

Though a punch was thrown by an All Black in the second line-out — G.L. Brown needed six stitches from a split above his eyebrow — most of the trouble erupted in the scrums.

B.L. Muller, in particular, raised tempers by boring across the tiny prop I. McLauchlan, and soon after the All Blacks had scored their try with an excellent piece of organisation involving Going, A. Wyllie as a decoy, M.G. Duncan and the scorer, W.D. Cottrell, trouble flared in a violent punch-up.

At that the referee, Mr J.P.G. Pring, the All Black captain, C.E. Meads, and some cooler-headed players in the two teams set out to restore order.

Before the scrum packed down again, Mr Pring spoke to the All Black front row and it was evident from the manner of his address that he was not passing the time of day or passing on the race results.

Muller remained an unhappy figure. It was he who conceded a penalty which gave the Lions the

The prospect of a draw was enough to keep some of the Eden Park crowd happy.

lead, 11–8, through raking in a ruck after the whistle had blown. It was Brown again who was injured, this time with a wound below the knee which needed 14 stitches.

In between the tempestuous start and the blazing finish, neither team developed the form it had hoped for.

The principal fault of the All Blacks was that they did not develop the stable forward platform of old.

One finds it difficult to recall a drive at the line out of the sort which so often wore down opponents of New Zealand in the sixties.

The substitution of running attacks was, especially in the first half, extremely well done.

Gross Errors

Gross errors by the Lions, not least in uncontrolled tapping of the ball to Edwards, not least, too, in the subjection of Edwards to yet another wearying time — how long will it take the British forwards to learn some of the simplicities — spurred the All Black forwards to fierce attacks. They were checked only because the Lions by and large were the faster over the ground.

It was another of life's little ironies that the All Blacks, the inferiors in attacking back play, frequently utilised their backs while the Lions, largely because of the tactics of Edwards and John, resorted principally to 10-man rugby.

These All Black attacks were made spiritedly. Going more than once weaved down the field; Cottrell, who handled extremely well, was ever the servant of his threequarters.

P.C. Gard once or twice stepped past his man with intuitive skill and M.G. Duncan in the centre used a hand-off which in one bright movement knocked C.M.H. Gibson clean off his tackle.

For all their number, the attacks only once yielded profit. Admittedly the Lions' defence was sound and in the second half reached brilliance.

For only a few tackles, each of which was crucially important, D.J. Duckham on the left wing could well be regarded as one of the brightest stars of the game.

Wings Starved

The trouble with the attacks was that the ball too seldom reached the wings furbished by the asset of the half-break.

This was a pity because K.R. Carrington, as ever, was a lively bundle of energy and B.G. Williams, unhappily thicker of thigh than when he was in South Africa last year, for the first time began to look like the wonder boy who bemused and delighted the South Africans.

It was a weakness that Mains was not an enterprising joiner of attacks in the manner of J.P.R. Williams, the fullback of the Lions.

However, one must be fair to the All Black backs. If they failed, it was certainly not for want of trying.

As to the All Blacks' forwards, the stars here were fewer and less bright than they are in the Southern Cross.

T.N. Lister attended to his tight-loose duties extremely well. R.A. Guy in the first half covered a great deal of ground at prodigious speed and as a result looked almost exhausted later.

Meads doggedly, rather than with the old flair, ran with the ball in hand in the second half.

I.A. Kirkpatrick a number of times looked to be breaking from tackles but each time was caught; and, overall, his contribution was smaller than expected.

Wyllie got no closer to John than any other forward, A.M. McNaughton in the second test and the Bay of Plenty game excepted.

The Lions rather let themselves down by the paucity of their attacking ploys and their addiction to 10-man Rugby.

Gibson and his fellow-centre, S.J. Dawes, for example, did not once handle the ball in a set-piece play in the second half.

They stood or chased while John crashed the ball down the field and so deprived them, and the brilliant wings, T.G.R. Davies and Duckham, of the chance to run the ball.

John was a consummately gifted director of the Lions' strategical plays and Williams gave everything in defence or attack.

But this was not the sort of Rugby the Lions had pledged they would play. Rather was it the sort they had condemned in New Zealanders.

McBride, as usual, was the very boiler in the engine-room of the Lions' forward effort.

T.M. Davies off the back of the scrum sustained a high level of effort. Dixon and J. Taylor of the flanks were extremely hard workers and McLauchlan, J.V. Pullin and J.F. Lynch in the front row worked hard.

Little Reward

But there were too many mishandlings, too many mistakes, too much effort for too little reward, by all of the Lions.

The team leaders said this was a natural consequence of the tension felt by the players.

One felt the tension was with the All Blacks; it ought not to have been in the Lions.

The tourists had nothing to lose. They should have played in this spirit.

Their failure to do so suggested that in their great achievement they had reached only the anterooms, they had not yet penetrated to the central hall, of really great Rugby.

---

21 August 1971

BIG NORM SCORES HIS LAST CATERWAUL
Gordon McLauchlan at Eden Park

Last Saturday I went to Eden Park to interview Big Norm, the last of the loud-mouth barrackers, who had been brought out of retirement by his cobbers to help the All Blacks to square the series.

A five-eighth fumbles and before the ball hits the ground, Big Norm lets him have it with: 'Ya couldn't catch a bus, ya mug.'

Then, in an aside, he says to me: 'The trouble with these poor lads in black nowadays is your genteel crowds. They've got no sting. The result is a meaningless roar. No wonder they're losing tests, even at home.'

'Why is it, Big Norm, that there are no loud-mouth barrackers coming on to fill in the gaps left by blokes like you and Whinger Smith and Nev the Howler?'

'Dunno. The kids just aren't interested. Television, I suppose, and all the other distractions. I've heard some promising kids but they don't stick with it. All the kids are good for these days are throwing beer cans and tepid "horrays". Your loud-mouth barracker is becoming a thing of the past, like happy drunks and short hair . . .'

An All Black doesn't find the line. 'Ya couldn't kick a habit, ya mug.'

'You shout against your own side then?' I asked.

'Too ruddy right. I'm no bigot. Look, there's a lot of great players out there on both sides and they deserve the best grandstand wit and abuse that's available.'

The play stops for injuries. A Lion and an All Black are both bending over waiting for attention. The Zambuck runs to the Lion first, 'Don't worry about the Pom, ya mug, look after Sid first.'

His face was 'Aw shucks' with pride when the crowd laughed its appreciation of that gem.

'I think my timing's coming back.' Then wistfully: 'There's no good kidding myself, age has turned down my volume.'

The halfback can't get the ball in and for the third time the referee blows up the scrum. 'Knock it orf, postie, the mail's been delivered.'

'I served my time here and on the western bank at Athletic Park, ya know, and at my peak I had forwards in the line-outs searching the crowd to remember my face, swearing to blazes they'd sort me out after the game. But the crowds are too big nowadays, and these concrete stand roofs are not a patch on the old corrugated iron for acoustics . . .'

'Go hard, ya little Pommie beaut, go hard. Siddown, hey you, siddown.'

A middle-aged chap in front turns round. 'Would yew maynd keeping it down a bit, old chap? You're upsetting the waif.'

'Don't you old chap me, granddad, or I'll have ya blazer for a mat. Take ya missus to the ballet next time.

'Orfside, ref, orfside. Where's ya white stick?

'See I'm not getting through except to the old dowager here. The acoustics are crook. I shouldda gone to the first test. I go great guns down in that Carisbrook stand. I couldda been a big help to the boys down there and put some fire in the belly of the pack . . .

'Go back to pommie-land, ya mug . . .'

'He's a great little player, that Barry John. He's a man deserving of the highest standard of loud-mouth wit but I can't get to him. Old Stringy Jones wouldduv reached him even in this crowd. He was the best ever heard on Eden Park. They reckon that when Old Stringy let go with a "Ya mug," yachties used to spin round out in the gulf.

'Get him round the knees. He's only Welsh, his vowels are twisted.

'Orfside. Hey, Lord Nelson, he's orfside.

'The Howler was also very talented with more volume than a force-five gale. He used to sit behind the posts down there and when he was at his best, captains winning the toss in club matches used to play with or into the Howler, never mind the wind.'

The game pauses for a Scot, injured on the ground. 'Get up, ya big plate of porridge.'

But his voice was going and he knew it. 'This'll be my last big performance, Mac, my last game.'

I put my hand on his arm. 'Save your breath for the big one, Norm,' I said quietly.

Ten minutes later, Barry John slips over and is caught in possession. Big Norm is on his feet in a flash: 'Ha-ha-ha. Crown 'im boys, crown the King. Ya mug.'

As his voice soared over the ground, he slumped back into his seat, his head down, his mouth working but silent. Big Norm had scored his last shoutdown.

———

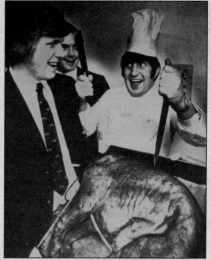

Top left: Lions coach, Carwyn James, meets the cast of
'The Country Wife' at Auckland's Mercury Theatre.
Above: J. McLauchlan and C.W. Rea prepare to carve a
wild pig shot by McLauchlan and J.F. Slattery.
Left: R. Hopkins, W.D. Thomas and G.O. Edwards pick up a
little light reading while waiting to fly out of Auckland.

2 October 1971

LIONS TOUR WAS A BONANZA

D.J. Cameron

WELLINGTON

Although the Lions takings fell below the 'magic figure' of $1 million, they produced a profit for the New Zealand Rugby Union of about $292,156, said the NZRU chairman, Mr J.L. Sullivan, yesterday.

Although some final returns had yet to be received, said Mr Sullivan, the gross tour proceeds were estimated at $993,023.

Immediate match expenses reduced this by $87,632. Of the remainder, $905,391, the various unions' share took $340,275. The New Zealand Rugby Union's share $565,116, as further reduced by expenses of $272,960, leaving the final figure of $292,156.

With Mt Egmont as a backdrop, the Lions took a plunge in their motel's heated pool. Fom left are:
Peter Wheeler, Trevor Evans, Graham Price, Brynmore Williams and Andy Irvine. Already in the pool is Nigel Horton.

1977

18 June – Wellington
9 July – Christchurch
30 July – Dunedin
13 August – Auckland

12 May 1977

NZ RUGBY FACING SERIOUS TIMES AS LIONS ARRIVE

T.P. McLean

It is chastening and melancholy that the visits of All Black teams to South Africa have had an aftermath of serious recession in the standard of New Zealand rugby.

For this reason alone, girding the loins for the Lions this week may pessimistically be reckoned as a time of morbid contemplation for New Zealanders.

This is deepened by a remark of the manager of the 1971 Lions, Dr D.W.C. Smith, in a recent letter that the forwards of the team which arrives in Auckland today are bigger and stronger than they were in his team.

Dr Smith acknowledges that the Lions' backs will not be of the standard of '71. There may be cracks in the line, he says. Comforting news. But if the forwards are, in fact, bigger and stronger, then New Zealand's task is formidable, if not desperate.

It is disturbing to remember that after the 1928 tour in South Africa, the All Blacks were beaten by the Wallabies in three tests in 1929.

In 1950, after the fateful tour of the Forty-Niners, the All Blacks scratched home against a Lions team which was demonstrably deficient at forward.

Dawes' Lions

The grossly ill-managed French team of 1961 was beaten by the aid of the worst conditions under which a test match has ever been played, and that the consequence of the 1970 visit to South Africa was the well remembered visitation by S.J. Dawes' Lions the next year.

Now, after the unfortunate expedition of last year, the leadership of A.R. Leslie has been lost precisely at the moment when, fortified by bitter experience, he might have been better equipped than ever before to captain his country.

Rumours too strong to be discounted as careless talk contend that such players as I.A. Kirkpatrick, H.H. Macdonald, S.M. Going and

D.J. Robertson are to be axed.

The talk is disturbing. It has undoubtedly affected the confidence of senior players.

P.J. Whiting's retirement is an incalculably severe blow. As the All Black coach, Mr J. Gleeson, in a just tribute remarked, Whiting was 'a true test-match footballer.' There are not many such.

Very Gloomy

The conjunction of retirements, disturbing rumours and the historical fact of a disturbance in the balance of New Zealand rugby after tours to South Africa — as well, naturally, as Dr Smith's assessment of the potential of the Lions' forwards — tends to make the girding of the loins a gloomy exercise.

Nor is it easy to clap hands in girlish delight about the composition of the teams in the national trials at Wanganui on Saturday.

There will be special interest in the five-eights M. Taylor, who was highly praised in the Argentine, and the goalkicking fullbacks, G. Rowlands and R. Wilson. Also to be watched will be the halfback M. Donaldson, whose form for the Barbarians in Australia was assessed by a famous practitioner, Mr P.L. Tetzlaff, as 'the best I have seen in a young bloke in this possie in years.'

Haden's Skills

Whether A.M. Haden will be as good as his reputation, which may perhaps have been extravagantly assessed, is a point of profound importance. The selectors will pay special attention, one may be sure, to the Taranaki brothers, John and Bryce McEldowney.

They have served their term as apprentices in an excellent provincial pack and undoubtedly will offer the severest competition to the ranking favourites, B.R. Johnstone and K.K. Lambert.

For the rest, the mixture is much as before. Dazzling geniuses are not abundant, back or forward. There is even a case for wondering whether trials in which players are thrown together higgledy-piggledy serve any other purpose than confusion.

Undoubtedly the luck of playing with the wind in the first half in the trials at Athletic Park last year determined the choice of C.L. Fawcett and L.W.

The Lions arrive in New Zealand. The Lions mascot is held aloft by Fran Cotton.

Mains as fullbacks for South Africa.

In the event, these selections were not a good advertisement for trials as such. There is even a point for wondering why selection committees — or at least the present incumbents — have not used trials as experiments in the fullest sense.

For want of encouragement at provincial level, two backs of considerable promise, B.M. Gemmell at halfback and E. Dunn at five-eighths, have disappeared and are unlikely to be resurrected — simply because their provincial selectors have not thought well of them.

Real Potential

Yet Gemmell proved to have international talent. Dunn had genuine potential. It is tragic that such players — and perhaps around the country there are many more — have been neglected.

What, then, is required to beat the Lions? First off, discipline.

The All Blacks in South Africa last year were champions at bitching, on the field, about rulings by referees and many times they were penalised, rightly, by another 10 yards.

This was indiscipline. It weakened concentration. It was a cancer of the tour.

There will be none of this in the Lions. The British are now the most ambitious players in rugby. In these last few years, they have become world champions and they are determined to stay as such.

Secondly, the All Blacks have got to be provided with a goalkicker and if he happens also to be a quality fullback, so much the better.

The selectors may even find it necessary to take a chance, as their predecessors did with D.B. Clarke in 1956, on a young, untried player, B. Wilson, of Otago, being the man in mind.

But someone has got to be found, or manufactured. In default, defeat, now a possibility of the series, could be turned into a certainty.

Third Need

Thirdly, the All Blacks must be turned into a harmonious combination of strength, speed, with high skill in the basics.

There is even a case for persuading the selectors to choose their squad of 21 players a fortnight before the first test at Wellington, naming the XV at a get-together training run, naturally at Wellington, on the Sunday beforehand.

The Welsh have built up their Triple Crown and Five Nations' championship teams of recent years precisely by this method.

Winning admittedly is not everything. It is excellent news, in this respect, that the Lions' manager, Mr G.M. Burrell, and the coach, Mr Dawes, have declared totally against any team tactics of intimidation based on physical assault.

Rugby at all levels, but especially in New Zealand, could not possibly countenance a campaign of violent play. But winning is still important — as Mr J.L. Sullivan sardonically used to observe to his players, it does make the beer taste better.

Deteriorated

It is especially desirable at this time when New Zealand rugby has deteriorated as an international force and has reached as low a standard as can be remembered.

The country, it is plain, is not gripped as it used to be by a fever of anticipation and excitement at the approach of the invader.

But that great old fervour, surely one of the most remarkable national phenomenons of world sport, will for a surety be awakened as and when the All Blacks by quality rugby devour the Lions.

---

28 May 1977

'LUNCH WITH THE LIONS' UNDER FIRE

T.P. McLean

Commercialisation of the British Lions rugby tour yesterday drew a protest from the tour manager, Mr G. Burrell.

In response to advertisements, a number of Taranaki rugby followers yesterday each paid $5 for 'Lunch with the Lions,' at the Westown Motor Hotel, at which the Lions are staying. An integral part of the smorgasbord meal was catchy interviews of both Lions and members of the public as they sat at table.

Various prizes, including seats to the match against Taranaki today, appeared to be offered from time to time — no one could have missed the answer to the question as to which member of the Taranaki team was playing his 148th game for the province today. But the Lions were not amused by these tableside interviews. The team captain, P. Bennett, said to Mr Burrell: 'We have come here to play rugby, not to get into this sort of act.'

'I am bound to agree with "Benny",' Mr Burrell said. 'If we can be of help to New Zealand rugby at all reasonable times, we will fall over backwards to do so.

'But this sort of thing is, I suggest, unfortunate, if not unfair, to the players.'

The 'Lunch with the Lions' meal was sponsored by Lion Breweries.

The general manager of New Zealand Breweries Ltd, Mr J. Macfarlane, said from Wellington last night he understood the special lunch had been organised by a local brewery representative. He did not know whether it had been advertised as an occasion on which people could meet and mix with the Lions.

But, he added, when anyone was staying in one of the brewery's hotels and wanted privacy, the company would see that they got it.

---

28 May 1977

ARRESTED LION IS NOT HELD

T.P. McLean

NEW PLYMOUTH

New Plymouth police were smartly on the job yesterday morning to make an arrest of a member of the touring British Lions rugby team.

But it was an 'arrest' with a difference.

The members of the force were intent upon securing the English lock-forward, N.E. Horton, who is to lead the Lions' pack against Taranaki at Rugby Park today.

As a member of the police in Birmingham for the last 10 years, Horton has been treated royally by the New Zealand police since his arrival.

Though still ranked a police constable, Horton spends most of his time training recruits.

He has had plenty of active service — he was to the forefront in chasing after the notorious Irish Republican Army zealots who bombed Birmingham pubs with killings and woundings a few years ago.

A tall, strong, powerful man, Horton has been identified as a principal cause of the

Lions lock Nigel Horton feeling the fit of Constable C.A. Francis's helmet during a visit to Taumarunui police station.

rejuvenation of English forward play in the recent home season.

The power of his shoulders and arms comes easily — he has represented England at waterpolo and in his time has swum 100 yards in 42 seconds, or thereabouts.

Having been concussed by an aimed punch in the first match with Wairarapa-Bush, Horton is now awake to the perils and dangers of forward play in New Zealand.

Like the New Plymouth police, he may be in on arresting actions today himself.

---

20 June 1977

WEATHER CONTRIBUTED TO POOR SECOND HALF OF RUGBY TEST

T.P. McLean

WELLINGTON

Rugby most decidedly was not the winner of the test, or rather, such was the ferocity of play, the contest at Athletic Park on Saturday in which the All Blacks (two goals and a try), beat the Lions (four penalty goals), by 16 points to 12, all of the points being scored before halftime.

The only reasonable excuse for a good deal of ineffective and unintelligent play, which, in fact, was standard through the second half in which the All Blacks were unable to breach a defence they held under siege, was the weather.

At 3 pm, a half-hour after kick-off, the south-east wind was blowing at an average velocity of 20 knots, gusting up to 25 and higher. The temperature was 6 degrees.

One of the busiest men in the game, W.M. Osborne, the All Blacks' second five-eighths, wore a singlet which hung out over his shorts. It looked like a trysail of a yacht riding out a force 10 gale.

8 June 1977

PLENTY OF DOUGH SURROUNDS LIONS

——

They might have to call in Julie Andrews, of 'Sound of Music' fame, to sing about 'Dough, the dough, the anything but female deer,' which is beginning to clutter the path of the touring British rugby Lions.

A Dunedin gentleman, name available on request, has laid $8000 to $400 that the Lions will be beaten at some stage of their New Zealand tour.

Heading the brave British bettors are M.R.C.C. Thomas, who represents the *Observer* in London, and Mr C. Lander, of the *Daily Mirror*.

Each has taken a quarter-share of the $400 of the wager. Other British journalists have laid out smaller sums and, at last report, about $30 was still there to be picked up.

The Lions were turning into rather a glum team at the Otago Racing Club's meeting at Wingatui on Queen's Birthday when, principally through a New Zealand press photographer, they were given the wheeze about Caladam in the last race.

The horse finished nine lengths behind the winner. Who cared? All but one of the Lions.

For third place, Caladam paid $18.65, largely as a result of which, 'the Duke,' otherwise the Welsh hooker, R.W. Windsor, departed the course with $200.

The Lion's captain, P.H. Bennett, traipsed off with $190 and most of the other players spent a 'hap-hap-happy' evening.

Two Irishmen, P.A. Orr, the loosehead prop, and Mr T.P. O'Connor, of the *Daily Mail*, both backed other than Lions' horses, on principle. They are still sorrowing.

It was a profitable day for some of the Lions at the Wingatui races. Here Clive Williams and Phil Bennett watch the running.

There were no other excuses. The New Zealand forwards in a number of respects played like an international unit.

They won 28 line-outs, 14 in each half, and held the Lions to only eight, four in each half.

The All Blacks also won the rucks and mauls by 23 (12 and 9 in each half) to 10 (6 and 4).

Lady Luck

But the fruits of this phenomenal superiority of possession were no more than three tries, each of them bounteously blessed by Lady Luck.

S.M. Going might work for a whole month of Sundays for another such try as the one with which he opened the All Blacks' scoring in the fifth minute.

He moved to his right, then swivelled to his left. The Lions were little more than a handspan distance. Going turned about and, facing the enemy, saw before him a golden road leading to rugby's Samarkand.

He sped down it for about 10 paces and, as the Lions' captain, P. Bennett, grasped at him, he dived to score. It was an extraordinary achievement beyond the reach, one would contend, of any other international scrumhalf. But, clinically, it was possible only because of a dreadful defensive weakness in the Lions' forwards.

The All Blacks' second try, scored by B.R. Johnstone next-door to the left-hand upright, was even simpler.

B.G. Williams' attempt at a penalty goal into the wind had gone so high that, as it descended, an unfortunate Lion caught the ball with his shoulder rather than his hands.

Keen Lad

Amid a flurry it fell over the tryline, with Johnstone, ever a keen lad, about an inch from it all the way.

The third try, two minutes from half time, was so fortuitous that it turned the game and caused the Lions' manager, Mr G. Burrell, to observe, reasonably enough, that it was worth 12 points.

The Lions, who by this time were leading by 12 to 10 from one huge penalty goal beyond halfway by A.R. Irvine in the first minute and three 'bull's-eye' shots by Bennett at later stages of the half, moved an attack to the left and, switching to the right, had the All Blacks' defence flummoxed as T.P. Evans offered a pass to Bennett.

Bennett had two men to his right, no more than two All Blacks, including G.B. Batty.

A try between the uprights and a half-time lead of 18 to 10 — enough, probably, to win the game — seemed certain. Batty took not Bennett. He took the ball. More than 50 yards distant loomed the tryline and, because Irvine had come into the attack, the area was untenanted.

Set Off

So Batty, travelling at much below his velocity before his knee was damaged, set off with Irvine and the prop, G. Price, tailing him.

He managed to hold the lead until he plunged down for the decisive event of the game.

B.G. Williams, not an effective goalkicker against or with the wind from any sizeable range, had no trouble with the goals to Johnstone's and Batty's tries. So what promised to be a goal for the Lions was turned, instead, into a goal for the All Blacks.

These 28 points of the half had produced a great deal of excitement and not, in all of my test-match experiences around the world, have I heard a salutation of such length and strength as greeted Batty as he walked back to his place. The crowd was all but hysterical.

The same crowd, as may be imagined, were in a ferment of expectation as the second half began.

Black Wave

Now were they to see, their mood suggested, the great unfolding, vivid flashes of genius by Going and among the threequarters, overwhelming rushes by the forwards, the scattering and shattering of Lions' defenders as the massive black wave moved relentlessly with the wind towards the shore which was the Lions' in-goal.

It was an entrancing prospect.

The play began. The All Blacks' forwards faithfully continued their task of winning the ball.

Their courage was unfathomable, their vigour prodigious, their application ideal.

But the yield, beyond one attempt at a drop-goal and another at a penalty, both by B.G. Williams, was nothing.

It was bewildering; it was tedious.

The explanation principally centred upon Going and his partner, D.J. Robertson.

Going was in one of those moods, so characteristic of his later days. He varied the extreme brilliance of his try and other similar efforts, including marvellous intelligent thrust on the blind-side, with handling and passing which would have earned a schoolboy in olden times six cuts with the cane, even if he received a shoddy ball at early line-outs.

Robertson could be excused if he had to stand and wait for a pass because he could have no clear idea of where the ball would go.

He could not so easily be excused his own mishandlings, his kicks, chip and long which imposed no strain upon the defence, or his attempts valorous but overdone, to skittle the defence on his own.

From the troubles of these two men, compounded by the eagerness of forwards to plunge through the defensive wall, it followed that the potentialities of the All Blacks' threequarters and of the new fullback, C.P. Farrell, as a helping agent, were never developed.

Other strong words will, in due time, be addressed, one surmises, to I.A. Kirkpatrick and other forwards whose fanatical ambition to pick up the ball and run with it into the fringe defence around the pack and ruck inevitably led to their being tackled and the attack strangled.

Kicked Away

The All Blacks kicked away possession 17 times in the first half, 18 in the second — the Lions' figures were 15 and 8. The All Blacks passed the ball beyond the first five-eighths four times in the first half, once in the second. The ball reached their wings twice in the game. This was doleful stuff. It offered no encouragement to B.G. Williams, who almost certainly was the All Blacks' best player, or to B.J. Robertson, who looked as fast as any Lion.

It did nothing to steady the nerves of Farrell, of whom it is enough to say that he will play very much better in the next test.

So the qualities of the All Blacks' display must be remembered as the excellent play of A.M. Haden in the line-out, of Kirkpatrick, L.G. Knight (an outstanding test debut) and K.A. Eveleigh as an amazingly industrious back row, of F.J. Oliver holding off the taller Irishman, M.I. Keane, at the line-out, and of the front row of Johnstone, R.W. Norton and K.K. Lambert. Norton's excellence as a captain would have been improved if he had chastised his halfbacks more vigorously.

Salutary

The experience was severe and salutary for the Lions. Their luck changed when their scrum-half, D.B. Williams, turned out to be their finest player, brilliant on the break and much more reliable with his hands than Going.

But A.J. Martin could not hold against Haden, T.P. Evans was overpowered by Kirkpatrick, playing his finest-ever game at the line-out for New Zealand, and W.P. Duggan at No. 8 and T.J. Cooper on the flank were compelled to defend all the time.

The outstanding Lions forwards were their front-row men, P.A. Orr, R.W. Windsor and G. Price, the last-named especially so. His tackle was ferocious. Bennett's early injury in tackling Going and the lack of ball cut down his effectiveness.

S.P. Fenwick was staunch and capable in midfield and P.J. Squires on the right wing might have won the game with a long fly-kick and chase in the second half. But there was little for Irvine to feed upon with his brilliant intrusions into the attack. There was, in fact, little joy for the Lions.

---

20 June 1977

LOUNGE COMFORT PREFERRED
T.P. McLean

Almost 3000 people who had paid for their seats stayed away from the rugby test match at Athletic Park on Saturday in which the All Blacks won the opening test match against the British Lions by 16 points to 12.

The absentees from the expected crowd of just on 44,000 presumably changed their minds because of the strong southerly wind, and the sharp temperature of 6 degrees in which the match had to be played.

Other points about the game:—

- The Lions suffered when their captain, P. Bennett, strained or tore muscles of his neck and left shoulder while attempting to halt S.M. Going in the fifth minute and aggravated the injury in the second half. A later X-ray discovered no fracture.

- Partisanship in the crowd was extreme. Jeers greeted Lions' attempts at goal, cheers the failures. It was the bitterest reception a Lions' team has had in a test match in New Zealand in the five tours since the Second World War.

- It is improbable that the All Blacks' team will be changed in more than one place, if in that, for the second test at Christchurch on July 9. The heart-in-the-mouth play of the Auckland fullback, C.P. Farrell, has been wisely accepted as the sufferings of a new boy. But there is anxiety that the new back-row man, L.G. Knight, may have severely ricked his right knee in a tackle 15 minutes from the end.

- An extraordinary event was the appearance of the All Blacks in black shorts bearing the white trademark of a sponsor.

1 July 1977

LABELLED GEAR RULED OUT

T.P. McLean

CHRISTCHURCH

The several All Blacks who wore black shorts bearing the insignia of a German sporting goods manufacturing firm while playing against the British Lions in the first test match are unlikely to do the same thing in the second test at Christchurch.

All of the All Blacks were issued with regulation gear 'which,' says the chairman of the New Zealand Rugby Union, Mr C.A. Blazey, 'was most decidedly not sponsored.

'We have no idea how some players came to be wearing gear of commercial firms.

'It will be my wish, and the wish of the council of the union, that only authorised gear, bereft of trade insignia, is worn by our players in all other tests.'

---

8 July 1977

DISTINCTIVE BOOTS TOO

If rugby shorts bearing a brand name are ruled out does this mean that boots with distinctive markings should also be outlawed?

Mr J.W. Hinton, manager of the Puma Sportswear Division, asks this question in commenting on the remarks of Mr C.A. Blazey, chairman of the New Zealand Rugby Union council.

Several All Blacks wore black shorts bearing the insignia of a sports firm while playing against the British Lions in the first test at Wellington on June 18.

Mr Blazey commented later: 'It will be my wish, and the wish of the council of the unions, that only authorised gear, bereft of trade insignia, is worn by our players in all other tests.'

Recognised Fact

Mr Hinton said: 'It is a recognised fact that manufacturers of sportswear and sports equipment consider the gifting of their products to prominent sportsmen and women to be an excellent way of presenting their products to the public. If you like, it is a form of advertising.'

This form of presentation had been occurring overseas for some time and at the Olympic Games in Montreal at least 80 per cent of the competitors had some form of brand insignia displayed on their uniforms.

'The particular shorts which have been mentioned,' he said, 'were given to the All Blacks, along with other apparel, during a visit they made to the Wellington branch of my company.

'That they chose to wear the shorts in the test was their own choice and my company in no way put the pressure on them to do so.

Same Gesture

'If shorts bearing a brand name are ruled out does this mean that boots with distinctive brand markings will also be outlawed?

'These boots, I would venture to say, have been presented to the players in the same gesture as the shorts,' said Mr Hinton.

'Because of these distinctive markings will the All Blacks be forced to play in bare feet?'

---

11 July 1977

SECOND TEST GAVE GAME OF RUGBY A HARD POUNDING

T.P. McLean

CHRISTCHURCH

Few moments of humour illumined the rugby match at Lancaster park on Saturday in which the British Lions beat the All Blacks by 13 points to 9 and rugby as a game took a terrible pounding.

Reviewing the game, the All Black selector, Mr J.J. Stewart, said with saturnine wit: 'As for myself,

Bill Osborne sets off on one of his slashing runs. Behind him is centre Bruce Robertson.

I would have much preferred the New Zealand Army band to have kept on playing for another hour and a half.'

The character of the game and the antipathy of the crowd toward the Lions, expressed in jeers when some of their men went to ground with injuries and cheers when, as an example, the Lions captain, Phil Bennett, failed with a vital kick at goal, recalled the bitter tests and fervent nationalism about which members of the All Blacks in South Africa last year expressed such strong criticism.

At one instance J.J. Williams, the Lions wing, who had tumbled over the dead-ball line after stopping an All Black try, was sprayed with beer by a nearby spectator as Williams lay on the ground.

At the final whistle as two Lions players were embracing each other at the moment of victory they were knocked to the ground by spectators who had rushed on to the field.

Old Hat

The chairman of the judicial committee of the Canterbury Rugby Union, Mr J. Mullins, said: 'We have worked hard on a campaign in our union to clean up rugby and I think most people have been on our side.

'But when young chaps of 18 and 19 see test men doing the sort of things that were done in this game and getting away with it, their reaction is to tell us "oldies" we are old hat, we are not in touch with the modern game, what is good for the big guys must be good for them.'

An All Black forward said after the game: 'Our object was to get anything in red.'

Bleeding

Bennett's scarred body yesterday testified to the getting. In an early run, he was collected by New Zealand forwards. He came out of the ruck bleeding at the mouth and obviously shaken.

Later, trying to run out of the Lions' quarter, Bennett slipped on the heavy, greasy turf and was overwhelmed in a ruck.

The ball had been well cleared toward the new cap on the left wing, Mark Taylor, but booting of Bennett continued.

A Lions prop, Graham Price, and the Aucklander, Brad Johnstone, figured in a distasteful episode early in the game.

As the two men fell to the ground, clutching each other, Price delivered a 'Liverpool kiss' — a butt of the head at Johnstone's jaw.

Bill Bush, Johnstone's partner in the All Black front row, rushed in upon the two men and kicked more than once at Price.

Price suffered an eye injury during the game.

He is having to wear a bandage over the eye for five days and will be unable to play for ten days.

In the worst incident, Bennett had long since cleared a kick to touch from his own quarter when he was struck down by Kevin Eveleigh.

Punching and counter-punching immediately developed and many players in the two teams were involved in a brawl.

While the crowd angrily — and, in the circumstances, accurately — jeered at the referee, Mr B. Duffy, for failing to notice a late tackle of Bryan Williams, All Blacks more often offended in this lamentable exercise.

Taylor three times was involved in late tackles. Williams was penalised for a dangerous tackle.

At another stage, however, the Southland lock,

Ian Kirkpatrick making a run, with Billy Bush in support. Terry Cobner is the Lions player preparing to make the tackle.

Frank Oliver, meaningfully pointed at two of the Lions' forwards and gestured with his foot to indicate that, in his opinion, they were transgressing.

Crowd Effects

Radio New Zealand's commentator, Mr John Howson, was stationed in his box above the tightly-packed terrace on the western side of the ground.

Desiring to get crowd effects to embellish his broadcast, Mr Howson let down a microphone to within a few feet of the gallery.

'After a few moments of listening,' Mr Howson said, 'I knew my idea was no go.

'The language was incredibly rough and foul. In my broadcasting experience, I have heard nothing to touch it.

'As a fact, however, the crowd in that area were not yelling against the Lions.

'Most of them were jeering at the All Blacks. Statements about their parentage were commonplace. It didn't make for good listening.'

No reference was made in speeches at the after-match gathering to the unfortunate qualities in the play.

The coach of the All Blacks, Mr J. Gleeson, declared it had been 'impossible' for his men to run the ball when so many Lions so often stood in offside positions.

Dirty Game

The complaints were a repetition of remarks made by the Lions coach, Mr S.J. Dawes, at the end of the preceding match against Marlborough-Nelson Bays at Blenheim last Tuesday.

Bennett told a radio audience it had been a dirty game. The captain of the All Blacks, Tane Norton, denied that this was so.

Perhaps Mr John Reason, of the London Daily *Telegraph*, was right when he quoted the remark of a Lions captain of the 1960s, A.R. Smith, of Scotland, who, discussing a match of similar character and violence, quietly observed: 'They were two wee bitie puir teams who had an off day.'

30 July 1977

ONE MISTAKE COULD BE DECISIVE IN BIG SERIES

T.P. McLean

DUNEDIN

Ten days of rain have so much saturated the Carisbrook pitch on which the British Lions and the All Blacks this afternoon are to play the third test of the tour that, in the opinion of the manager of the All Blacks, Mr R.M. Don, 'one mistake could determine the series.'

This is a pretty fair estimate. When the All Blacks yesterday morning held their wind-up training run, which was intended to be light, just over the dune from St Clair beach, the new wing threequarter, Brian Ford, rushed to the sideline to put on his tracksuit.

'They want me to practice throw-ins,' he said.

'I had better make sure I don't catch cold. It was hailing out there just now.'

It had, indeed. But the captain of the All Blacks, Tane Norton, was sanguine.

Slumped

'Before the second test,' he said, 'everything felt right up till the moment we took the field.

'In the dressing-room, the players seemed to be right in their attitudes. I had no worries.

'Then we missed our first kick at goal in the first minute of the game and you could feel the whole side slumping, losing zest.

'I think, in fact I am sure, this will not happen again. I feel the All Blacks will be keyed up to win.'

On the Lions' side, a sentiment assured of universal approval was uttered by the coach, Mr S.J. Dawes.

'I hope,' Mr Dawes said, 'that the bad memories of the second test will be erased by a good display by both teams.'

One most hearty supporter of this sentiment was the famous coach of Otago teams of a generation ago, Mr V.G. Cavanagh.

13 July 1977

QUIT THEIR JOBS TO FOLLOW THE LIONS

Carol Dixon (bottom left) has a prematch drink with other members of the Lions' support party.

Resigning a job and travelling over 12,000 miles to follow a rugby tour might seem crazy to some people, but not to a party of English, Welsh, Irish and Scottish supporters now in New Zealand.

The Scottish representative is 23-year-old Miss Carol Dixon, who hails from Edinburgh. Like the men, she is not a member of an organised supporters' tour and has had to make her way as cheaply as possible around New Zealand.

Accommodation for the group has ranged from youth hostels to grandstands, but they have a good way of keeping in touch. They meet on the halfway line after matches.

Two of the men from Wales have spent the past five years in Canada and are trying to get more support for the game in that country.

The supporters are very pleased with the way the tour is going, although they had a few anxious times when the Lions lost the first test and the match against New Zealand Universities.

Although they feel the 'inconsistent' decisions from referees must be causing misunderstandings, the supporters naturally expect that the Lions will win the test series.

Their only regret is that some of the men do not as yet have tickets for the last test in Auckland.

Only Game

'If I were to see many more games like the second test,' he said, 'I think in the future I would just stick to watching my old club having a go every now and again.

'I really don't think I would be bothered watching the big boys.'

Mr Cavanagh's opinion was supported by a famous All Black captain who preferred not to be identified.

'You can lose a match,' this man said, 'and it seems to be the end, calamity, catastrophe.

'But after a time, you remember that, really, the match has only been a game, the result is not really seriously important.

'The difficulty occurs when a game like rugby loses goodwill because of one bad match.

'Overcoming this is a tremendous problem. It may take a long time.'

Changes

From these various and varied opinions, it may be deduced that, while the outcome of the match is important, the consequences to rugby of a well-played match are much more serious.

The Lions are fielding a team proficient in forward play, especially in scrummaging, mauling and at the line-out, but with certain deficiencies in the backline, where the Newport players, David Burcher and Gareth Evans, appear to be deficient in top-line international quality.

In fact, the Lions' backline, as an attacking unit, appears to depend too greatly on the employment of the brilliant fullback, Andy Irvine.

The several changes made by the All Black selectors may be beneficial, and victorious, but only if the backs, who look better qualified than the British, can utilise their pace and superior attacking qualities.

Hard Tussle

Here, the suitability of the pitch may be the determinant. No blame can be attached to Carisbrook. Even the centre court of Wimbledon could not withstand, as a grass surface, the day in, day out attacks of the rain and mist which have overlain Dunedin in the last fortnight.

The match could turn into blind-man's bluff or, perhaps, blind-man's duff — as Mr Don has said, one mistake could cost the game.

On the whole, new boys and all, the odds seem to favour the All Blacks.

But it will be a desperate tussle. Errors could cost a kingdom. The hope is, as Mr Dawes has said, that the two teams produce, under difficulties, such a match as will give everyone cause to renew their faith in rugby as one of the greatest of team games.

---

1 August 1977

OBVIOUS PARADOX IN NOTABLE THIRD TEST WIN OF THE ALL BLACKS

T.P. McLean

DUNEDIN

All hail to the All Blacks for their victory, by 19 points to 7, over the British Lions in the rugby test match, the third of the series, which was played at Carisbrook on Saturday — and now, let's set about righting the dreadfully low quality of the New Zealand forward effort, which in scrummaging was surely the worst in the country's history.

All hail to the Lions for being courageous — and clean — in play and gracious in defeat, and now let's see about restoring in the team those virtues in back play which have been the hallmark of British rugby since the dawn of time.

That was the paradox of an extraordinarily interesting and fascinating match — that the All Blacks, who according to tradition cannot run the ball, won the match because they did, while the Lions, who according to tradition can most decidedly run the ball, lost it because they did not.

The All Black forwards were beaten in the line-outs by 24 to 14 and, in this contest, conceded five penalties while being awarded three.

The forwards were also beaten twice on their own head at critical scrummages of the second half and at many stages, starting with the first scrum of the match, were rolled back as if they were paperweights in a heavyweight league.

By traditional New Zealand standards, these deficiencies were staggering, quite unbelievable.

By traditional British standards, the quality of the Lions' forward effort was also staggering and quite unbelievable.

Yet there was no question of New Zealand's superiority, which yielded a goal, two penalty goals, a try and a drop goal against a try and a penalty goal.

The explanation was that for the first time in a long, long time — much too long a time — the New Zealand backs ran with such spirit, such speed, such sureness in passing and support that the Lions, despite their massive and magnificent forward performance, were undone and outplayed.

At the end, praise was lavishly heaped upon the coach of the All Blacks, Mr J. Gleeson, and his captain, Tane Norton, and indeed all of it was deserved.

A Thought

But perhaps a thought might have been spared for the coach who was axed, Mr J.J. Stewart, because it was he who for several seasons tried to persuade New Zealand's backs that they had the ability to believe in themselves.

Round about the year 2000, in New Zealand rugby, people assuredly will be fixing perfect strangers with glittering eyes to recount how the All

Willie Duggan goes over for a try in the tackles of Graham Mourie and Bryan Williams in the first minutes of the third test at Carisbrook.

Blacks scored their first points, by a try by Ian Kirkpatrick, and a goal by the whiz kid from Omaku, Bevan Wilson, within the first minute of play and their last points, by a drop goal by Bruce Robertson, in the last second before no-side was blown by Mr D.H. Millar.

Indeed, the beginning and the end could not have been more blissful. There were many other blithe moments, too — brilliantly sure handling by the All Blacks, from Lyn Davis through Doug Bruce to Bill Osborne and that shining star, Robertson.

Hectic charges down the left touch by the new cap, Brian Ford, who looked as if he was willing to wrestle the whole Lions team, en masse; and on the other side, one huge chase by Bryan Williams also set the crowd into a frenzy of anticipation.

And, behind them all, playing like a dream, Wilson, a young man whose technique, whose sense of position, fielding and kicking left a special, unforgettable imprint upon the match.

But not all of the All Blacks' rugby was fit for Cloud Nine. Brilliant as was Robertson's drop at goal, the pleasures of a final try — which looked a stone-cold certainty, so much was the Lions' defence disarrayed — would surely have been greater; and at an earlier attack, when the Britons were again spreadeagled, Bill Bush played the ball instead of Davis at halfback and a vital moment of time was lost.

Concern

What to do about the scrummaging? That is the great concern for the final test. Loosely though Bush played, the fault in the packing was not his.

The whole New Zealand scrum was gripped and tossed backwards. Not, perhaps, since 1928, when the All Blacks in South Africa were dominated, has a New Zealand pack been so decisively overwhelmed.

Fullback Bevan Wilson playing his first game in the All Black jersey kicks one of his two penalty goals in the third test.

A novel grandstand outside Carisbrook during the third test gave the occupants a clear view of the whole ground.

Whether it might have been better to play Brad Johnstone for his line-out skills rather than John McEldowney for power and drive may be argued, but the latter, too, was imbued with the total wish for total committal asked for and demanded by Norton.

As a first summing-up, the failure of the Lions seemed to rest upon the inability of the captain, Phil Bennett, and the fullback, Andy Irvine, to place goals. Between them, they missed six of seven attempts — but a thought had to be spared for the difficulties of the two men on the sludgy surface which most definitely did not favour their instep-style of kicking.

Big Factor

As a second summing-up, Bennett's inability to direct and control the plays made available by the possession won by the forwards seemed to be a critical factor in defeat.

Yet it might well be reckoned, on deeper analysis, that the Lions' forwards were so consumed with the ambition to overpower the All Blacks in the set-piece plays that they neglected to spread their loose men in cover-defence roles which might more severely have pressed and oppressed Bruce and Osborne and sucked in Mourie and Knight from their foraging.

In the set plays, especially the scrummage, the Lions were magnificent. Peter Wheeler hooked with instantaneous reaction and Graham Price and Fran Cotton each played a role like Atlas in taking the weight of the All Blacks on their shoulders. Moreover Brown and Beaumont were superb in their crushing strength.

Not Equal

But the role of the Lions' loose-forward attack was in a narrow channel of a few yards' width. Had Davis been agitated by the attentions of Terry Cobner, Willie Duggan and Derek Quinnell, these attacks might have yielded profit. But Davis, under pressure or free from it, cleared and cleared; and not even Cobner was equal to the chase.

The Lions' backline had a harrowing time which became the more dreadful when John Williams with a thigh injury and Brynmor Williams with a recurrence of his left hamstring trouble had to leave the field.

Yet there were abundant compensations. Graham Mourie so intelligently anticipated, so severely tackled, so cleverly controlled the ball, that he ranked as the outstanding forward of the match.

Kirkpatrick, in the last quarter, scorned the fatigue which was gripping at every man after running so much on that heavy field and became, as he used to be, powerful, dominating.

Like Mourie, Lawrie Knight hunted incessantly and tackled men at their shins and ankles, hurling them to the ground. Andy Haden and Frank Oliver were held and outplayed by Gordon Brown and Bill Beaumont at the line-out, but a tremendous solo run by Haden staggered the Lions and he and Oliver were never far from the ball.

The dice were loaded against the backs even before Ian McGeechan and Doug Morgan came on as substitutes. For want of a cool decision in planning attacks and/or pressuring the All Black defence, the Lions' attacks were either individual runs by Bennett, Irvine and Steve Fenwick or distraught and haphazard efforts in which combination spluttered and attacks were soon killed.

For the All Blacks, Kirkpatrick and Haden with tries, Robertson with his drop goal and Wilson with a conversion and two fine penalty goals were the scorers. For the Lions, Duggan slipped easily past the defence for a try four minutes after Kirkpatrick had scored and Irvine placed a penalty in the second half.

Question

Happiness abounded at, and surrounded the All Blacks. But not everything in their garden was entirely lovely. 'What are we to do about our scrum?' said one of the selectors.

What indeed. But, quite obviously, something needs to be done — the Lions may yet discover their best team and as and when they do, they will be the harder to beat in the final test at Eden Park on Saturday week.

---

11 August 1977

TICKETS MAY BE 'HOT'

There is a hot demand for tickets for the fourth Lions–All Black test on Saturday — and late buyers might beware that their tickets may, in fact, be 'hot.'

Recently a club and a school were burgled and about 40 test tickets stolen.

'The police have been notified about the thefts,' said Mr Barry Smith, deputy-chairman of the Auckland Rugby Union, yesterday.

'We have reissued tickets with the same seat numbers, so buyers should beware buying tickets that might not have come from a recognised source.

'Officials at the Eden Park gates will know the numbers of the stolen tickets,' said Mr Smith, 'and people with those tickets may be questioned.'

---

13 August 1977

TOO ROUGH FOR LIONS
T.P. McLean

Few of the British Lions who are to play the All Blacks in the Rugby test match at Eden Park this afternoon would want to return to New Zealand to play rugby.

'This is a fact. I find it very sad,' said the Lions' coach, Mr S.J. Dawes, yesterday.

'Our players have been disturbed by the physical contact aspect of New Zealand rugby.

'They feel that this reduces the enjoyment of the game — and, frankly, I have always considered that one plays for enjoyment.

Only a Game

'First, last and all of the time, rugby is only a game.'

If the Lions, wearied by a long slog through an abundance of vile weather, have rather lost their joy in life Down Under, the supporting parties which have homed in on the tour in recent weeks are finding plenty of it.

'The hospitality of Kiwis has been overwhelming,' said the famous Springbok fullback of the 1960s, Mr Lionel Wilson. 'My party of 17 South Africans has been treated so royally that when we arrived at Hamilton airport, the widow of "Has" Catley had a dozen people waiting to transport us to Taupiri for a bang-up banquet.

Great Experience

'Our tour has been a fabulous experience — friendships everywhere.'

The hundreds from the British Isles, especially the very large contingent from Wales, echo Mr Wilson's sentiments.

---

15 August 1977

CHANCES WERE THERE, BUT MISSED BY LIONS

T.P. McLean

It could be reckoned that the lamentable figure of military history General Incompetence was in command of both sides in the rugby battle at Eden Park on Saturday in which New Zealand beat the British Isles by 10 points to 9 and so won the series by three matches to one.

It could also be reckoned that the Lions in a military sphere would have been put on charge for the serious crime of SIW — self-inflicted wounds.

Even in the dying moments, when they were responding to Lawrie Knight's match-winning try five minutes from no-side with a hectic attack on the All Blacks' goal line, their Number 8, Willie Duggan, could not control his patience long enough to establish beyond any doubt whatever a pushover try.

His irresistible urge to pick the ball up and plunge had a death-wish aspect. It was an act of indiscipline quite out of place in a team winding up a long, long tour.

Many other acts of folly disfigured the Lions' attempt to win.

Mix-up

As for the appalling mix-up involving Gareth Evans, Fenwick and Peter Wheeler in pure melodrama from which Knight scored, it could be said that their reactions were, if not hysterical, then at least frenzied.

Test matches, said the Lions' coach, Mr John Dawes, are determined by luck. And the Lions, he said, did not get their share.

Doug Bruce, the All Black first five-eighths, searching for a space as he is challenged by Ian McGeechan (13) and Phil Bennett (10) during the fourth test at Eden Park.

Duggie Morgan scores a try for the Lions in spite of All Black fullback Bevan Wilson's desperate tackle.

Bluntly, they did not deserve to. Their lead at half-time of 9 points to 3 from a penalty goal by Duggie Morgan in answer to Wilson's first goal and, near the break, a brilliant Morgan try — which he himself converted — should have been enlarged in the second half when Morgan twice had shots at goal, once from 40 yards, the other time from 30.

The slight wind was behind him, the pitch — easily the firmest and finest of the test-match grounds of the tour — was level, the grass short.

But these great chances were not taken. Who could call that luck? Great golfers do not miss their putts from four feet. Great kickers — and Morgan is outstanding — do not miss from the equivalent distance of 30 yards or thereabouts.

One must acknowledge, naturally, that Wilson also missed shots at goal from, in the second half, 45 yards, 46 and 30.

But then Wilson is not yet a great kicker, he needs the advice of an expert like Don Clarke to tidy his approach to the ball.

One must acknowledge, too, that the All Blacks did stick at the game and that in the last quarter, despite an awful hammering in the forward play of the first hour, they were running harder and faster than the Lions.

But they, too, lacked real international quality and, failing some substantial improvement at forward, one fears that the team chosen for the tour of France will have a very hard time indeed.

Many of the problems for both teams developed at halfback.

In the first hour, Lyn Davis was mercilessly harried. The Lions in this period were dominant at the line-out, in which, overall, they had superiority by 26 possessions to 14, and outstanding players like Graham Price, Fran Cotton and Peter Wheeler breached the New Zealand wall with staggering ease.

Morgan's problems were fewer. In fact, you could say he had only one problem. This was Duggan.

Morgan could never be sure whether the heel would come to him fast or slow — Duggan always

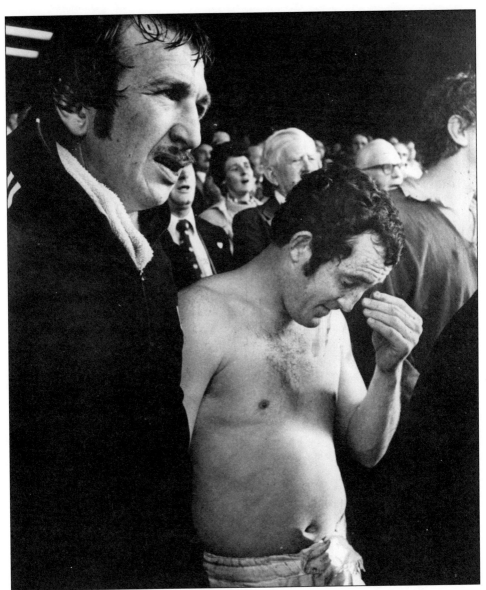

Lions captain, Phil Bennett, showing the weariness not only of a test defeat but also of a three month tour. He is joined by All Black captain, Tane Norton, in the main stand at Eden Park after the fourth test.

seemed to be pondering this problem — nor could he be certain that Duggan would allow him to exercise his role as the servant of the backline.

Fine Day

Thus, though Phil Bennett, defensively speaking, played easily his finest game of the test series, he was never given, for want of a swift pass, time and space to exercise his unqualified genius in attack.

And when Fenwick, outside him, tried to turn himself into a battering-ram, the Lions' backline was no more effective than that of the All Blacks.

So a glorious day for rugby, sunny and nearly calm in the first half, and a glorious turn-out of about 57,000 spectators — a section of whom, sad to say, vehemently booed one of Mr David Millar's later decisions — did not yield a glorious game.

Such a pity. Had the Lions played memorably well and yet lost, the event would still have given character to their tour. Grace, too.

One surmises that the forwards must have felt like weeping as they trooped into the team's dressing-room after the game.

Outmatched

Gordon Brown and Billy Beaumont had outmatched Andy Haden and Frank Oliver at the line-out, the pack, though better held than in the earlier tests, was still powerful enough to march the All Black pack back towards the goal line in the last fateful seconds and Tony Neary and Jeff Squire relentlessly hustled and hassled the All Black backline.

To what end but defeat? Once, late, Andy Irvine cleared out from his own in-goal area, screaming past Graham Mourie, who is no sluggard, as if he were standing still, and with a great towering punt putting the All Black defence under strain at halfway, or beyond.

Here, surely, was an attacking weapon capable of cutting to pieces even the All Blacks' fine defence. But it was not used more than a time or two.

Morgan did his best and considering the distractions his was a presentable performance. Bennett kicked well but kicked once too often; for it was from his kick that Bill Osborne hoisted a huge counter-punt which descended at about the Lions' quarter-line and which involved Evans, Fenwikh and Wheeler in the maelstrom of mistakes leading to Knight's try.

The Auckland Supporters Club named Ian Kirkpatrick as their All Black of the match. It was a touching, sentimental gesture which was not quite deserved.

If a forward had to be chosen, perhaps the choice could have been between Kent Lambert for steady scrummaging and Tane Norton for fast heeling, once, amazingly, when at his command the New Zealand scrum consisted only of himself, Lambert and Billy Bush — Bush got about the loudest cheer of the day when he replaced the injured John McEldowney 14 minutes into the second half.

The deficiencies of Oliver and Haden at the line-out and the need, every so often, to post Knight to Number 3 in the hope of winning possession must now place a strain on the selectors.

Mr Millar hit the Lions hard with nine penalties in the second half and in all Williams and Wilson struck penalties for goal six times against Morgan's four. Brown argued one decision at the cost of a double penalty and the Lions with boyish gestures of delight tried to persuade Mr Millar that Duggan scored in the last minute.

---

15 August 1977

SOME TIME BEFORE IT SANK IN

Tane Norton never really realised he had led the All Blacks to a series victory over the British Lions until he appeared in front of the official enclosure a few minutes after the 10–9 victory.

'Hell's bells, it was tremendous to see all those thousands of people standing down on the field,' he said.

'As I went up the stairs I thought that all the crowd would have gone rushing off to the local — it was tremendous to see them all there . . . then it really sank in that we had won the rubber.

'I didn't really get a chance to talk to Phil Bennett, the Lions' captain, straight after the match. I felt a bit sorry for him, as we have been in the same position.'

The three-man scrum the All Blacks used while John McEldowney was injured and before Bill Bush took the field was not an impromptu move.

'We had actually practised the move a couple of times, but I was reluctant to use it — it is a defensive measure and I don't like to give the impression I am giving in,' said Norton.

'But with a forward off the field we would never have hooked the ball from a proper scrum, so we decided to try it.'

Top: Jet-boating down the Wanganui River provided some light relief for the tourists. Enjoying the break are Lions props Clive Williams and Graham Price.

Left: A broken thumb did not prevent Lions lock Nigel Horton enjoying one of the specialities of the deep south — Bluff oysters.

A day's hunting in the Lees Valley proved a success for a group of visiting Lions. They are (l to r) Terry O'Connor, Dusty Hare, Trevor Ringland, Roy Laidlaw and Jim Calder.

1983

4 June – Christchurch
18 June – Wellington
2 July – Dunedin
16 July – Auckland

4 June 1983

LIONS MUST FIGHT HISTORY AS WELL AS FAILINGS

D.J. Cameron

CHRISTCHURCH

The British Lions will be battling history, tradition and their own failings when they play the All Blacks in the first rugby test at Lancaster Park this afternoon, so much so that the easy prediction is that the All Blacks will win decisively.

Barring the 3–9 loss to the British Lions in 1971, the All Blacks over recent years have a very high proportion of wins in the first tests of series.

The history of the last few weeks suggests that the Lions are still short of their full potential, that they have flirted with various attempts to use New Zealand-style forward methods, and to run their threequarters.

Economic

None of these experiments has succeeded, so the Lions have, judging by their team selection, reverted to type and are ready to take up the sprawling economic style so often used by the British teams in the Five Nations championship.

This calls for a strong forward effort, tactical kicking to the opponents' half of the field and there the collection of points either by place-kicking for goal, or the snapping up of some chance left by a lazy defence.

It is, as Andy Dalton, the All Black captain, said on Thursday, test-style rugby.

However, it reduces the Lions' scoring options, and very likely will not allow for a long-range attack bringing the fullback and threequarters into the game. Rather it calls for sniping near the forward mass, either by Terry Holmes, the strong halfback, or his back row, Iain Paxton, Jeff Squire and Peter Winterbottom.

And there is always the prospect that from 40 metres or so Ollie Campbell will kick the goals.

Micheal Kiernan about to try a Bluff oyster while Robert Norster, David Irwin and John Beattie watch in disbelief.

The Lions' front row for the first test look formidable in training: (l to r) Graham Price, Ciaran Fitzgerald and Ian Stephens.

Austere

These are austere tactics, but they are international rugby in the modern European manner and the Lions will be happier playing in that style, rather than developing some hybrid of the more fluid New Zealand game of the moment.

At least it gives the All Blacks a simple aim. They must contain, and if possible, dominate the Lions' pack.

Once that threat is removed, the Lions may well be stranded and even Campbell should not be able to kick them home.

The All Blacks have the height at the line-out, and very likely in Dalton the more accurate thrower-in. Their scrum looks sturdy enough to win their own ball, and perhaps to wheel the Lions and mess up their possession.

Once the Lions' pack has been held, the All Blacks should be able to open up rather more attacking options than the Lions. The Lions' back row are strong and clever, but they need a measure of command before they can operate their set moves.

Spontaneous

The All Blacks, on the other hand, can call on more spontaneous thrust from David Loveridge at halfback, supported by Murray Mexted and Mark Shaw. And if these three can contrive the break then the Lions may be staggered, as were the Wallabies at Eden Park last year, by the powerful running of Gary Whetton, Andy Haden and Gary Knight.

The Lions have not yet met a pack strong enough to split their defence with such dynamic charges of the heavy infantry.

Auckland came close, but the wet conditions there did not encourage the thundering close-passing bursts of the big forwards.

The Lions have gone for strength rather than elusive speed in their backline and may well play a straight forward running game should Campbell occasionally free the ball.

Quick

Again the All Blacks should have more attacking options in the outside backs. Stuart Wilson and Bernie Fraser look very fit, fresh and willing to try the surprise move, possibly in collusion with their fullback, Allan Hewson.

All these suggestions of All Black superiority infer that the All Blacks will quickly pick up their form of last season, and promote a style of speed and movement which the Lions may find difficult to match.

However, the All Blacks will need some caution. There is always the threat of Campbell's boot. There is the danger that the All Black forwards, if they do not strike form quickly, may be dragged into a trench-warfare battle by the Lions, with the loss of attacking thrust from their loose forwards.

And there is the prospect that Francis Palmade, the French referee, may regard the Lions' style of play more warmly than the All Blacks'.

Mr Palmade does get excited by the sight of flashing boot studs at the ruck, and if he should penalise the All Blacks for their rucking methods in the early forward battle the All Blacks will lose one of their most potent weapons.

At the same time the Lions, who favour the maul and the pile-up, may find themselves more in tune with Mr Palmade's refereeing.

Should the crystal-clear Christchurch weather of yesterday continue today, with clear sunny skies following an overnight frost, the conditions should be fair and unlikely to make the toss important.

Thick Sole

Lancaster Park is carrying a thick sole of grass and, after a trim, has seldom looked in better condition. It will, however, be a little soft on top and one supposes that the inevitable curtain-raiser will not improve the quality of the ground.

But there is not likely to be a strong wind, nor rain, and so there is little chance of conditions dictating the flow of the match.

Provided they knit together quickly and do not offer Campbell too many early points, the All Blacks should win.

If they can keep up the speed of the game, and bring their running forwards into the game, they should win decisively.

---

6 June 1983

ALL BLACKS REPEL LIONS CHALLENGE

D.J. Cameron

CHRISTCHURCH

The Lions of British rugby had the All Blacks within their jaws at Lancaster Park on Saturday, and let them wriggle clear, scarred but spared a mortal wound, by 16 points to 12.

This represented, as Andy Dalton, the All Black skipper, graciously remarked afterwards, a fortunate win for the All Blacks.

They had been confounded by the Lions, if not rampant, then certainly less couchant than they have appeared lately.

Last Roar

New Zealand had struggled to keep in contact, 6–9 at half-time, and between the 11th and 16th minutes of the second half, were quick-witted enough to find a third penalty goal from Allan Hewson and a long-range try, with the build-up a mixture of skill and good fortune, by Mark Shaw.

Ollie Campbell, who haunted the All Blacks on Saturday and very likely will continue to do so during this series, kicked the Lions to 12–13 and then, in a desperate last-minute punt from in-goal upfield, presented the remarkable Hewson, who if nothing else has a touch of the dramatic, with the 40-metre drop goal which muffled the last Lions' roar.

Under a clear and frosty sky, and on a pitch not quite as firm as it looked, the close scoring and the occasional dramatic touch offered high drama and excitement.

Chances Lost

Unfortunately, this did not also coincide with a match of high quality. Both teams were so tense the first half consisted of nervous, jittery rugby, full of short sharp movement, and twitching mistakes.

Yet it was during this 40 minutes that the test was decided, that the Lions cast away the chances that would have put them eight or 10 points clear, and roaring away to a famous victory.

After 20 minutes of staccato attack and counter-thrust the score stood at 6–all, two penalty goals to Hewson, a penalty goal and dropped goal taken expertly by Campbell.

The All Blacks were poised to strike, but Ian Dunn fumbled a pass, the Lions broke clear and between the 24th and 32nd minutes the Lions seemed sure to make the decisive thrust.

At one stage they won four rucks in succession within the All Black 22, with Campbell twice jinking clear, but they lacked the cool-headed man to make the critical break and score the try.

Then Graham Price thundered away from a line-out peel to the goal mouth and from the ruck the Lions swept right, the All Black defence strained. Yet Robert Ackerman, the slowest of the Lions backs, decided that he rather than his wing was the man to score the try and the defence just smothered him, and won a clearing penalty on the goal line.

Another promising Lions thrust to the left foundered because Roger Baird was on his heels, and slipping, as the critical pass came to him. From all this frantic activity the Lions acquired only another effortless penalty goal from Campbell, and a three-point lead as the All Blacks tried to gather their wits at half-time.

Had the Lions taken a converted try, perhaps two, in those nerve racking minutes they would have taken a lead which the All Blacks would have found extremely difficult to cut back.

Past Campbell

However, the lack of real pace of the decisive thrust in midfield which let these winning points slip away, remained to haunt the Lions in the second half.

Once the ball was past Campbell, so much the hinge of all the Lions' hopes, mistakes were likely to happen, and usually did.

David Irwin, the second five-eighths, again became obsessed with kicks, which went any old where, or trying to break Warwick Taylor's gritty and secure tackling.

Ackerman lacked real speed, and Baird and Trevor Ringland, let alone the fullback Hugo MacNeill, superbly safe on defence, were seldom brought into the play.

So the steadfast work of the Lions' pack, extremely competitive through Maurice Colclough and Iain Paxton at the line-out, and not at all shy in meeting and stifling the occasional massed charge of the All Black heavy artillery, was wasted.

Kicked Goals

The Lions' forwards did enough to win the game. The halfbacks, Terry Holmes and then his replacement Roy Laidlaw, were quick and aggressive.

Campbell kicked goals and slid gracefully through the defence. The other backs wasted all this gold, so dutifully mined and delivered.

The All Blacks received some salutary lessons. Andy Haden in the middle and John Ashworth at the front won important line-outs when they mattered, and Gary Whetton worked hard in the middle, and made two highly important tackles on the goal line.

The others seemed to work fitfully — Shaw continually busy, Jock Hobbs most promising in pursuit and acquisition of the loose ball, and Murray Mexted clever from the base of the scrum. But they seldom joined together on attack, for the Lions kept them engaged in the tight.

Loveridge was consistently steady, but seldom allowed to break and Dunn had a nervous start, dropping a key pass on attack, missing a high catch, until he settled down and worked steadily on defence.

Wide Attack

Taylor's tackling of Irwin became of critical importance in the second half, Stephen Pokere had his moments in broken play, but one waited in vain for all hands to work smoothly into a series of backline attacks.

Much of this was caused by the economical attacking plan, and when Dalton found this was not working he asked for the wide attack 10 minutes after half-time.

The reward was immediate, and rather fortunate. Whetton won the line-out, Pokere went half through a tackle before putting Stuart Wilson away down the right flank, with Taylor and then Dunn continuing the thrust.

Lions' halfback Terry Holmes leaves the Lancaster Park field with torn ligaments during the first test.

As Dunn was tackled the ball sprung loose, shuttled this way and that and into Shaw's arms who bolted to his backs on the left. Pokere again, Hewson, Bernie Fraser with room, but as he was taken by Ringland he flung the ball infield.

Well Taken

It bounded off a Lions' shoulder and lay there until Shaw charged up, accepted the gift and scored in a tackle.

It would not rank among the great test-match tries, but it was well taken, and sufficient to put the All Blacks clear and within sight of victory.

So the Lions returned to their lair, licking their self-inflicted wounds caused by their faulty selection of their midfield backs. They played far above recent form. They may well play better. The All Blacks certainly will have to, for this was a test the Lions lost rather than the All Blacks won.

---

7 June 1983

FUN FOR SOME …
Staff Reporter

GREYMOUTH

Willie John McBride, the British Lions' rugby manager, yesterday celebrated his 43rd birthday and received a most unusual present — a live, wild and not at all amused piglet.

Some of the Lions went pig shooting on Sunday and dropped two pigs, mainly through the keen eye of Terry O'Connor, the baggage man, who, as president of the Pukekohe Club, keeps an even keener eye on the Counties club scores.

Along the way the party captured a pig and decided it would make the right sort of birthday present for the Irish manager, for it was immediately christened 'Paddy'.

The pig was presented to Willie John at a team meeting before the side left for the West Coast yesterday. The pig was not amused. It escaped from his hands and darted round the players, who took hasty avoiding action.

'I am not sure what happened to the pig,' said Mr McBride, 'but I think it was let loose back in Christchurch.'

---

7 June 1983

… BUT AGONY FOR OTHERS
NZPA

CHRISTCHURCH

Lions' halfback Terry Holmes lay in a Christchurch hospital bed yesterday cursing fate, which has once again intervened in his career.

He nursed the severely twisted right knee which in the first test on Saturday ended his part in the 1983 British Isles tour of New Zealand and which may jeopardise his playing career.

The first-class and international career of the 26-year-old Welshman has been riddled with injury.

In two tours for the British Isles, to South Africa in 1980 and then here, Holmes has played only four games, has missed four others through injury and has been forced home prematurely on both occasions.

His test career for the British Isles lasted only 29 minutes — his time on the field on Saturday. As his first Lions cap it was to have been his greatest rugby moment.

A heavy fall shattered ligaments in his right knee, stretcher bearers bore him from the ground, his tour was at an end. His lot now is one of long and intensive recovery while he hopes to play again for Wales.

He will remain in Christchurch Hospital until Sunday, rejoin his team-mates until the second test at Wellington and then head home to Cardiff.

---

16 June 1983
TEST FAVOURITISM DISPUTED
D.J. Cameron

WELLINGTON

The psychological battle for the second British Lions–All Blacks test at Athletic Park on Saturday was warming up nicely yesterday, with both coaches maintaining the other side would start as favourites.

'The All Blacks will have to be favourites for the second test,' said Jim Telfer, the Lions' coach, after naming his side yesterday for the test.

'We have improved, but the All Blacks will be stronger than the first test. Their record at home must make them favourites on Saturday.'

In contrast, Bryce Rope, the All Black coach, said the New Zealanders would have to accept the fact that they will enter the test as underdogs.

'The Lions have obviously improved and they have had some very good wins since the first test.

'I don't suppose we could have avoided being favourites for the first test,' said Mr Rope, 'but we did not play very well. We made so many errors and did not play up to form.

'Now the Lions are building up to challenge us in the line-out and the scrums.

'However, the All Blacks will be more confident now the first test is behind them. Any first test in the series is something of a psychological barrier, but our players are through that now and will be better for the experience.'

Mr Rope said the Lions second test team was as much as he had expected. Mr Rope said he was pleased with the All Blacks' training yesterday, even though he did not have a full squad in operation.

Jock Hobbs, who has a groin strain, and Bernie Fraser, who is suffering from a slight bout of influenza, did not train yesterday.

'Bernie is not very sick, but we thought it wise to give him a rest and let him get rid of his influenza,' said Mr Rope.

Warwick Taylor, the Canterbury second five-eighths, missed the Canterbury–Marlborough match on Tuesday, also because of influenza, but

he trained yesterday and Mr Rope said afterwards that he was in good health.

---

17 June 1985
DISPARITY EASILY EXPLAINED
Staff Reporter

WELLINGTON

The All Blacks outpointed the British Lions by about 150 to 2 during their second test training yesterday morning.

In view of the controversy building up surrounding the invitation of seven All Blacks to play in South Africa late next month, the Wellington police took some precautions yesterday.

They found the location of the Lions' training, and sent two policemen there in case of trouble.

The only problem there was the icy blast of the Wellington weather which had the Lions, and police, moving to warmer places after a little more than an hour. In contrast, the All Blacks had long lines of policewomen and policemen watching their training at Porirua, where they were spared the rain, but still had a bitter southerly to add to their discomfort. The disparity of protection came because the Lions trained at Wellington College and the All Blacks at the National Police School at Porirua.

---

20 June 1983
SUPERB ALL BLACK PACK EXCEL IN EPIC SECOND HALF
D.J. Cameron

Fortunate is the New Zealander, who, once in a decade, can watch a sporting event which uplifts the heart, stirs the blood, and makes the spirit soar with the nobility of the enterprise.

All Black scrum half Dave Loveridge scores the only try of the second test at Athletic Park. In the background are Lions' centre Michael Kiernan and All Black flanker Mark Shaw.

Last January there was one such occasion when, in the searing cauldron that was the Adelaide Oval, the New Zealand cricketers, with splendid defiance, ignored the impossible and defeated England 297 to 296.

So doubly fortunate then, when on Saturday the All Blacks came out of the shadows of defeat which hung about them when they led 9–0 at half-time after playing with a stiff breeze and, with forward play of heroic proportions, defeated the British Isles in the second rugby test by the same score.

Swept Aside

All the odds demanded that the All Blacks, whose play downwind in the first half had jerked along without the domination of the points which a lop-sided match demanded, should be swept aside by the Lions once their forwards, and Ollie Campbell's boot, came within range of the New Zealand goal line.

And once the inevitable happened, once the Lions had won, everyone would have turned on Andy Dalton for his gamble in taking first use of the wind; on the All Blacks who had made far too many mistakes and had conceded far too many penalties, without building the 15- or 16-point lead which Dalton's temptation of fate demanded.

Instead, they had only a cleverly taken try from a ruck by David Loveridge, and the conversion and a penalty goal by Allan Hewson, who had earlier tried downwind for goal from 60 and 70 metres.

But Dalton, who was in the middle of giving quite his finest display in a test, turned his piercing eyes upon his team-mates at half time and told them that if they held out the Lions, if they could smash ahead in the forwards and keep things tidy in the backs, they would achieve one of the great rugby test victories.

Drew Breath

They could, and they did. The forwards, who had gained some measure of control over the Lions' pack in the first half but had fumbled and fidgeted away too many scoring chances, drew breath and launched into the Lions with total determination.

The All Black backs, whose handling and tackling in the first half had been an invitation to cardiac arrest, caught their passes, found touch and through Allan Hewson covered expertly the occasional long punt into their country.

And in the middle David Loveridge played the kind of game which confirmed, if such was necessary, that he is very likely the best all-round scrum half to pull on an All Black jersey.

Loveridge played the second half like a maestro, and played his team like a finely tuned orchestra. He sometimes flicked the violins of his backline into action, but mostly he turned towards the brass and thundering percussion of his forwards.

So this marvellous 40 minutes of rugby surged on — Loveridge guiding his valiant forwards yard by yard closer to the Lions' line, being thrown back by a long punt, and then leading the remorseless charge back into the Lions' lair.

It was a superb, totally enthralling display of stamina, spirit and control. Especially control, for in those breath-taking 40 minutes the All Blacks (who had been laced 10–4 by Francis Palmade in the first half) conceded only two penalties, and both beyond the range of Campbell's boot.

In fact Campbell, whose merciless boot had destroyed so many teams, had only one kick at goal in the match, a drop-kick in the first half which the wind whisked away from the posts.

All the New Zealand forwards came triumphantly home with glory thick upon them. They had won the great victory and re-established the benchmark of All Black forward style.

But the honour was specially with Dalton, who not only played THE game of his All Black life, but drew from his men such a marvellous response.

And so once again the Lions were within sight of victory only to have the prize snatched away, and now they have but four weeks, and two more tests, from which to rebuild the confidence and character which they took into Saturday's test.

But while the Lions lost the first test because of their own sins of omission, they did not win the second because they were out-played by those unforgettable All Black forwards.

Danger Spot

The Lions had their problems. Iain Paxton wrenched his leg in the first movement of the game, and was replaced by John Beattie in the 52nd minute. Robert Norster damaged his back which might partly explain why the All Black scrum could toy with the Lions on their loosehead in the second half.

But as the almighty All Black forward drive went on and on in the second half too many of the Lions were slow to rally to the danger spot. Too often reduced to a trot crossfield while the All Black forwards, whether smashing forward or making important covering tackles, played with the elan given to those who know they are taking part in something special and precious.

In one crucial aspect of the game the All Blacks cracked the hinge of the whole Lions battle-plan at Roy Laidlaw and Campbell.

If Loveridge was not sniping at Laidlaw round a wheeled scrum the All Blacks were darting through the line-out a foot or two behind the ball hopefully slapped or tapped in Laidlaw's general direction.

So what possession found its way to Campbell placed him under pressure. Really, even from his own line, Campbell only needed two consecutive pieces of quick possession to put the All Black line or posts under pressure. He never had that luxury.

So now the Lions, demolished at what they regarded as the bulwarks of their play at scrum, line-out and halfback, must try to pick up the pieces of their teamwork which the All Blacks scattered over Athletic Park.

They can now only play for a draw in the series, when they had such high hopes of standing one–all. If they can rebuild, and like the All Blacks refuse to accept the impossible, they might yet make a fight of the series. If they do not, their last four weeks will be an ordeal.

---

20 June 1983

BLAZER OF LION STOLEN IN HOTEL
NZPA

WELLINGTON

For the second time on its tour of New Zealand, the British Lions rugby team has fallen victim to over-enthusiastic souvenir hunters.

In Invercargill last week a Lions blazer belonging to the English lock Steve Boyle disappeared after a party at the team's hotel. Appeals by the manager, Mr Willie John McBride, on radio and in newspapers pricked the thief's conscience and the jacket was returned.

Now a second Lions blazer, this one belonging to the Irish centre David Irwin, has disappeared and Mr McBride is again appealing for its speedy return. The blazer was removed from Mr McBride's room in the team's Wellington hotel on Saturday night after the team's second test loss to New Zealand.

'David is very upset that his blazer has gone missing,' Mr McBride said, 'and he is dearly hoping that if someone knows where it is they will do all they can to see it is returned to the team.

'These things are very special. They cannot be replaced.'

---

30 June 1983

SOCIAL WHIRL REDUCED BEFORE TEST
Staff Reporter

DUNEDIN

The British Lions have cut out all social engagements, except visits to schools, in the three days before the crucial third test against the All Blacks on Saturday.

Willie John McBride, the Lions' manager, said yesterday that some of the players had answered requests to appear at rugby clubs — 'where they sometimes talk to half-drunk people' — but these were rather demanding, especially before a test.

'However, we will keep up the school visits. The players really enjoy them.'

Mr McBride referred briefly to his earlier comment that the New Zealand media was conducting 'character assassination' of his players by claiming that he was not blaming all the New Zealand media.

'My criticism does not apply right across the board,' said Mr McBride.

His criticism was sparked by media reference to the head-butting of the North Auckland lock, Alastair Robinson, by a Lions' player, Steve Bainbridge, last Saturday.

'If I had seen the incident,' said Mr McBride, 'I would have condemned it, for it is sad when a game sometimes contains an incident like that.'

It will be scrum time for both the Lions and All Black teams today.

Following his training before the second test, Bryce Rope, the All Black coach, has arranged for two packs to work against the All Black scrum when they train at the small town of Outram today.

Now the Lions will follow suit, bringing in a local pack to join with the Lions' reserves in action against their test forwards.

---

1 July 1983

SHAW FIGHTS FLU ON EVE OF TEST

D.J. Cameron

DUNEDIN

Mark Shaw, the loose forward most feared by the British Lions and rated New Zealand's most effective forward last year by the Wallabies, is very unlikely to play in the third rugby test at Carisbrook tomorrow.

While the All Blacks trained amid sleet and snow at Outram yesterday, Shaw remained in his hotel bed, suffering from a sharp attack of influenza. 'Mark said he felt a bit sniffy after training on Wednesday evening,' said the All Black coach, Bryce Rope, yesterday, 'and he was not at all good this morning.

Doctor's Report

'Mark is not one to complain and he maintains he has never had influenza before, but the chances must be less than 50–50 that he will be fit to play.'

The All Black management will obtain another doctor's report this morning and if that is favourable they may wait until tomorrow morning before deciding whether Shaw will play, or Geoff Old will take his place as the blind-side flanker.

Old took on this role for the third test against the Springboks in 1981. If there is no improvement in Shaw's condition by this morning, Old will definitely play, and train with the test team this morning. As a precaution, Frank Shelford, the former All Black and Bay of Plenty loose forward now playing for Hawke's Bay, will be included in the All Black squad.

Shelford had been chosen, said Mr Rope, because he could handle the No 5 position in the line-out, a position he played in the Prince of Wales Cup match earlier this month.

The Lions are preparing themselves for a muddy battle on Carisbrook.

2 July 1983

BLAST OF WINTER PUTS LIONS TACTICS ON ICE

D.J. Cameron

DUNEDIN

Neither the All Blacks nor the British Lions could take any comfort from the wintry blast which continued to snarl about Dunedin yesterday and which threatens to turn the third test at Carisbrook today into a storm-tossed mud-wallow.

In normal times the All Blacks might smile wickedly at playing a wet-weather test for they have the forwards, and the web-footed wonder of David Loveridge at halfback to make the most of bad conditions.

That estimate might still apply today, but the All Blacks are some distance below the level of preparation demanded by what must be a hard-fought low-scoring test.

Blizzard

The All Black's training at Outram on Thursday did wonders for the local rugby folk, but the blizzard conditions did not allow the All Blacks to put in the solid two hours' work they needed.

Yesterday they chose a closer venue, Hancock Park along the sandy strip of grounds bordering on the Dunedin beaches, and this gave a quite reasonable footing.

However, the temperature was close to zero, there were showers of sleet and a half-gale turned the training into a short ordeal.

The All Blacks warmed up indoors, tried some combined movements for about 20 minutes, but the stinging cold was too much for even well-upholstered and thick-clothed All Blacks to bear.

So the main part of the training run became a mile run back to their hotel, leaving the real down-to-earth tactical training undone.

There was a sense of urgency about some of the All Blacks' work and Gary Knight, in particular, was cracking the whip among the forwards.

But really the All Blacks needed some precise

training, especially at setting up defensive screens to counter the expected tactical kicking bombardment which Ollie Campbell and John Rutherford will aim at Allan Hewson.

In conditions as difficult as they should be at Carisbrook today the prudent team prepares for defence rather than attack, for tactics to use when the other side has the ball.

This may seem a negative aspect but a slip-and-slither game often makes set-forward possession an embarrassment, and the realistic tactics are those designed to mess up the opponents' possession.

The Lions have had a rather better preparation for they are at the point of no return. They are 0–2 in the series, they have lost in total four of 13 tour games, and they know that they must win today otherwise they will disappear from the world rugby map.

Betrayed

Yet the weather has dealt them a harsh hand. They had, after the firm field on Lancaster Park and the hint of fine weather on Wednesday, picked a side geared to backline attack through the introduction of Gwyn Evans, the enterprising fullback, and the playing of the nimble Rutherford in midfield.

The Lions forwards are geared up, so much so that Maurice Colclough sees his immediate destiny as the demolition of Andy Haden near the front of the line-out — and Colclough has even shaved off his beard in an effort to change his luck.

The playing of both Jim Calder and Peter Winterbottom will also serve the Lions well in a muddy forward battle. Calder, especially, is a valiant fighter and the slow pace of the ground will cover up his own lack of real speed.

Jock Hobbs outpointed Winterbottom in the second test and again at Lancaster Park last Tuesday, but he may have to try to counter both Calder and Winterbottom today.

Targets

The loose forwards will hold the key and the halfbacks will be their main targets.

Should the All Blacks break up the Lions by overwhelming Roy Laidlaw as they did in Wellington, then the Lions face a difficult and unhappy afternoon.

Loveridge is rather more resilient and can expect more protection, but he will have to be very quick to escape the Calder–Winterbottom loose forward pincer.

The great pity is that Carisbrook, after being rested for five weeks, has never had such a lush coating of emerald/green grass.

However, the Siberian blast has made the ground very spongy. It will cut up rapidly and make running and dodging very hazardous.

The locals huddled in draughty corners yesterday and predicted a clear frosty day today, while the temperature display in the middle of the city showed eight degrees, which is either a public relations trap, or someone forgot to add the minus sign.

On Wednesday when conditions were merely cold they practised all sorts of backline manoeuvres designed to bring Evans and the blind-side wings into midfield attacks.

Now the Lions have been betrayed, and they must face a game that is unlikely to allow any frilly or frothy midfield tricks.

Still, the placing of Rutherford at second five-eighths should still be a bonus, for he still reacts like a first five-eighths, he has a powerful punt, and he could take off some pressure that is likely to fall on Campbell.

Crucial

So the test will be a kick-and-chase affair, and even more a lottery than a wind-swept game at Athletic Park. The All Blacks should win and if they can keep their grip on the Lions forwards they will win.

But one lucky kick, one lusty speculator at the crucial time, one fumbled catch could turn the course of this game.

Good teams generally make their own luck, but the ground conditions will be so chancy today that both teams will start at the same level — and the lucky one will win.

4 July 1983

ALL BLACKS FIND ONE CORNER TO THEIR LIKING

D.J. Cameron

DUNEDIN

Rugby test grounds have their sacred spots — at Cardiff Arms where Bob Deans did or did not score that try, at Twickenham where Obolenski did score for England, at Eden Park where Peter Jones found glory in 1956.

Now can be added to those sanctified places an area about 20 metres square in the scoreboard corner of Carisbrook where on Saturday the All Blacks defeated the British Lions, 15–8, and so took the test rubber, 3–0.

It took a lot of very hard work, a lot of agony for the players and 28,000 spectators benumbed by wind and rain and bitter cold, before the All Blacks found that special piece of ground.

The Lions, full of spirit and energy at the start, struck an equally numbing blow in the eighth minute when John Rutherford and Steve Bainbridge hacked the ball through the defence and little Roger Baird made a brilliant one-point landing on the ball before it sloshed away into touch in-goal.

Good Kick

The All Blacks battled back, seldom with cool or consistent control, and found two penalty goals to Allan Hewson, the first an extremely good kick against the wind, to take them to half-time at 6–4.

Then in the second minute of the second half the Lions struck again with a try of such speed and daring and sublime control that any other team might have been demoralised by the blow.

Jim Calder broke away from his own country, led the raid deep into the All Black twenty-two at the right, then the ball moved with dry-weather mastery out to Baird on the left who ran and then reached round Stuart Wilson's tackle to find Gwyn Evans, who nipped inside John Hobbs' tackle.

Rutherford roared up for the pass, the dive and perhaps, the double-movement on the tackle as he reached the line.

A pedantic referee might have questioned that final surge but Dick Byers, the Australian, was there, nicely in tune with the flow of the match, to see the justice to a regal move was done.

Just Wide

Ollie Campbell, short with his first conversion, was just a shade wide with his second, and the All Blacks were only 6–8 astern.

They had problems. They were not in command at line-out or scrum, and Hobbs had a battle keeping both Calder and Peter Winterbottom away from control of the loose ball.

Wayne Smith had gone with a groin injury, and Steve Pokere at first five-eighths and Arthur Stone at centre tried some fair-weather Maori mischief in midfield which allowed the Lions to smother and break clear. Words were said, mainly from Andy Dalton, who again was an effective and inspiring leader. So Pokere teased the Lions with tactical kicks, the Lions began to wilt at the scrum, and the All Blacks began to chip away at Roy Laidlaw as he struggled to control line-out possession.

Slowly, steadily, the All Black forwards began to heave the Lions back, and by either good luck or good management, headed for the scoreboard corner. There were the deepest and iciest puddles, the most treacherous turf, the place where cool defence was the most difficult.

Imprisoned

And there the All Blacks stayed, each forward content to smash and charge at the Lions, sure in the knowledge that his close-knit band of brothers would only be a foot or two behind.

The Lions were imprisoned, their forwards hanging on by spirit alone. Laidlaw continually harassed, Campbell like a nervous and tired fox, cornered by the baying hounds of the All Black loose forwards.

The break had to come, and curiously at the right corner. Loveridge ran toward the posts, Wilson came hurtling across against the flow of attack and three Lions could only wave a desperate hand as he raced across for the try, which Hewson converted.

The Lions kicked off deep. From inside his twenty-two Hewson, who could do no wrong, smashed a huge

Lions' loose forward Jim Calder is caught in possession by All Blacks Dave Loveridge (at rear) and Stephen Pokere during the third test in Dunedin.

Lions' winger Roger Baird dives on the ball for the first Lions' try in the test in Dunedin.

punt which soared and then slithered into touch, putting the All Blacks again back in that fateful corner.

Hammered

And there they stayed for most of the last 20 minutes, the Lions sometimes wriggling clear, only to be hammered back by an All Black pack sodden, half-frozen, completely magnificent in their urgent charge into the Lions.

Fittingly enough, Hewson added the death-thrust three minutes from the end when Winterbottom was offside and he had the penalty goal.

Hewson, without fault or fear, played superbly. The Lions thought that through Hewson might lie the road to victory. Instead he destroyed them.

And so did the All Black pack, always together, growing in power with every frozen minute, and with Loveridge both the complete servant to his pack and the constant menace to the Lions.

It could not, in such Siberian conditions, be a game of great rugby, but it was bravely played by an All Black side which grew in strength and confidence as they built that prison in the left corner, and by a Lions side which fought with spirit to the bitter end.

At the end the Lions stood as a guard of honour for the All Blacks as they went back to the warm comfort of their dressing room. It was a distinctive and gracious act. The Lions now have a fortnight to endure, but they now seem to have the right balance to their test side.

They offered a muted roar at Carisbrook and the test series left them without a whimper. They might still be good enough to trumpet the roar that precedes the kill at Eden Park on Saturday week.

Africa this winter, and the little effort by the Government to stop the New Zealanders.

'We are not opposed to the game [at Eden Park],' Mr Minto said. 'There is no reason for that.'

Mr Don said, 'We must be cautious, and we have withdrawn from sale to the public those seats that are close to the playing area.'

He described the action as quite a minor matter.

12 July 1983

BLAZEY COMES OUT SWINGING
McLean on Sport

Too bad British Lions' manager Willie John McBride couldn't hang on in New Zealand for a few more days after his team winds up with the final rugby test against the All Blacks on Saturday.

Too bad he couldn't publicly debate with New Zealand Rugby Union chairman Ces Blazey the merits of one particularly savage charge he delivered against Kiwi refereeing standards after the Lions had battled to victory over Counties on Saturday.

In that charge, which followed his generalised statement that the refereeing encountered throughout by the Lions had been 'very disappointing,' McBride alleged that his players had found they needed to play twice as hard to win in New Zealand as they would need to in their home countries. Deserting, for once, his lifelong attachment to fair, reasoned and diplomatic argument in controversy, no matter how violent and bitter the issues, Mr Blazey yesterday came out swinging.

'If Willie John,' he said, 'is suggesting that New Zealand refereeing does not compare in quality with that which is standard in the British Isles, I reject his contention totally.

'I have seen sufficient of the refereeing in the two communities to be absolutely sure I am right.'

Strong words from anyone; confrontational words from as well-disciplined a man as Chairman Ces. By begging off his homeward-bound flight for

8 July 1983

PROTEST PLANS REDUCE RUGBY GATE

One thousand tickets have been withdrawn from public sale for the fourth rugby test at Eden Park tomorrow week because of a demonstration planned by the anti-apartheid organisation Hart.

The Auckland Rugby Union had planned to offer 2000 tickets for sale to the public.

The chairman of the union, Mr R.M. Don, said last night that the 1000 tickets going on sale on Monday would be well away from the playing area for the final match between the All Blacks and the Lions.

Hart representative, John Minto, said the march would highlight invitations to several All Blacks and British Lions to play in a match in South

a few days, McBride at Wellington next Wednesday could attend a gathering which has been called by the Council for Recreation and Sport.

The topic is the problem confronting all adjudicatory officials in all sports — in plain language, referees and umpires. The response to the invitation, which has gone out to all sports, has been, according to the council director Bob Stodart, 'excellent'.

Certainly the Rugby Union, according to Mr Blazey, will be there, with bells on; and one imagines its leadership will be supported by most other sports who are troubled, in Mr Stodart's words, 'by the influence on kids in sport caused by bad-mouthing of officials'.

The congress is the outcome of a study done by the international cricket umpire Stan Cowman — who has also done his whack in hockey — as part of his qualifying for a council diploma.

Cowman discovered a significant erosion of cricket umpires was occurring in the Hutt Valley because of the amount of abuse voluntary, unpaid officials acting for the love of the game were suffering on field and off.

Basketball has also had its fair share of sore-heads and controversies; and however profound their love of the game, sensitive souls in rugby might not care to expose themselves to the kind of criticisms Willie John McBride and Ciaran Fitzgerald made on Saturday and which, it seems, have been a running sore of the tour.

Studies done by Cowman and the soccer celebrity Barrie Truman, who is running the council's congress, tend to establish that television in the United States is sheering away from concentrated coverage on punch-ups and foul incidents in sport and coincidentally is cheering up officials who are confronted with these unpleasantnesses. There might also be a lesson for somebody — guess who? — in Ces Blazey's comment, the smoothness of which did not entirely conceal the tartness, that the Lions 'might have a good look, not at officials but at their own failings.'

---

16 July 1983

LIONS NEED WIN TO ESCAPE FROM OBLIVION

D.J. Cameron

If spirit and ambition mean anything in sport the British Lions should start with a handy advantage over the All Blacks in the fourth test at Eden Park this afternoon.

The Lions have the spur that although they have already lost the test series 0–3 they have one last chance to take home a little glory.

If they lose they will join the almost forgotten Lions of 1966, of which Willie John McBride and Jim Telfer were both members, who lost all four tests. In fact should the Lions lose today it will be their sixth loss in 18 games which would make them inferior, by the odd decimal point or two to the 1955 team which lost eight of 25 matches.

Incentive

If such a lugubrious fate does not spur on the 1983 Lions (the 1966 manager Des O'Brien years later said the 1966 side had never had a reunion because they could find no real wish to be reunited) then nothing will. By all appearances the All Blacks have not had the same kind of incentive within reach.

They have already won the series. Their preparation has been affected by the loss of Wayne Smith, by the conjecture about which players will fly off to South Africa tomorrow night, and by their demands for more tickets. These things suggest a team without the desperate ambition which should put some steel in the Lions' backbones today.

But at training yesterday, when the forwards went off by themselves to work on their line-out while the backs had a busy, breezy time elsewhere, there was a hint that the right kind of attitude was building among the All Blacks.

Seniors

Especially was this so among the members of 'the club,' the senior group among the New Zealanders who have been through so many battles together, and sometimes won against bigger odds than the

Lions will present this afternoon.

This, in fact, may be the last hurrah for many of the All Blacks for several of the senior players. Allan Hewson, Bernie Fraser, Stuart Wilson, David Loveridge, Murray Mexted, Andy Haden, Mark Shaw, Gary Knight, John Ashworth and Andy Dalton may not tread Eden Park in a test match again. The All Blacks drew deep on this inspiration when Graham Mourie led them for the last time at Eden Park last year. Mourie has gone, but the All Blacks' pride in performance remains.

The Lions have strength in their pack and abundant attacking ability in their inside backs. But the one man who stands between the All Blacks and victory is Ollie Campbell, the Lions five-eighths and goal-kicker.

Artist

Campbell is a perfectionist, an artist who has not been able, yet, to reach his self-appointed goals in a country whose rugby he respects so much.

Campbell has it in him to be the dominant man of the match, the one man whose accurate boot and nimble brain could take the game away from the All Blacks. All this supposes that he is not affected by his hamstring injury, and that he has a firm enough field on which to show his art.

A hamstring strain, however slight, can sap the confidence, and the Lions will need Campbell, and his inside partner, Roy Laidlaw, in their sharpest form today. The field was still soft yesterday and if there is no rain today should give a reasonably firm footing.

Special

Eden Park has produced some marvellous final tests in recent years. It might be too much to expect full-scale attack from start to finish, although Fraser and Wilson at training have hinted that they will produce something special today.

Rather, the test should be close fought until the forward battle stabilises. Then the game should open up. The Lions have nothing to lose but their chains. The All Blacks have nothing to lose but their pride. The All Blacks are the better balanced side. They should win.

---

18 July 1983

POLICE PART MARCH, SPECTATORS

Anti-apartheid marchers were stopped by about 70 police after a skirmish with rugby supporters who were heading for the test on Saturday.

The 300 protestors were in Cricket Ave, behind Eden Park, when two rugby supporters tried to take a banner from those at the head of the march. A scuffle broke out and the supporters were moved on — but they tried to take another banner from marchers further back. When the marchers reached the place where most of the rugby supporters had congregated they were booed and abused.

Scuffles

About 50 police moved in to escort them around the corner into Reimers Ave where the march was stopped. A further 20 police were put in place at the front of the group.

Chief Inspector Ross Dallow said the scuffles had prompted the move. He had decided to prevent any escalation by holding the protesters at that point until most of the rugby supporters were in the park. The protesters were held for 20 minutes, and then moved on to Sandringham Rd where they attached anti-apartheid messages to the Eden Park fence.

Slogans Shouted

In Walters Ave the protesters stopped outside Gate E to shout slogans at the nearby crowd. They continued on to Dominion Rd and returned to Potters Park, from where the march had started at 1 pm.

Detectives are investigating the reported discovery of two Molotov cocktails in a hedge in Marlborough St, near Eden Park, on Saturday.

The national chairman of the anti-apartheid group Hart, Mr John Minto, said yesterday that the bombs had nothing to with Saturday's protest and were not the work of protesters. The protesters had marched past Marlborough St but had not gone into it.

---

18 July 1983

ALL BLACKS LEAVE NO ROOM FOR ANY EXCUSES

D.J. Cameron

With the cool, calculating skill of a surgeon the All Blacks cut through the flim-flam, the might-have-beens, the 'if onlys' of this British Lions tour as they surged unerringly on to their 38–6 win in the fourth test on Saturday at Eden Park.

This time there could be no argument about Lions' chances not taken in the first test, nor the unequal struggles in the gale of the second test and the icy swamp of the third.

This time there was no need for a Danie Craven to say afterwards: 'It's all yours, New Zealand.'

This time the All Blacks, on a firm field and under conditions which insisted on a fair contest, played as close as they have come in recent years to total rugby.

Shaken

From the first seconds when Andy Haden plunged through the Lions' forwards as he caught the first kick-off and sparked a withering series of All Black attacks in the first 10 minutes, the Lions were shaken, almost shattered.

That brilliant opening, even if it brought only two penalty goals to Allan Hewson on a field which must be his idea of paradise, set the test and the All Blacks alight.

From then onward they were in almost total control — clever in the line-out, strong at the scrum, meshing together nicely in the loose forwards . . . a devastating mixture of cool skill and raw power.

And nicely blended with a free and joyful spirit

Lions' No 8 Iain Paxton breaks with the ball, supported by Peter Winterbottom (rear) and John O'Driscoll. All Black halfback Dave Loveridge looks on.

Lions' flanker Peter Winterbottom makes a break during the fourth test at Eden Park.

Lions' prop Graham Price is tackled by All Black Andy Haden during the fourth test at Eden Park.

All Black centre Stephen Pokere makes a break with the ball during the All Blacks' 38–6 win over the Lions at Eden Park.

among the backs as Dave Loveridge, again the maestro, let his backs away through the soundness of Ian Dunn and Warwick Taylor in midfield, the sheer magic of Steven Pokere at last off the leash, the exuberance of Stuart Wilson and Bernie Fraser on the wings.

Sublime

Here at last were the All Blacks reaching the sublime quality which this band of brothers so often seek, but, being human, seldom achieve — each man knitting perfectly into a pattern which put their game into a dimension the Lions were not good enough to reach.

Within the first 15 minutes the All Black control was so complete that Loveridge was presented with the ball 13 times, while Roy Laidlaw received it three times, and even then he and Ollie Campbell, already suffering from the hamstring injury he had taken into the match, were under such pressure they could not clear it.

Inevitably the Lions had to crack. First the All Black forwards screwed, with almost insolent ease, a Lions loosehead on their own line, the ball squirted clear and Jock Hobbs had a simple pick-up for the try.

The Lions answered with a Campbell break, and a penalty goal — which further damaged his leg, and he was a wan and stiff-legged wanderer until he retired soon after half time — and then 10 minutes later came the classical try which took the test completely beyond the Lions' reach.

Reach

Gary Whetton, his line-out work honed by his pre-match practising against Haden, won the line out, a long cut-out pass found Fraser who, just as he half-committed Roger Baird to the tackle, slipped the ball to Wilson who glided away to the corner and into the record books.

That, taking the score at half time to 16–3, was the end of the Lions, and they had to endure another 40 minutes of agony in a game they could never win.

First Fraser hacked on downfield from his own country, Loveridge put the backs clear, Pokere floated a lovely chip in front of Wilson and that was that.

Hewson glided up, flicked a kick ahead and as it bobbled up between Campbell and Gwyn Evans, Hewson slipped between the two, the ball flipped into his hands and he was away to the posts.

Indignity

A massive All Black forward charge to the line somehow delivered the ball back and Haden plunged between the posts.

As the final indignity, not at all eased by a late penalty goal by Evans, the Lions tried to run from their twenty-two, Hugo MacNeill's flip went behind Robert Ackerman, and Wilson was offered the gift of a careful kick ahead and the try.

The Lions made errors in the backs, they were outplayed in the pack, and once again their scrum gave Laidlaw an impossible task. All the Lions could do was to tackle and this they did bravely, especially David Irwin in midfield and Baird, at the cost of concussion, on the left wing.

No wonder, then, Andy Dalton, the All Black captain, still had a starry look in his eyes 40 minutes after the finish. He has never played so well, nor had his leadership borne such fruit.

Tackles

He had a team perfectly geared for attack, yet superbly strong in tackling, especially by Taylor and Hobbs. He had that wondrous blend of aggression and finesse in his pack, Loveridge in command, and a backline of burgeoning confidence and flair.

He had, after winning the series at Carisbrook, promised a great performance at Eden Park. Seldom has a promise been so blissfully fulfilled.

Rival captains Andy Dalton and Ciaran Fitzgerald after the final test.

Representatives of the four British nations rehearsing at Eden Park before the third test. From left: Murdo MacKenzie (Scotland), Ann Cribbens (England), Carmen Painter (Wales), Brian Sheridan (Ireland).

1993

12 June – Christchurch
26 June – Wellington
3 July – Auckland

7 June 1993

DOWD AND CLARKE SECURE VACANT TEST POSITIONS

Herald staff, NZPA

The All Black selectors yesterday named a predictable line-up for the first rugby test against the British Isles, in Christchurch on Saturday.

Auckland pair Craig Dowd and Eroni Clarke have nailed down the two vacant places. Loosehead prop Dowd, who has played 18 games for his province, will pack down with fellow Auckland frontrowers Olo Brown and captain Sean Fitzpatrick.

He takes over the place left open by the suspension of Waikato's Richard Loe.

Clarke, who has played at centre and on both wings for Auckland this season, will be on the right wing against the Lions, stepping in for John Kirwan, who did not play in the All Black trials.

All Black team: John Timu (Otago); Eroni Clarke (Auckland), Frank Bunce (North Harbour), Va'aiga Tuigamala (Auckland), Walter Little (North Harbour), Grant Fox (Auckland), Ant Strachan (North Harbour), Zinzan Brooke (Auckland), Michael Jones (Auckland), Robin Brooke (Auckland), Ian Jones (North Auckland), Jamie Joseph (Otago), Olo Brown (Auckland), Sean Fitzpatrick (captain, Auckland), Craig Dowd (Auckland). Reserves: Matthew Cooper (Waikato), Jon Preston (Wellington), Arran Pene (Otago), Mark Cooksley (Counties), Mark Allen (Taranaki), Graham Dowd (North Harbour).

Meanwhile, the Lions have been forced to risk captain Gavin Hastings in tomorrow's match with Southland leading into the vital first test of the series against the All Blacks.

Injuries to midfielders Scott Hastings and Will Carling meant the selectors had to choose playing either Hastings or Jeremy Guscott tomorrow and Hastings opted to play.

In naming their side the Lions have indicated that blind-side flanker Mike Teague's opening test chances may have disappeared under the challenge from Ben Clarke.

Clarke, who has played in all three loose forward positions on this tour with a high degree of success, was rested for the Otago game and again for tomorrow. That suggests he has done enough to play at Lancaster Park on Saturday.

In the halves, Rob Andrew and Robert Jones are paired again and after the mixed effort of the other duo against Otago, a strong showing tomorrow could clinch their test places.

The selectors have resisted trying utility forward Mick Galwey at lock tomorrow with both Martin Bayfield and Wade Dooley unavailable.

Instead they will use both Damian Cronin and Andy Reed, perhaps with the view that one or even both will have to play in the test. While the side has a distinctly second-string look it will not want for motivation with several places still open for the test.

Lions: Gavin Hastings (capt), Richard Wallace, Scott Gibbs, Tony Underwood, Tony Clement, Rob Andrew, Robert Jones, Mick Galwey, Richard Webster, Andy Reed, Damian Cronin, Mike Teague, Jason Leonard, Brian Moore, Peter Wright.

---

10 June 1993

LANDMARK FOR SKIPPER

Wynne Gray

Sean Fitzpatrick becomes the fourth All Black to play 50 tests this Saturday at the same Lancaster Park ground where he made his debut for the 'Baby Blacks' in 1986 and where he led New Zealand for the first time last season.

Fitzpatrick's predecessor as national captain Gary Whetton, holds the record with 58 caps, Colin Meads is next with 55 then John Kirwan, too late home from Italy to be chosen for this test, having 54 caps.

'I am just happy to be out there and want to have the same excitement I had in the other 49 tests,' Fitzpatrick said yesterday about his feelings coming into the opening international with the Lions.

'Obviously Lancaster Park has special memories for me.

'It seems a bit more stable than playing for the Baby Blacks in my first test. I think the feeling is the same even though I have been around I still have got to have the same excitement as Craig Dowd [debut All Black prop].'

Fitzpatrick mentioned that the new loosehead prop and Auckland team-mate had great potential for a lengthy career with the All Blacks. While the captain has scored out on the 'wing' for the All Blacks he mentioned that the pace of the Lions' threequarters was an obvious asset his team would have to shut down on Saturday.

'They have shown good ability to spread the ball wide and score tries which is good for them,' he said.

Fitzpatrick's milestone appearance is his 48th test in succession, his run only broken by Hika Reid's two tests against the Australians in 1986.

Another player with a record in sight is first five-eighths Grant Fox, the only member of the All Blacks to have played against the Lions when he drop-kicked Auckland to a victory a decade ago. The leading All Black points-scorer has 573 test points and 995 in all games for New Zealand. It would be ironic if he could reach the 1000 points with a try, a result which would only be his second touchdown for the All Blacks.

---

10 June 1993

ALL BLACKS DETERMINED NOT TO FALL PREY TO FIRST-TEST VULNERABILITY

Wynne Gray

CHRISTCHURCH

The All Blacks have dismissed suggestions they may fall victim to the first-test blues which, in recent years, have often hit New Zealand in the opening international of a domestic series.

Through the 1980s and into the '90s the All Blacks have carved out a tradition as slow first-test starters, usually winning but with some considerable difficulty.

Saturday's opponents, the British Isles, have won only five and drawn two of the 28 internationals they have played here since 1930 but two of the victories and one draw have been in the first test of a series. All Black coach Laurie Mains said the first-test bogy was not a concern for his squad. That part of All Black history was just that.

Under Mains for the first time last season, the All Blacks lost the opening game to the World XV at Lancaster Park and then only squeaked home 24–21 at Carisbrook against Ireland.

'We are very determined not to allow the things that have disrupted us last year in our first test to be repeated this time,' Mains said yesterday.

'The players are very aware of that and we have identified the areas we need to be good at to avoid that happening.'

Mains was confident that with 13 of the side who won the test against the Springboks in the side for Saturday, preparations would run much more smoothly.

'They basically know what we are talking about,' he said. Mains believed the Northern Hemisphere rugby players had closed the gap on their Southern Hemisphere counterparts, with the evidence coming in the last World Cup tournament and the manner the Lions had played on this tour.

He would not accept that either side was entitled to be favourites for the opening Lancaster Park test. There were advantages for both sides.

A team on tour had the chance to mould their patterns and get into a rhythm for their style while the All Blacks had the assistance of a home ground and a home crowd.

Since 1981 the All Blacks have won all but two of the 18 opening games in domestic series but there have been some extraordinarily tight and sketchy performances.

Those included the 1983 16–12 win against the Lions at Lancaster Park, the 10–9 win over France at the same venue the following year and a year later the 18–13 win over England on the back of six Kieran Crowley penalties.

Captain Sean Fitzpatrick said the first-test bogy

had not yet played a major part in team discussions though the squad was aware of the All Blacks' patchy record. Those who played last year in the narrow win against Ireland just had to remember the changes wrought out of that dissatisfaction for the next test.

After the side trained yesterday at Rugby Park in Christchurch, Fitzpatrick said having the strong nucleus of the end of last season's side was most beneficial in getting organised quickly. There was also a strong reserves bench, players most capable of moving into the All Blacks should the initial selection not perform.

There was only one minor alarm at training, with reserve Jon Preston straining a calf muscle doing a series of 150m sprints. The medical staff said the problem was only minor, his treatment more precautionary than anything else.

Further adjustments to the laws would not have a significant effect in the test, Mains said. The developing maul after a kick was coming more into play but it was not making a major difference.

While the Lions' management had spoken this week about some difficulties with local referees not penalising players going to ground, Mains said the test would be a case of adapting to the rulings of Australian official Brian Kinsey.

'The problems are not just with the players here, it is the referees as well. We will have the discipline to adapt to and play to the interpretations of the referee on the day.'

---

12 June 1993

PACE CRUCIAL ELEMENT IN TRIAL OF TACTICS
Wynne Gray

CHRISTCHURCH

Among the many critical areas of today's opening rugby international between the British Isles and the All Blacks in Christchurch, pace will be paramount.

If the Lions can play the match in the forwards at their speed and then offer their outside backs adequate space they should sniff the try-line and give this test a real shake.

Conversely, the All Blacks will be wanting their pack to up their work rate, to increase their mobility, to run the Lions pack ragged.

If neither team can play the match at their momentum, the outcome will be the toss-up it has seemed since this ninth Lions tour began to take shape.

The All Blacks will play to a pattern that has been determined under the new reign of Laurie Mains and Co — there will be little deviation from the organisation used in Australia and South Africa last season.

But the key component will be whether either side can exert their pattern sufficiently to create the breaks that are generally scarce at this level of rugby.

If the play is scrappy and penalties numerous, the shootout between rival goalkickers Gavin Hastings and Grant Fox will be absorbing.

Both kickers have shown sound form in recent weeks and while Fox has rare off days, Hastings has shown in more than a few critical games, like Scotland's World Cup semifinal defeat, that pressure can disrupt his operations.

Any All Black march to quick points will have the Lions playing catch-up rugby, the type they were allowed to play against the New Zealand Maoris, but there will not be that leeway today from the more efficient All Blacks.

All Black coach Laurie Mains believes his team will have to counter a few Lions surprises but not a whole range of different tactics.

'The pace of their wings is a concern, they are as fast as there are around, but we just have to make sure they do not get many chances,' he said yesterday.

He had been concerned earlier in the week that some of the All Black combinations were not gelling as quickly as they should, but those had been fixed and there should be no typical first-test dramas.

After both sides had gentle runs yesterday Lions' captain Gavin Hastings, like most in his team, nominated his backs to inflict the damage today.

Lions' second-five Will Carling tries to dodge the tackle of All Black Walter Little during the first test in Christchurch.

'There is no question our backs are more potent, more dangerous than they [the All Blacks] are and given the right ball they can bring us the win,' he said.

But, if the Lions started slowly and played to some of the form they showed against the provinces, a victory was not possible. The strong suspicion remains that the Lions' pack, particularly at tighthead prop, are vulnerable. Under the new laws that may not hurt them too much as scrums play less of a part in rugby now.

But any defensive scrums near their line will determine if they have been foxing about their prowess in this area.

To former national coach Brian Lochore, and most observers, the line-out possession and control will have a huge bearing on the test.

'That is the most critical area of the test, where the Lions have Martin Bayfield with lots of ability and ball skills, too,' Lochore said.

While the Lions have not yet exposed any desire for short line-outs on this trip, that method would provide Bayfield and Co with more room for their talents and also a better view for referee Brian Kinsey of Australia to patrol interference.

The Lions, through Dewi Morris' kicks to the box and the punting of Rob Andrew, will test the All Black back trio's defensive communication while the All Blacks will target the Lions' halves from forays off the rucks and mauls.

If the visitors can collect several phases of continuity their potent switches of play will stretch the defence. The All Black counter will be a barrage of runners hammering the inside lines to eliminate fringing.

The forecast is for some rain but that should not stop a hefty crowd watching this enthralling prospect.

14 June 1993

REF CERTAIN ABOUT DISPUTED DECISIONS
Wynne Gray

CHRISTCHURCH

Test referee Brian Kinsey had no doubts about two controversial decisions which went the way of the All Blacks to help to clinch Saturday's first test, 20–18, against the British Lions.

For the first-minute try to Frank Bunce he was unsighted but on the advice of linesman Andrew Cole made his decision.

Then with a minute remaining of the combative Lancaster Park international he ruled Lions No 8 Dean Richards was lying over the tackled player and not allowing the ball to come free.

It is now history that Grant Fox, who brought up his 1000 points for the All Blacks during the game, nailed the 42m penalty kick for the narrow victory.

The Lions' camp were most critical of both decisions, manager Geoff Cooke asking why his side would want to hold the ball in the final minute when possession was coming back to his team.

'We wanted it, it was a strange decision. But the whole game was full of inconsistencies, the players were off their feet all the game,' he said.

Of the game's single try, Cooke said there had been considerable dressing room debate with Iuean Evans saying both he and Bunce held the ball as they fell over the Lions' line.

Evans later expanded: 'I went up for the ball, caught it and then Bunce wrapped himself round me and we went down. The guys have told me that if anything I might have got it down first but neither of us let it go as we crossed the line.

'I was surprised the referee came from where he was and gave the try,' Kinsey said. Bunce obstructed his view but linesman Andrew Cole 'was in a very good position in-goal and gave me the nod.'

For the final crucial Fox kick, Kinsey said Richards tackled an All Black, lay over the player and because of that New Zealand could not get at the ball.

'There had been penalties against New Zealand earlier for exactly the same thing so, therefore, for consistency, I had to make the award,' Kinsey said.

'As a tackler, his obligation is to get off the player where possible, but he made no attempt and just lay there.

'Michael Jones was penalised at least two or three times for doing it. Zinzan Brooke was penalised. The Lions probably got six to nine points for similar penalties and unfortunately that, from my memory, was the only time a Lions player lay over the ball.

'They were making every attempt to clear it or roll away.'

Kinsey said the players made the opening international easy to administer. They had played in 'such a marvellous spirit.'

He had not noted any great problem with players joining from the side rather than coming from behind the last feet as required under the amended maul law.

'So long as the player makes an attempt to come round the back we are going to be reasonable. The way the law is written it is very easy to destroy a game so we want to be able to referee reasonably liberally.'

The Australian test referee said the coaches from both sides had been to visit him on the eve of the match to discuss interpretations and how he would officiate.

---

24 June 1993

THE BOTTOM LINE IS WINNING THE TEST

Disappointment with their play in the first test may have the All Blacks treading a fine line between wanting to offer a more appealing spectacle and resorting to percentage rugby in Saturday's crucial second rugby international with the British Isles.

While rugby officials and administrators do not like to compare their game with the concurrent league test series, it could be said that the opening Kiwi–Kangaroo league test had much more action than the initial All Blacks–Lions international.

All Black coach Laurie Mains said what happened in league was of no concern to him but he wanted his team's play to be a model for New Zealand rugby players.

However, he was 'extremely disappointed at the quality of our play and the way the game went in the first test and we would be certainly looking to play a better game,' Mains conceded yesterday.

'Last year, pretty well all the test matches we played in were damned good spectacles.'

That thinking would be taken to Athletic Park in Wellington but it would not be allowed to overshadow the importance of winning the test and the series.

'Often you get the situation where, if you talk about playing attractive rugby by passing the ball to the wings all the time, you are fooling yourselves because that is not a reality,' he said.

'It is more by playing with quality and keeping the mistakes to a minimum and what you do, you do well,' Mains said.

That philosophy came through later with captain Sean Fitzpatrick, who said there was an All Black responsibility to promote rugby but at the end of Saturday the side who won the test would be remembered.

The All Blacks held a sharp and intensive training session yesterday, their only open practice before the test.

Reserve halfback Ant Strachan seemed to be much more comfortable with leg and shoulder problems which have disrupted his preparation.

He is likely to be fit for a place on the bench, though Stu Forster will stay with the squad until tonight as a precaution.

One other problem appeared, however, with new lock Mark Cooksley complaining of some leg muscle soreness and being excused some of the drills. Mains said the Counties lock would be fit, there were no long-term problems.

The tension within the camp has risen markedly from the first-test week with a number of the players off-limits yesterday in any official discussions with the media. That group included John Kirwan, Craig Dowd, Eroni Clarke, Jon Preston, and Cooksley.

While the Lions have lost two of their three games since the narrow first-test defeat, Mains said those results were irrelevant in the context of the international matches.

The Lions were most difficult opponents with their line-out, switches of play and aggressive midfield backs being particular areas of danger. Fitzpatrick mentioned the Lions would be like the All Blacks were last season, hungry and eager to atone for a miserable midweek loss to a Sydney XV.

Saturday's referee and the final test official as well, Patrick Robin of France, had been an alert and constructive arbiter, Mains said, when the All Blacks had him for two tests in Australia last season. He had allowed fair rucking.

---

25 June 1993

LIONS LOOK TO JOHN BULL FOR TEST INSPIRATION

Wynne Gray

WELLINGTON

The British Isles have gone for an overload of England players in their bid to square the rugby test series with the All Blacks in Wellington tomorrow.

The selectors have placed their faith in the experience and combination of those players who have taken England to two Grand Slams but fell away with some sluggish efforts in this year's Five Nations competition.

A total of 11 England players, including all but Irish loosehead prop Nick Popplewell in the pack, have been charged with salvaging the tour at Athletic Park.

No 8 Dean Richards has been passed fit despite his calf muscle damage, though there are still some worries about the hamstring injury captain Gavin Hastings is trying to overcome.

Had the second test been scheduled for yesterday, Lions' coach Ian McGeechan said his skipper might have played but he felt the 48 hours left before the international would give Hastings every chance of taking his position.

'He did more than half a session, the medics are happy with him,' the coach said. A final decision on Hastings' playing may be left until tomorrow morning.

The Lions' changes from the slender first-test loss are at second five-eighths, where Scott Gibbs replaces Will Carling, Brian Moore is the hooker instead of Ken Milne, Martin Johnson comes in at lock for Andy Reed, while the experiment at tighthead prop continues with Jason Leonard in for Paul Burnell.

The four changes match the numbers switch by the All Blacks in a selection manager Geoff Cooke said was no more difficult than any other final decision.

The choice of players like Leonard and Ben Clarke out of their original positions, said McGeechan, was made partly on form and the way the tour had developed.

'I think Ben Clarke has come out, in particular, to be an outstanding forward and he has shown out here he can play in all three back-row positions — very successfully. And I think his development out here has been a real bonus for us,' he said.

The Leonard-for-Burnell swap was a reflection of encouraging form, said Cooke.

'He has had a couple of games at tighthead and we feel he is up to it, as simple as that.'

In making the decisions, Cooke said there had to be choices and they were only ever accepted by the media if the team won. Clearly this match will determine the reputation of the Lions, who have somehow to string together a full game of concentration rather than the patchy performances they have so far.

Their incentive will be to save the tour and then possibly win the test series.

The All Blacks are equally determined to atone for a moderate first test and finish off the tourists. All the All Black injury niggles had cleared yesterday in a private training session at Fort Dorset, with Ant Strachan fit to take his place on the reserves bench and lock Mark Cooksley in the pack.

Coach Laurie Mains labelled the final workout 'satisfactory' with the emphasis on line-out variations and honing moves. While the weather closed in on Wellington yesterday morning, it later cleared and the prospect for tomorrow is for fine but breezy conditions.

The All Blacks were not focused on the Lions changes — whatever combination they chose the task would be immense, Mains said. It was plain that the test series was the priority for the tourists.

'They have made it clear they are only worried about the tests and that came through in the first match. Nothing has altered in between.'

———

28 June 1993

PENALTY CHAIN BROKEN
NZPA staff

———

It rates as one of the rarest events in world rugby, but it happened in the 20–7 British Lions win over the All Blacks at Athletic Park in Wellington on Saturday.

All Black goalkicking machine Grant Fox failed to kick a penalty as the Lions levelled the three-match series.

That is the first time since the 52–3 win over Wales at Lancaster Park in 1988 that an All Black test has gone by without at least one Fox penalty. He was playing his 43rd test yesterday.

His sole contribution to the All Black points was a conversion of Eroni Clarke's first-half try, although he did hit an upright with one penalty shot at goal.

In that Welsh test, the All Blacks scored 10 tries, and Fox converted six of them.

Since taking over as the All Blacks' undisputed first-choice goalkicker in 1987, that was the only time he had not kicked at least one penalty in a test, until Saturday.

In 75 matches for New Zealand, Fox has scored 1012 points, including one try.

———

All Black centre Frank Bunce attempts to burst upfield as he is tackled from behind by Peter Winterbottom and Rory Underwood during the second test at Athletic Park.

28 June 1993

TACTICAL FAULTS PROVE FATAL

Wynne Gray

It was hard to apportion individual blame for the All Black second rugby test problems, more a case of questioning the game plan and tactics.

There were many individual errors like spilled ball and ill-discipline giving away penalties and momentum. But statistics would reveal the All Blacks had enough ball to win the game, or at least make a much closer contest of it than they did.

The Lions shaded the line-outs (20–17), rucks and mauls (37–35), penalties (14–7) and scrum feeds (14–7), yet those were not comprehensive margins. But what they did with that ball was far more authoritative, organised and convincing than the All Black counter.

And like the first test, there have to be questions about the thinking and patterns devised for the backline. Jon Preston was a more than adequate link but without any other weapons to his armoury, Grant Fox was often too static and Eroni Clarke and Frank Bunce cut-back culprits.

The lack of a playmaker made the defensive operations once again tackle-bag practice for the Lions, who have showed a forward tenacity to match the All Blacks.

John Kirwan was too often given the ball on the inside channel, John Timu was not changing any angles of attack from the back and was struggling with his kicking game, though Va'aiga Tuigamala was in charge of his own inimitable steamroller operations.

Questions must be asked about what instructions Earle Kirton is giving to his backs. We hear about gas and flair but in two tests so far those terms have counted for zilch.

And in the pack revision had to be contemplated. If Otago and Auckland could impose their pattern against largely test combinations why could not the All Blacks?

---

29 June 1993

SELECTORS DO ABOUT-FACE OVER STENSNESS

Wynne Gray

Propulsion into the All Black rugby midfield has finally come for Lee Stensness after the selectors appeared to find any number of objections earlier this season.

The 22-year-old Stensness' test debut this Saturday will be a pressure-cooker beginning as the series decider between the All Blacks and British Isles at Eden Park.

'Our motivation was we wanted to give ourselves more options in midfield,' coach Laurie Mains said yesterday.

'There were chances in the [second] test in midfield, Eroni Clarke played well, but we need to expand it a bit more on what he gave us.'

The selection of Stensness is one of three changes to the starting XV, so soundly beaten at Athletic Park. Arran Pene is preferred to Zinzan Brooke at No 8 while Mark Cooksley goes back to the reserves with Ian Jones reunited as lock with Robin Brooke.

Stensness' play this winter has provoked much comment. His move to Auckland to play outside Grant Fox has given that team an extra dimension, especially during the Super 10 series.

Out of that play Stensness won an early All Black trial but was overlooked for the final selection. Test incumbent Walter Little kept his place but when he was injured, Stensness was still ignored.

The reservation among the panel was about his tackling, though Mains would not make any comment on that subject yesterday.

Now with Clarke lacking any great vision or kicking skills at Wellington, the panel have moved for Stensness to fill the awkward second five-eighths spot.

His problem now will be of expectation, with the public looking for a saviour after the weekend disappointment. For the new marketing representative in just his second week of work with Placemakers, the midday radio news meant a

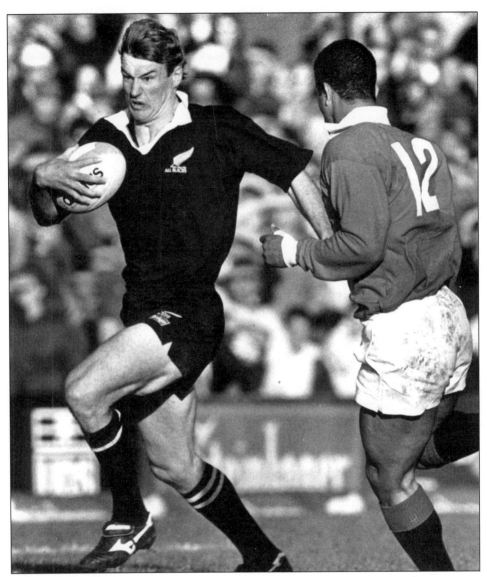

All Black winger John Kirwan shows determination in trying to evade Jeremy Guscott during the All Blacks' loss to the Lions in Wellington.

quick request for the rest of this week off.

Mind you, he did not have to look far as the news came as he was heading back to work in the car with his boss.

'It was like a bolt out of the blue, but it feels good, it's excellent,' Stensness said of his elevation.

'I thought I had a better chance of being selected for the second test,' he added. 'I hadn't given it much thought this time.'

Moving from second-division Manawatu this season, Stensness has slotted in neatly beside Fox at Auckland where, he said, the higher standard of rugby gave him the confidence to play at the top level.

That change of union has also meant a change of position for Stensness, who is still learning the vagaries of second five-eighths play.

'But I think it helps me with the skills I have of running, passing and backing up rather than first five where I had to do more kicking which is not my strength.'

Meanwhile, Mains spoke yesterday of his belief that the line-out troubles could be remedied at Eden Park. Hopes that Cooksley would give Martin Bayfield some problems did not eventuate, though he was probably hampered on two accounts — his bruised hamstring and the inaccurate throwing of skipper Sean Fitzpatrick.

'Our advice was he was fit to start but his hamstring may not have helped the situation,' Mains said.

Brooke had paid the price for not reaching last season's form since returning from Italy.

'We haven't seen Arran on the field for a couple of weeks because he has been reserving for us, but he showed earlier he had gone up a notch on last year's effort,' Mains said.

Pene showed great drive and thrust for Otago and the New Zealand Maoris against the Lions and must have been a close selection for the second international as well.

In making seven alterations already in just two tests, the selectors will be desperate to halt the form slide this Saturday. A repeat of their Lancaster and Athletic parks' form will not be tolerated by a demanding audience and would make the one-off Bledisloe Cup test with Australia a most traumatic week.

Both the captaincy and coaching will come under the most intense scrutiny after the directionless second-test effort. There will be demands for pliable tactics, for all the side to think and operate plans rather than letting just one or two players be in command.

Sensible variety, keeping the ball in play and an allowance for individual expression can help redress the balance.

New Zealand backs: John Timu (Otago), John Kirwan (Auckland), Frank Bunce (North Harbour), Va'aiga Tuigamala (Auckland), Lee Stensness (Auckland), Grant Fox (Auckland), Jon Preston (Wellington).

Forwards: Arran Pene (Otago), Michael Jones (Auckland), Robin Brooke (Auckland), Ian Jones (North Auckland), Jamie Joseph (Otago), Olo Brown (Auckland), Sean Fitzpatrick (capt, Auckland), Craig Dowd (Auckland).

Reserves: Ant Strachan (North Harbour), Graham Dowd (North Harbour), Mark Cooksley (Counties), Matthew Cooper (Waikato), Mark Allen (Taranaki), Zinzan Brooke (Auckland).

---

2 July 1993

IMPRESSIVE VICTORY DEMANDED
Wynne Gray

Word from the All Black camp this week has been about impressive trainings but the New Zealand public's concern will be whether that can be translated into victory tomorrow against the Lions.

Their key worries will be about acquiring usable line-out possession, knitting the tight five together and seeing some penetration from the backs.

A common theme in discussions among rugby fraternities has been to ask why provincial sides can give the Lions the run-around while the All Blacks cannot.

What has been the difference?

'It should be nothing, I can't pinpoint it,' national lock Robin Brooke said yesterday.

'I think we have it sorted out though. Most of us in the forwards play together in Auckland and if we can be more aggressive at line-outs, and get combinations at the mauls, we should go better.'

Brooke and his colleagues got some special line-out tuition yesterday when former All Black line-out ace Andy Haden was called in to assist.

His task was to find some remedy for the battle of the air with Brooke and Ian Jones facing Martin Johnson and Martin Bayfield.

Bayfield has been the principal danger with his height and spring giving him a huge advantage in the middle of the line-out.

Both the Lions and All Blacks trained in private yesterday, the All Blacks at captain Sean Fitzpatrick's old school Sacred Heart. Neither side revealed any mishaps with both teams as selected to take to Eden Park.

'This is the do or die game and we are pretty focused,' Brooke said. 'It would be great to get some of the crowd support though like the Lions get.'

While the All Blacks worked hard on their line-outs, backs' coach Earle Kirton would have been thrashing the variations with his charges.

A key man will be second five-eighths Lee Stensness, a runner, a man with backing-up vision and good distribution skills. He and Grant Fox will have to engineer a much straighter line than the one which played at Athletic Park.

Their mission will be to find ways through, over and round the Lions' drift defence.

---

2 July 1993

ALL BLACK JERSEY BRINGS NEW REWARDS

NZPA

All Blacks may not earn the astronomical sums of top overseas professional sportsmen but they are handsomely remunerated compared with their predecessors.

The average payment for a player from All Black Promotions Ltd for the year ended March 31, 1992, was $20,241 but the actual amount pocketed by some was considerably more.

All Blacks receive an allowance of $66 a day for home rugby tests. If they assemble on Tuesday and disperse on Sunday that is regarded as a week for which they receive $482, tax free.

They receive the same while on tour but if they are not being paid by their employer — and that applies to the majority — they also receive a hardship allowance that enables them to earn $964 a week.

The allowances do not include their earnings from All Black Promotions Ltd and the recently formed All Blacks' Club.

So just how much does a leading All Black made a year?

There is no straightforward answer. The incomes of John Kirwan and Zinzan Brooke, who regularly spend the off-season in Italy for the 'pasta and lifestyle,' vary considerably from those of Sean Fitzpatrick, who spends his summers in New Zealand.

It is believed one leading Auckland All Black, who did not play overseas apart from for his country, earned about $70,000 from rugby in 1991, World Cup year.

However, without the promotional opportunities generated by the World Cup, it is understood his earnings were considerably less last year.

With the formation of the All Blacks' Club and the involvement of big business, this year should be the most lucrative yet.

'Once you're an All Black in the year you're entitled to equal participation in the distribution of the scheme,' the deputy chairman of the New Zealand Rugby Football Union, John Dowling, said. 'The All Blacks themselves decided that.

'We've had people who have played in all the tests voting that people who played in one test receive the same as them. It's a team game and that's the way they want it. The income for the company is determined by the money which comes in.'

Some All Blacks work harder and are more adept at capitalising on marketing opportunities than others.

'Obviously, there is more scope for players to gain promotional and marketing opportunities in Auckland than there is, say, in Invercargill or on the West Coast,' Dowling said.

'Players who obtain commercial opportunities, the proceeds of which go to All Black Promotions Ltd, get a special percentage of the deal for the use of their initiative. This is another incentive for them to stay in New Zealand.'

A recent development is that All Black Promotions Ltd has appointed Harvard Sports Marketing Ltd (New Zealand agent) and Carnegie Sports Ltd (British agent) to obtain further marketing opportunities.

As well, All Blacks travel business class, stay in five-star hotels and receive 'civvy' clothing and accessories to the value of more than $5000.

The All Blacks' Club is designed not only to further reimburse the players in the short term but to create job opportunities when their rugby careers end.

'What has to be appreciated,' Dowling said, 'is that most All Blacks put on hold professional career opportunities so they can continue to play rugby.

'The lot of an All Black is now such that a convert to league was heard to say the biggest mistake he had made was to leave rugby union.'

Certainly, times have changed since Gary Knight, the powerful prop, was forced to pull out of the second test against the Springboks in 1981 because he could not afford to leave his farm.

'The whole aim of the All Blacks' Club, and rugby administrators, is to provide a climate in which top players can get on with the game without financial worries,' Dowling said.

Payments to players from All Black Promotions Ltd for the year ended March 31, 1993, are not yet available but, according to sources, they will be down considerably on the previous year.

However, with the recent initiatives, the payout for the year ending March 31, 1994, should be a record.

---

3 July 1993

FOX: REVISION NECESSARY

Wynne Gray

All Black points-scoring machine Grant Fox considers the test series with the Lions has underlined the problems and need for further revision of the ruck and maul laws in rugby.

When Lions' defenders have made effective tackles their colleagues, said Fox, can then fan out off the rucks and mauls waiting to deal with the next attacking wave. And they can assist a backline who are very adept at operating a drifting defensive screen.

'If there is ball freed and we are trying to send it through the backline it is often seven against 10,' the five-eighths said. 'This is why I bring into question the new ruck and maul law.'

Fox's queries are ironic at the end of a fascinating series with the Lions when there were early season objections from the All Black coaching staff to any law alterations.

That attitude was taken to a meeting of international coaches at the Hong Kong sevens tournament and a subsequent IRB meeting allowed the law to stay as it was. Now after two tests against the Lions, Fox has greater reservations about the usefulness of the current rules.

'Last year the two sides [Australia and New Zealand] were maybe more aggressive with the ball in hand and more willing to use the ball,' he said.

'This season the Lions have shown they will use the ball sparingly and I feel there is an attitude difference compared with Australia.

'We have tried to use the ball, not well I accept, but we have tried to maintain the positive attitude we had last year, but the Lions have concentrated very much on disruption and feeding off our errors.'

Fox agreed that this series had been the toughest for his backline for some time.

But he would not concede the All Blacks had the problems they had in 1990 and 1991. Breaching the defence was difficult, a fact shown up by the Lions' concession of just two test tries — both to up and unders — in the first two tests.

Mitigating factors for that lack of a try tally was the Lions' forwards ability to slow down play and their backs' well-organised drift defence.

It was a defence built on the speed of the backs allowing them to shepherd the All Blacks towards the sideline or back into the waiting loose-forward cover.

'We also have not had the luxury of quick second-phase ball but if we can get that it might be a different story with the Lions on the back foot,' Fox said. He and his outsides had stood too deep at Athletic Park. That line would be flatter today to make the Lions work harder and faster in their defence.

'Certainly we have got to have more eyeball-to-eyeball stuff to commit them but we can only do that if the possession is not too static.

'We have to be more confrontational.'

He added with some vehemence: 'I get the feeling some people think the series is over. Well, like hell it is over.'

---

3 July 1993

DEFEAT UNTHINKABLE FOR BOTH

Wynne Gray

It is a measure of the confusing rugby test series between the All Blacks and the British Isles that New Zealand's 12th international under coach Laurie Mains today may be the toughest to call.

At Athletic Park the Lions succeeded with their mission to keep the tour alive. Now the pendulum of pressure has swung back heavily on the All Blacks. It is a situation accepted by Mains, a by-product he says that comes with home-series expectations and a factor which can be used to advantage.

The major debate today will be whether the All Blacks have been able to generate the passion and commitment the Lions brought to the second test and ally it to sufficient skill to take out the series decider.

Should they fail, they will be remembered as only the second All Black team to have lost a test series to the Lions in eight visits. John Dawes' 1971 side holds the single honour at the moment — a triumph topped off with a 14–all draw in the final test at Eden Park in which Mains played at fullback.

A Lions series victory would be a remarkable transformation for a side written off at home and widely scorned in New Zealand before they played.

Conversely a loss will leave labels like disastrous on the tour and give the tourists a seven-win, six-loss record. They would then perhaps rue not paying more attention to some provincial fixtures.

In Wellington the Lions had the yearning which demanded, then achieved, the win. Some of that fire may have eased, with the All Blacks now feeling the heat and expectation. But do they have the armoury, aside from the clinical kicking of Grant Fox, to take the series before a packed house of 45,000 at Eden Park?

The suspicion is that these two sides of no more than steady ability offer the prospect of three results.

The All Blacks could sneak a win by a few points, the Lions likewise or achieve a decent margin. It is too difficult to envisage how the All Blacks could cobble together a substantial win.

There has been little in their forward play to suggest they can dominate the Lions pack, who have been more agile and destructive than expected. With trump line-out man Martin Bayfield in exceptional form a steady supply of quality possession is almost guaranteed.

Neither backline has operated with any great pizzazz, choosing to play percentage rugby rather than risk mistakes in their pursuit of tries.

While the All Blacks have outscored the Lions two tries to one, both have come from 'bombs,' an indication of the difficulty there is in breaching the Lions' defences.

Sure, the Lions have scored only that crucial Rory Underwood touchdown but they have looked exceedingly dangerous on other occasions.

Coach Ian McGeechan spoke about that as he contemplated what may be a parallel of the Lions team he coached in Australia in 1989.

'We should have killed them [All Blacks] off by now and this third test will be a different ball game altogether,' he said yesterday.

'It will be an aggressive and tense match. We have got to match them for desperation because their reputations are on the line.

'We have got to match their passion, match their heart.'

In 1989 in Australia the Lions came back from a first-test loss to win the next two and the series when winger Ieuan Evans pounced on David Campese's celebrated in-goal fumble.

'I have got a déjà vu feeling about this game,' Evans said.

If his crystal-ball gazing is correct the result would provide an epic swansong for flanker Peter Winterbottom, the only Lion playing today who has announced his retirement.

Both sides went for quiet strolls yesterday, the All Blacks to Eden Park and the Lions to the Teachers-Eastern club. It was the lull for both before today's fury in conditions which should be great for rugby.

Mains and his side watched several videos last night to generate the spirit needed for this tour finale.

There had been no discussion among the

selection panel, Mains said, that players were also competing for their All Black careers today — 'those sort of things get discussed after games.'

The Wellington loss had not shaken the team confidence, the task of the coaching staff was to work on the All Black strengths.

There had been a brief discussion with match referee Patrick Robin, an amicable chat about his attitude towards several laws.

3 July 1993

TEST FEVER PRODUCES A TRUE RUGBY UNION

Staff Reporter, NZPA

A week of debates, bets and rugby fever culminates at Eden Park today with the decisive test match between the All Blacks and the Lions.

Fine weather and a capacity crowd of 48,000 are expected in Auckland for the test, which starts at 2.30 pm.

About 3000 fans of the touring side will descend on the park with high hopes of a Lions win to clinch the three-match series.

The touring team's 20–7 win over the All Blacks last Saturday has spurred the British side to match their forebears of 1971 — the only time the Lions have won a series against the All Blacks.

A former Lions player, Mr Alan Phillips, will be cheering from the stands today with the tour group he has escorted from Britain.

The former Welsh representative said in Auckland yesterday that the comradeship of the English, Scottish, Irish and Welsh fans during the tour has equalled the spirit on the field.

'It's the one thing about Lions tours — it unites the whole of Britain. There has been no jealousy. We have all mixed together on the tour.

'We came to win the tests, not the provincial games.

'When the Lions won the second test they gained instant respect from New Zealanders,' said the former test player, who toured South Africa with the Lions in 1980 and played for Wales during the 1987 World Cup in New Zealand.

The Lions' management has paid tribute to the fans, saying their support has been of immense value to the team.

Although outnumbered more than 10 to one, the British spectators' at times out-shouted the muted home crowd last weekend.

Another Welsh rugby fan, who thought he might miss today's test, will be there after all, thanks to the mercy of a High Court judge in Auckland.

Mark Griffiths Jones, a butcher from Powys, flew into New Zealand three weeks ago on a supporters' tour.

The closest he has been to the rugby action, however, is a prison television set, after sniffer dogs got a whiff of the eight grams of hashish in the pocket of his jeans at Auckland Airport on June 12.

The 35-year-old admitted having the drug and said it was for his own use.

After hearing pleas from his lawyer that he be allowed to see at least one game of the tour and then leave the country, Mr Justice Temm sent him on his way with a $1000 fine.

'I think you have suffered a severe enough penalty already,' the judge said. 'I don't want to deliver a speech. Good luck, off you go.'

The park gates open today at noon, and before the scheduled kick-off, a 200-voice choir will take to the field to sing English, Scottish, Welsh and Irish songs. The Meteorological Service has forecast a fine day with light winds after frost and fog in some areas clears by late morning.

An Auckland Rugby Union spokesman, Mr Rocky Patterson, said that because most match tickets had been handled through clubs or tour groups, there was little chance for scalpers to get their hands on them to sell at the gates.

The match was sold out, meaning a capacity crowd of 48,000, he said.

Many New Zealanders appear to be backing the Lions to win the test.

Centrebet, an Australian sports betting agency, gives odds of 4 to 7 on an All Black victory. That means that for every $7 bet punters will get $11 back if the All Blacks win.

Big Lions loose-forward Ben Clarke makes a heavy load for winger Rory Underwood in training.

Robin Brooke (5) gets some help from Craig Dowd while Jamie Joseph looks astounded. The leaping Lions are Dean Richards (8) and Martin Bayfield.

A Lions victory is at slightly shorter odds.

A Centrebet spokesman, Mr Gerard Daffy, said more than 300 New Zealanders in Australia had placed bets. Most were picking an All Black loss.

'They are more worried about their pockets than their hearts,' said Mr Daffy.

Even the bookmakers remain edgy about the All Blacks' prospects.

'I personally think the Lions will roll them,' Mr Daffy said.

---

5 July 1993

PUGNACIOUS ALL BLACKS RESCUE SERIES WITH STYLE

Wynne Gray

Faced with a career-threatening series loss, the All Blacks provided some vital pugnaciousness and tactical revision for a 30–13 final test victory over the British Isles to send a capacity Eden Park throng into delirium.

This time there was the appetite for work from the tight-five forwards, the quicker ball movement and the en bloc approach rather than the one-out efforts seen in the opening two internationals. From the initial minutes the urgency was evident, though some of the work slightly off-key as the All Blacks battled their inner frenzy.

Perhaps it was that over-excitement which caused some of the early indiscipline, too, with four double penalties given against the home team and another reversed.

But there was an inner fire on Saturday, a flame which had flickered all too briefly at Christchurch and Wellington. This time the flicker became a flame stoked by the fear of failure.

There was too much to lose.

Who could bear being branded as just the second All Black team to lose a series to the Lions, the first side since 1949 to lose two successive tests at home?

It was an All Black side and coaching staff operating under excruciating pressure, but they survived and in the best traditions of New Zealand rugby did so in rousing fashion.

It all had to be done after the Lions had raced to a 10-point start through a fortuitous try. But the signs were there, even then, that the All Blacks were not going to be denied while the Lions were not urgent enough to record the victory to raise their tour record from poor to good.

Laurie Mains later reflected it was the most intense, demanding week in his coaching career.

'We had a responsibility to New Zealand rugby and we really felt that,' he said.

The fightback began through debut midfield back Lee Stensness as the All Blacks regrouped facing the point deficit and the loss of experienced lock Ian Jones. A Stensness chip kick led to a Frank Bunce try, then four minutes later Sean Fitzpatrick was over after a traditional All Black rumble. The clawback had swiftly assumed the style of a shutout.

The half time lead was 14–10 and although the Lions made valiant counter-attacking moves in the second spell it seemed to be just a matter of waiting for the All Blacks' death thrust.

It came from a try to halfback Jon Preston assisted by a dummy run by John Kirwan after Grant Fox had earlier lacked the conviction to score one, perhaps two tries.

The Preston touchdown sealed the victory which had been assured by an octopus-like defence, some of the fiercest tackling imaginable. It was a match of many errors but some rich, raw-blooded aggression with the All Blacks' desperation matching that of the Lions at Athletic Park.

The line-out was repaired, the scrum was too strong, the backs even had a crack or two.

It was a gutsy All Black effort containing some outstanding individual contributions.

Robin Brooke was supreme at kick-offs and worked aggressively round the park, Jamie Joseph and Michael Jones a pair of thunderous flankers as they were given the opportunity to work a wider pattern. In midfield Stensness revealed the attacking talents he has consistently displayed for Auckland this year, vision for the half chance and also an ability to conform to a pattern when needed.

He also offered the defence the selectors had

been dubious about. Stensness' performance should make it too hard for the panel's original series preference, Walter Little, to be chosen for the Bledisloe Cup.

John Kirwan was back with aggression if not extreme pace while Bunce and John Timu were defensive tough nuts, an impenetrable duo.

With such a winning margin it may be seen as picky to find fault. Mains nominated the discipline problem. He could add several others like still needing to fire Fitzpatrick to the form of last season, remedying the two-stage passing action of Preston, praising Fox for his overall control but encouraging him to release his backline even more and placing emphasis on Timu's further positional play.

Those may be quibbles but if a team and coach seek to be professional those aspects will be addressed for the next clash with the world champion Wallabies.

---

5 July 1993

'FEAR' THE SPUR
NZPA

Fear of failure inspired the All Blacks to victory over the Lions in a test match of great tension, British newspapers reported yesterday.

'The prospect of being hanged high from Mt Eden this morning with most of New Zealand looking forward to the ceremony concentrated the minds of the All Blacks as nothing else can,' John Reason wrote in the *Sunday Telegraph*.

'The urgency they produced as a consequence was too much for the British Isles.'

Former Welsh international Eddie Butler, in the *Observer*, said the test was played on as tense a day in rugby as there had ever been.

'In the end, fear of failure in the All Black camp — that dread of shaming the famous dark jersey with its silver fern — proved stronger than

Lions' skipper Gavin Hastings (kicking) and All Black captain Sean Fitzpatrick.

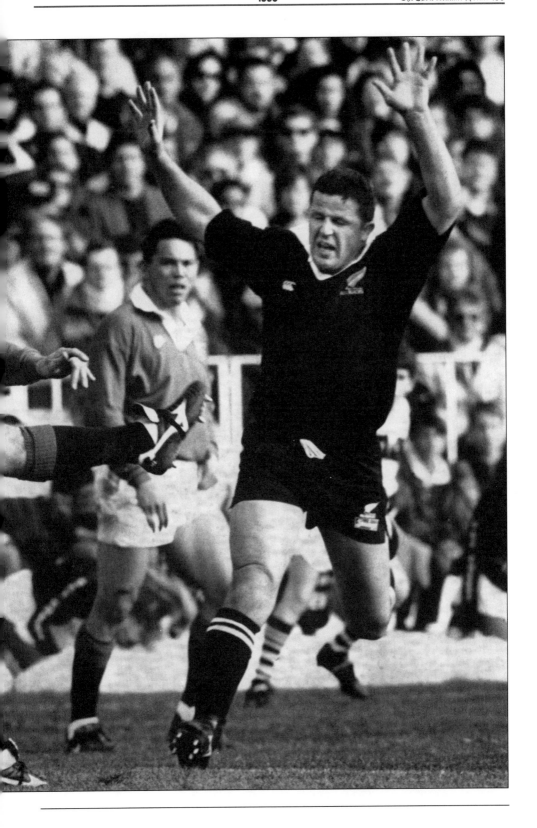

Lions' captain Gavin Hastings pushes off the tackle of debutante All Black Lee Stensness at the third test at Eden Park. John Kirwan and Jeremy Guscott move in to assist.

the will of the Lions to throw a little light on a grim [British] sporting summer.'

British Lion Wade Dooley, writing in the same paper, said beating the All Blacks was one thing, but beating them and history was another.

'They hadn't lost successive games at home for almost 50 years,' said the England lock, who returned home midway through the tour after the death of his father.

'You could see the fear in their eyes as they came out of the tunnel.'

In the *Sunday Times*, Stephen Jones said the Lions committed too many errors, while their 'superior backline malfunctioned.'

Meanwhile, the All Blacks were revitalised by the introduction of No 8 Arran Pene, 'the best forward the Lions have met on tour,' and second five-eighths Lee Stensness.

All Black captain Sean Fitzpatrick lifts the spoils of victory at Eden Park.

Statistics

1930 Matches

MANAGEMENT
All Blacks: Manager – A.J. Geddes
Lions: Manager – James Baxter

	Played	Won	Draw	Lost	For	Against
Non-Tests	17	14	0	3	507	153
Tests	4	1	0	3	48	51
Total	21	15	0	6	555	204

21 May 1930	Lions vs Wanganui	19-3	Wanganui
24 May 1930	Lions vs Taranaki	23-7	New Plymouth
28 May 1930	Lions vs Manawhenua	34-8	Palmerston Nth
31 May 1930	Lions vs Wairapapa Bush	19-6	Masterton
3 Jun 1930	Lions vs Wellington	8-12	Wellington
7 Jun 1930	Lions vs Canterbury	8-14	Christchurch
11 Jun 1930	Lions vs West Coast/Buller	34-11	Greymouth
14 Jun 1930	Lions vs Otago	33-9	Dunedin
21 Jun 1930	**Lions vs New Zealand**	**6-3**	**Dunedin**
25 Jun 1930	Lions vs Southland	9-3	Invercargill
28 Jun 1930	Lions vs Ashburton/South Canterbury/North Otago	16-9	Timaru
5 Jul 1930	**Lions vs New Zealand**	**10-13**	**Christchurch**
9 Jul 1930	Lions vs NZ Maori	19-13	Wellington
12 Jul 1930	Lions vs Hawkes Bay	14-3	Napier
16 Jul 1930	Lions vs Poverty Bay/East Coast/Bay of Plenty	25-11	Gisborne
19 Jul 1930	Lions vs Auckland	6-19	Auckland
26 Jul 1930	**Lions vs New Zealand**	**10-15**	**Auckland**
30 Jul 1930	Lions vs North Auckland	38-5	Whangarei
2 Aug 1930	Lions vs Waikato/King Country/Thames Valley	40-16	Hamilton
9 Aug 1930	**Lions vs New Zealand**	**8-22**	**Wellington**
12 Aug 1930	Lions vs Marlborough/Nelson/Golden Bay/Motueka	41-3	Blenheim

1st test — Carisbrook, Dunedin, Saturday, 21 June 1930
Attendance: 27,000
Conditions: Weather: rain and snow showers. Ground: muddy
Half-time: New Zealand 0, British Isles 3
Full time: New Zealand 3, British Isles 6

2nd test — Lancaster Park, Christchurch, Saturday, 5 July 1930
Attendance: 32,000
Conditions: Weather: fine. Ground: soft
Half-time: New Zealand 8, British Isles 5
Full time: New Zealand 13, British Isles 10

3rd test — Eden Park, Auckland, Saturday, 26 July 1930
Attendance: 40,000
Conditions: Weather: fine with late rain. Ground: greasy
Half-time: New Zealand 5, British Isles 5
Full time: New Zealand 15, British Isles 10

4th test — Athletic Park, Wellington, Saturday, 9 August 1930
Attendance: 40,000
Conditions: Weather: fine. Ground: firm
Half-time: New Zealand 6, British Isles 3
Full time: New Zealand 22, British Isles 8

1950 Matches

MANAGEMENT
All Blacks: Manager – T.C. Morrison
Lions: Manager – Surgeon Captain L.B. Osborne

	Played	Won	Draw	Lost	For	Against
Non-Tests	19	16	0	3	400	128
Tests	4	0	1	3	20	34
Total	23	16	1	6	420	162

10 May 1950	Lions vs Marlborough/Nelson/Golden Bay/Motueka	24-3	Nelson
13 May 1950	Lions vs Buller	24-9	Westport
16 May 1950	Lions vs West Coast	32-3	Greymouth
20 May 1950	Lions vs Otago	9-23	Dunedin
23 May 1950	Lions vs Southland	0-11	Invercargill
27 May 1950	**Lions vs New Zealand**	**9-9**	**Dunedin**
31 May 1950	Lions vs South Canterbury	27-8	Timaru
3 Jun 1950	Lions vs Canterbury	16-5	Christchurch
6 Jun 1950	Lions vs Ashburton County/North Otago	29-6	Ashburton
10 Jun 1950	**Lions vs New Zealand**	**0-8**	**Christchurch**
14 Jun 1950	Lions vs Wairapapa Bush	27-13	Masterton
17 Jun 1950	Lions vs Hawkes Bay	20-0	Napier
21 Jun 1950	Lions vs East Coast/Poverty Bay/Bay of Plenty	27-3	Gisborne
24 Jun 1950	Lions vs Wellington	12-6	Wellington
1 Jul 1950	**Lions vs New Zealand**	**3-6**	**Wellington**
5 Jul 1950	Lions vs Wanganui	31-3	Wanganui
8 Jul 1950	Lions vs Taranaki	25-3	New Plymouth
12 Jul 1950	Lions vs Manawatu/Horowhenua	13-8	Palmerston Nth
15 Jul 1950	Lions vs Waikato/King Country/Thames Valley	30-0	Hamilton
19 Jul 1950	Lions vs North Auckland	8-6	Whangarei
22 Jul 1950	Lions vs Auckland	32-9	Auckland
29 Jul 1950	**Lions vs New Zealand**	**8-11**	**Auckland**
2 Aug 1950	Lions vs NZ Maori	14-9	Wellington

1st test — Carisbrook, Dunedin, Saturday, 27 May 1950
Attendance: 35,000
Conditions: Weather: fine. Ground: firm
Half-time: New Zealand 0, British Isles 3
Full time: New Zealand 9, British Isles 9

2nd test — Lancaster Park, Christchurch, Saturday, 10 June 1950
Attendance: 43,000
Conditions: Weather: fine. Ground: heavy
Half-time: New Zealand 8, British Isles 0
Full time: New Zealand 8, British Isles 0

3rd test, Athletic Park, Wellington, Saturday, 1 July 1950
Attendance: 45,000
Conditions: Weather: overcast. Ground: heavy
Half-time: New Zealand 0, British Isles 3
Full time: New Zealand 6, British Isles 3

4th test, Eden Park, Auckland, Saturday, 29 July 1950
Attendance: 58,000
Conditions: Weather: fine. Ground: firm
Half-time: New Zealand 8, British Isles 3
Full time: New Zealand 11, British Isles 8

1959 Matches

MANAGEMENT
All Blacks: Coach – R.A. Everest, Manager – Tom Pearce
Lions: Coach – O.B. Glasgow, Manager – A.W. Wilson

	Played	Won	Draw	Lost	For	Against
Non-Tests	21	19	0	2	540	209
Tests	4	1	0	3	42	57
Total	25	20	0	5	582	266

Date	Match	Score	Venue
20 Jun 1959	Lions vs Hawkes Bay	52-12	Napier
24 Jun 1959	Lions vs Poverty Bay/East Coast	23-14	Gisborne
27 Jun 1959	Lions vs Auckland	15-10	Auckland
1 Jul 1959	Lions vs NZ Universities	25-13	Christchurch
4 Jul 1959	Lions vs Otago	8-26	Dunedin
8 Jul 1959	Lions vs South Canterbury/Mid Canterbury/North Otago	21-11	Timaru
11 Jul 1959	Lions vs Southland	11-6	Invercargill
18 Jul 1959	**Lions vs New Zealand**	**17-18**	**Dunedin**
22 Jul 1959	Lions vs West Coast/Buller	58-3	Greymouth
25 Jul 1959	Lions vs Canterbury	14-20	Christchurch
29 Jul 1959	Lions vs Marlborough/Nelson/Golden Bay/Motueka	64-5	Blenheim
1 Aug 1959	Lions vs Wellington	21-6	Wellington
5 Aug 1959	Lions vs Wanganui	9-6	Wanganui
8 Aug 1959	Lions vs Taranaki	15-3	New Plymouth
11 Aug 1959	Lions vs Manawatu/Horowhenua	26-6	Palmerston Nth
15 Aug 1959	**Lions vs New Zealand**	**8-11**	**Wellington**
19 Aug 1959	Lions vs King Country/Counties	25-5	Taumarunui
22 Aug 1959	Lions vs Waikato	14-0	Hamilton
25 Aug 1959	Lions vs Wairapapa Bush	37-11	Masterton
29 Aug 1959	**Lions vs New Zealand**	**8-22**	**Christchurch**
2 Sep 1959	Lions vs New Zealand Juniors	29-9	Wellington
5 Sep 1959	Lions vs NZ Maori XV	12-6	Auckland
9 Sep 1959	Lions vs Bay of Plenty/Thames Valley	26-24	Rotorua
12 Sep 1959	Lions vs North Auckland	35-13	Whangarei
19 Sep 1959	**Lions vs New Zealand**	**9-6**	**Auckland**

1st test — Carisbrook, Dunedin, Saturday, 18 July 1959
Attendance: 41,500
Conditions: Weather: fine. Ground: soft
Half-time: New Zealand 6, British Isles 9
Full time: New Zealand 18, British Isles 17

2nd test — Athletic Park, Wellington, Saturday, 15 August 1959
Attendance: 53,000
Conditions: Weather: fine. Ground: firm
Half-time: New Zealand 6, British Isles 0
Full time: New Zealand 11, British Isles 8

3rd test — Lancaster Park, Christchurch, Saturday, 29 August 1959
Attendance: 57,000
Conditions: Weather: fine. Ground: firm
Half-time: New Zealand 14, British Isles 8
Full time: New Zealand 22, British Isles 8

4th test — Eden Park, Auckland, Saturday, 19 September 1959
Attendance: 60,000
Conditions: Weather: overcast after rain. Ground: slippery
Half-time: New Zealand 3, British Isles 3
Full time: New Zealand 6, British Isles 9

1966 Matches

MANAGEMENT
All Blacks: Coach – Fred Allen, Manager – Ron Burk
Lions: Coach – John Robins, Manager – Des O'Brien

	Played	Won	Draw	Lost	For	Against
Non-Tests	21	15	2	4	268	202
Tests	4	0	0	4	32	79
Total	25	15	2	8	300	281

11 Jun 1966	Lions vs Southland	8-14	Invercargill
15 Jun 1966	Lions vs South Canterbury/Mid Canterbury/North Otago	20-12	Timaru
18 Jun 1966	Lions vs Otago	9-17	Dunedin
22 Jun 1966	Lions vs NZ Universities	24-11	Christchurch
25 Jun 1966	Lions vs Wellington	6-20	Wellington
29 Jun 1966	Lions vs Marlborough/Nelson/Golden Bay/Motueka	22-14	Nelson
2 Jul 1966	Lions vs Taranaki	12-9	New Plymouth
6 Jul 1966	Lions vs Bay of Plenty	6-6	Rotorua
9 Jul 1966	Lions vs North Auckland	6-3	Whangarei
16 Jul 1966	**Lions vs New Zealand**	**3-20**	**Dunedin**
20 Jul 1966	Lions vs West Coast/Buller	25-6	Westport
23 Jul 1966	Lions vs Canterbury	8-6	Christchurch
27 Jul 1966	Lions vs Manawatu/Horowhenua	17-8	Palmerston Nth
30 Jul 1966	Lions vs Auckland	12-6	Auckland
2 Aug 1966	Lions vs Wairapapa Bush	9-6	Masterton
6 Aug 1966	**Lions vs New Zealand**	**12-16**	**Wellington**
10 Aug 1966	Lions vs Wanganui/King Country	6-12	Wanganui
13 Aug 1966	Lions vs NZ Maori XV	16-14	Auckland
17 Aug 1966	Lions vs Poverty Bay/East Coast	9-6	Gisborne
20 Aug 1966	Lions vs Hawkes Bay	11-11	Napier
27 Aug 1966	**Lions vs New Zealand**	**6-19**	**Christchurch**
31 Aug 1966	Lions vs New Zealand Juniors	9-3	Wellington
3 Sep 1966	Lions vs Waikato	20-9	Hamilton
6 Sep 1966	Lions vs Counties/Thames Valley	13-9	Papakura
10 Sep 1966	**Lions vs New Zealand**	**11-24**	**Auckland**

1st test — Carisbrook, Dunedin, Saturday, 16 July 1966
Attendance: 43,000
Conditions: Weather: overcast. Ground: soft
Half-time: New Zealand 8, British Isles 3
Full time: New Zealand 20, British Isles 3

2nd test — Athletic Park, Wellington,Saturday, 6 August 1966
Attendance: 44,425
Conditions: Weather: overcast. Ground: muddy
Half-time: New Zealand 8, British Isles 9
Full time: New Zealand 16, British Isles 12

3rd test — Lancaster Park, Christchurch, Saturday, 27 August 1966
Attendance: 52,000
Conditions: Weather: overcast. Ground: greasy
Half-time: New Zealand 6, British Isles 6
Full time: New Zealand 19, British Isles 6

4th test — Eden Park, Auckland, Saturday, 10 September 1966
Attendance: 58,000
Conditions: Weather: fine. Ground: firm
Half-time: New Zealand 10, British Isles 8
Full time: New Zealand 24, British Isles 11

1971 Matches

MANAGEMENT
All Blacks: Coach – Ivan Vodanovich, Manager – Ernie Todd
Lions: Coach – Carwyn James, Manager – Dr. Douglas Smith

	Played	Won	Draw	Lost	For	Against
Non-Tests	20	20	0	0	507	162
Tests	4	2	1	1	48	42
Total	24	22	1	1	555	204

Date	Match	Score	Venue
22 May 1971	Lions vs Counties/Thames Valley	25-3	Pukekohe
26 May 1971	Lions vs Wanganui/King Country	22-9	Wanganui
29 May 1971	Lions vs Waikato	35-14	Hamilton
02 Jun 1971	Lions vs NZ Maori XV	23-12	Auckland
05 Jun 1971	Lions vs Wellington	47-9	Wellington
09 Jun 1971	Lions vs South Mid Canterbury/North Otago	25-6	Timaru
12 Jun 1971	Lions vs Otago	21-9	Dunedin
16 Jun 1971	Lions vs West Coast/Buller	39-6	Greymouth
19 Jun 1971	Lions vs Canterbury	14-3	Christchurch
22 Jun 1971	Lions vs Marlborough/Nelson Bays	31-12	Blenheim
26 Jun 1971	**Lions vs New Zealand**	**9-3**	**Dunedin**
30 Jun 1971	Lions vs Southland	25-3	Invercargill
03 Jul 1971	Lions vs Taranaki	14-9	New Plymouth
06 Jul 1971	Lions vs NZ Universities	27-6	Wellington
10 Jul 1971	**Lions vs New Zealand**	**12-22**	**Christchurch**
14 Jul 1971	Lions vs Wairarapa Bush	27-6	Masterton
17 Jul 1971	Lions vs Hawkes Bay	25-6	Napier
21 Jul 1971	Lions vs Poverty Bay/East Coast	18-12	Gisborne
24 Jul 1971	Lions vs Auckland	19-12	Auckland
31 Jul 1971	**Lions vs New Zealand**	**13-3**	**Wellington**
04 Aug 1971	Lions vs Manawatu/Horowhenua	39-6	Palmerston Nth
07 Aug 1971	Lions vs North Auckland	11-5	Whangarei
10 Aug 1971	Lions vs Bay of Plenty	20-14	Tauranga
14 Aug 1971	**Lions vs New Zealand**	**14-14**	**Auckland**

1st test — Carisbrook, Dunedin, Saturday, 26 June 1971
Attendance: 45,000
Conditions: Weather: fine. Ground: greasy
Half-time: New Zealand 3, British Isles 3
Full time: New Zealand 3, British Isles 9

2nd test — Lancaster Park, Christchurch, Saturday, 10 July 1971
Attendance: 57,500
Conditions: Weather: fine. Ground: muddy
Half-time: New Zealand 8, British Isles 6
Full time: New Zealand 22, British Isles 12

3rd test — Athletic Park, Wellington, Saturday, 31 July 1971
Attendance: 50,000
Conditions: Weather: fine. Ground: soft
Half-time: New Zealand 0, British Isles 13
Full time: New Zealand 3, British Isles 13

4th test — Eden Park, Auckland, Saturday, 14 August 1971
Attendance: 56,000
Conditions: Weather: cloudy. Ground: firm
Half-time: New Zealand 8, British Isles 8
Full time: New Zealand 14, British Isles 14

1977 Matches

MANAGEMENT
All Blacks: Coach – Jack Gleeson, Manager – Ron Don
Lions: Coach – John Dawes, Manager – George Burrell

	Played	Won	Draw	Lost	For	Against
Non-Tests	21	20	0	1	545	241
Tests	4	1	0	3	41	54
Total	25	21	0	4	586	295

Date	Match	Score	Venue
18 May 1977	Lions vs Wairapapa Bush	41-13	Masterton
21 May 1977	Lions vs Hawkes Bay	13-11	Napier
25 May 1977	Lions vs Poverty Bay/East Coast	25-6	Gisborne
28 May 1977	Lions vs Taranaki	21-13	New Plymouth
1 Jun 1977	Lions vs King Country/Wanganui	60-9	Taumarunui
4 Jun 1977	Lions vs Manawatu/Horowhenua	18-12	Palmerston Nth
8 Jun 1977	Lions vs Otago	12-7	Dunedin
11 Jun 1977	Lions vs Southland	20-12	Invercargill
14 Jun 1977	Lions vs NZ Universities	9-21	Christchurch
18 Jun 1977	**Lions vs New Zealand**	**12-16**	**Wellington**
22 Jun 1977	Lions vs South Mid Canterbury/North Otago	45-6	Timaru
25 Jun 1977	Lions vs Canterbury	14-13	Christchurch
29 Jun 1977	Lions vs West Coast/Buller	45-0	Westport
2 Jul 1977	Lions vs Wellington	13-6	Wellington
5 Jul 1977	Lions vs Marlborough/Nelson Bays	40-23	Blenheim
9 Jul 1977	**Lions vs New Zealand**	**13-9**	**Christchurch**
13 Jul 1977	Lions vs NZ Maori XV	22-19	Auckland
16 Jul 1977	Lions vs Waikato	18-13	Hamilton
20 Jul 1977	Lions vs New Zealand Juniors	19-9	Wellington
23 Jul 1977	Lions vs Auckland	34-15	Auckland
30 Jul 1977	**Lions vs New Zealand**	**7-19**	**Dunedin**
3 Aug 1977	Lions vs Counties/Thames Valley	35-10	Pukekohe
6 Aug 1977	Lions vs North Auckland	18-7	Whangarei
9 Aug 1977	Lions vs Bay of Plenty	23-16	Rotorua
13 Aug 1977	**Lions vs New Zealand**	**9-10**	**Auckland**

1st test — Athletic Park, Wellington, Saturday, 18 June 1977
Attendance: 43,000
Conditions: Weather: overcast with light rain. Ground: soft
Half-time: New Zealand 16, British Isles 12
Full time: New Zealand 16, British Isles 12

2nd test — Lancaster Park, Christchurch, Saturday, 9 July 1977
Attendance: 50,000
Conditions: Weather: cold and clear. Ground: very heavy
Half-time: New Zealand 6, British Isles 13
Full time: New Zealand 9, British Isles 13

3rd test — Carisbrook, Dunedin, Saturday, 30 July 1977
Attendance: 34,000
Conditions: Weather: fine. Ground: soft
Half-time: New Zealand 10, British Isles 4
Full time: New Zealand 19, British Isles 7

4th test — Eden Park, Auckland, Saturday, 13 August 1977
Attendance: 58,000
Conditions: Weather: sunny. Ground: firm
Half-time: New Zealand 3, British Isles 9
Full time: New Zealand 10, British Isles 9

1983 Matches

MANAGEMENT
All Blacks: Coach – Bryce Rope, Manager – Paul Mitchell
Lions: Coach – Jim Telfer, Manager – Willie John McBride

	Played	Won	Draw	Lost	For	Against
Non-Tests	14	12	0	2	452	198
Tests	4	0	0	4	26	78
Total	18	12	0	6	478	276

Date	Match	Score	Venue
14 May 1983	Lions vs Wanganui	47-15	Wanganui
18 May 1983	Lions vs Auckland	12-13	Auckland
21 May 1983	Lions vs Bay of Plenty	34-16	Rotorua
25 May 1983	Lions vs Wellington	27-19	Wellington
28 May 1983	Lions vs Manawatu	25-18	Palmerston Nth
31 May 1983	Lions vs Mid Canterbury	26-6	Ashburton
4 Jun 1983	**Lions vs New Zealand**	**12-16**	**Christchurch**
8 Jun 1983	Lions vs West Coast	52-16	Greymouth
11 Jun 1983	Lions vs Southland	41-3	Invercargill
14 Jun 1983	Lions vs Wairapapa Bush	57-10	Masterton
18 Jun 1983	**Lions vs New Zealand**	**0-9**	**Wellington**
25 Jun 1983	Lions vs North Auckland	21-12	Whangarei
28 Jun 1983	Lions vs Canterbury	20-22	Christchurch
2 Jul 1983	**Lions vs New Zealand**	**8-15**	**Dunedin**
6 Jul 1983	Lions vs Hawkes Bay	25-19	Napier
9 Jul 1983	Lions vs Counties	25-16	Pukekohe
12 Jul 1983	Lions vs Waikato	40-13	Hamilton
16 Jul 1983	**Lions vs New Zealand**	**6-38**	**Auckland**

1st test — Lancaster Park, Christchurch, Saturday, 4 June 1983
Attendance: 44,000
Conditions: Weather: fine. Ground: soft
Half-time: New Zealand 6, British Isles 9
Full time: New Zealand 16, British Isles 12

2nd test — Athletic Park, Wellington, Saturday, 18 June 1983
Attendance: 40,000
Conditions: Weather: fine but windy. Ground: firm
Half-time: New Zealand 9, British Isles 0
Full time: New Zealand 9, British Isles 0

3rd test — Carisbrook, Dunedin, Saturday, 2 July 1983
Attendance: 30,000
Conditions: Weather: cold with cross-wind. Ground: heavy and wet
Half-time: New Zealand 6, British Isles 4
Full time: New Zealand 15, British Isles 8

4th test — Eden Park, Auckland, Saturday, 16 July 1983
Attendance: 54,000
Conditions: Weather: fine. Ground: greasy
Half-time: New Zealand 16, British Isles 3
Full time: New Zealand 38, British Isles 6

1993 Matches

MANAGEMENT
All Blacks: Coach – Laurie Mains, Manager – Neil Gray
Lions: Coach – Ian McGeechan, Manager – Geoff Cooke

	Played	Won	Draw	Lost	For	Against
Non-Tests	10	6	0	4	263	228
Tests	3	1	0	2	51	57
Total	13	7	0	6	314	285

Date	Match	Score	Venue
22 May 1993	Lions vs North Auckland	30-17	Whangarei
26 May 1993	Lions vs North Harbour	29-13	Auckland
29 May 1993	Lions vs NZ Maori XV	24-20	Wellington
2 Jun 1993	Lions vs Canterbury	28-10	Christchurch
5 Jun 1993	Lions vs Otago	24-37	Dunedin
8 Jun 1993	Lions vs Southland	34-16	Invercargill
12 Jun 1993	**Lions vs New Zealand**	**18-20**	**Christchurch**
16 Jun 1993	Lions vs Taranaki	49-25	New Plymouth
19 Jun 1993	Lions vs Auckland	18-23	Auckland
22 Jun 1993	Lions vs Hawkes Bay	17-29	Napier
26 Jun 1993	**Lions vs New Zealand**	**20-7**	**Wellington**
29 Jun 1993	Lions vs Waikato	10-38	Hamilton
3 Jul 1993	**Lions vs New Zealand**	**13-30**	**Auckland**

1st test — Lancaster Park, Christchurch, Saturday, 12 June 1993
Attendance: 38,000
Conditions: Weather: fine. Ground: firm
Half-time: New Zealand 11, British Isles 9
Full time: New Zealand 20, British Isles 18

2nd test — Athletic Park, Wellington, Saturday, 26 June 1993
Attendance: 39,000
Conditions: Weather: fine. Ground: firm
Half-time: New Zealand 7, British Isles 9
Full time: New Zealand 7, British Isles 20

3rd test — Eden Park, Auckland, Saturday, 3 July 1993
Attendance: 47,000
Conditions: Weather: overcast. Ground: firm
Half-time: New Zealand 14, British Isles 10
Full time: New Zealand 30, British Isles 13